WAR

WAR

Ends and Means

PAUL SEABURY

and

ANGELO CODEVILLA

Basic Books, Inc., Publishers

NEW YORK

Library of Congress Cataloging-in-Publication Data

Seabury, Paul.
  War: ends and means.

  Bibliography: p. 288
  Includes index.
  1. War. 2. Military art and science. I. Codevilla,
Angelo M., 1943–   . II. Title.
U21.2.S43 1989   355′.02   88–47897
ISBN 0–465–09067–2

CONTENTS

ACKNOWLEDGMENTS

THE AUTHORS acknowledge the encouragement and sage advice of our editor, Martin Kessler, and his assistant, Charles Cavaliere. Michael Whitticar of Stanford and Daniel Berman of the University of California, Berkeley, helped with the endnotes. We were first persuaded that a contemporary book on this stark subject was possible, needed, and long overdue by Glen Gendzel, who produced a graceful set of lecture notes from Professor Seabury's undergraduate course on war and politics for *Blacklightning*, a note-taking service for Berkeley students.

We do not regard ourselves as disciples of any school of political or international theory. Yet we acknowledge our intellectual debts to Niccolo Machiavelli, Carl von Clausewitz, Abraham Lincoln, Winston Churchill, and, in our times, to Raymond Aron—a humane scholar who in dangerous times defied the intellectual dishonesty of many fashionable theorists.

WAR

INTRODUCTION

ARMA VIRUMQUE CANO—"Of arms and the man I sing." Thus Virgil began his *Aeneid*, recounting the splendor and excitement of the founding of Rome in war.

Our book does not celebrate epic heroism, much less war. Rather, it addresses the generic properties of war—its causes, character, and conclusions. We may thus preface it: "Of arms and the man we study." But why study war? Our answer begins with the one that John Adams, among America's first statesmen, gave to his wife during the American Revolution:

> I must study politics and war, that my sons may have liberty to study mathematics and philosophy, geography, natural history, and naval architecture, navigation, commerce and agriculture, in order to give their children a right to study painting, music, architecture, statuary, tapestry and porcelain.

But Adams ignored an eternal question that realists might then have posed to him: "What knowledge of war should his grandchildren require when, as legatees of the comforts, safety, and endowments that Adams's generation had won for them, they spend much of their time studying the higher and gentler arts?" How long would this cruel world allow a people of painters and porcelainmakers to enjoy themselves freely if it had also forgotten the art of war that had made possible that refined way of life? If Adams had read back into the wisdom of the Renaissance, he might have come upon an inscription that the Commonwealth of Venice—tiny, rich, and independent for one thousand years—engraved upon its armory:

> Happy is the city which in time of peace thinks of war.

This book means to reintroduce a generation of Americans that has come to think of peace as its birthright to thoughts about war: why nations fight, what happens to them when they do, how they fight, and how they make peace.

For Whom We Write

This book is not written for strategic theorists, military professionals, or historians who devote themselves to the nature of organized violence and its relation to politics. It is written for a generation of Americans whom the absence of the military draft has trained to live as if military matters were a spectator sport, whose popular culture gives the impression that violence belongs exclusively to the past or to lower forms of life, and whose university curricula make it well-nigh impossible to put one's self in the shoes of history's protagonists—or of those caught in the middle. This book would not be understood in the Communist world or in much of the Third World, where violence is endemic and discourse on this subject is deformed or nonexistent. It would be superfluous in, say, Switzerland or Israel, where personal involvement in military matters goes hand in hand with sober discourse, as it would have been superfluous in America prior to the 1950s. But in the magic kingdom of modern upper-middle-class American life, it is as necessary as it was two thousand years ago for the slave who sat behind the conquering hero in Rome's triumphal processions and whispered in his ear: "All glory is fleeting." We write to break the spell of ignorance about war and to bring some of the least palatable aspects of reality into contemporary American minds through the gentle medium of the printed page lest someday these aspects intrude of their own accord.

When Adams's colleague, Thomas Jefferson, put forward the case for liberal education in America, and founded the University of Virginia, he defined that education as one that would "enable every man to judge for himself what will secure or endanger his freedom." He certainly meant to include the military arts in his curriculum. He did not think that the American Revolution had implanted liberty once and for all, but rather that the tree of liberty must be perpetually watered by the blood of patriots and tyrants. The authors of this book agree with him, as also with Adams and the wise Venetians: knowledge of the necessary conditions for human freedom entails an appreciation of the nature of war because freedom can only be enjoyed by people ready, willing, and able to fight for it.

Knowledge of war is especially required in peacetime, just as knowledge of surgery and disease are most fruitfully gathered in good health. Neglecting war's somber reality as a tool of political leaders, or rejecting it as an unmentionable reversion to barbarism, or disregarding it as an apocalyptic threat to biological survival ignores one of the constituent parts of politics. People overlook such basic features of reality only at their own peril.

Our Context

In 1985, Europeans and Americans commemorated the fortieth anniversary of the end of World War II. At that time, some observers, in wonder, pointed out that not since the long Victorian era had this world so long been spared the scourge of general war. They had the advantage of hindsight; the "general peace," commencing in 1945, also had been what John F. Kennedy in 1961 described as a "long twilight struggle." Others before and since have called it the Cold War, "neither war nor peace" or "low intensity warfare." This peace, this absence of general war, has been jolted many times by thunderclaps of crisis, and accompanied by many "peripheral wars," of which the Korean and Vietnamese conflicts—vivid in American memories—have been but two. The daily newspapers carry stories of American servicemen blown up in their bunks and of American civilians kidnapped and murdered on airlines, on the high seas, or in foreign capitals by people who choose to make war on us. War has been no stranger to us in our time of long peace.

More ominous than even this loss of life is the disappearance during this long period of the older traditions and distinctions concerning the relationship of war and peace that the intellectual heritage formerly passed on to generations of future leaders. Meanwhile, the furious clashes of our time between incompatible ideologies about how we shall live our lives, between totalitarian and free societies, have formed the background of our uneasy existence. In this twilight zone of discomfort and uncertainty, the navies, armies, and air forces of the contending powers watch each other warily, even as their proxies, and their proxies' proxies, wage fitful and inconclusive battles. Perhaps the most dangerous feature of this condition of no peace, no war has been the confusion generated in democracies. In particular, this strange condition has spawned unrealistic ideas that have gained uncritical acceptance: Nuclear war is unimaginable; limited conventional war is unwinnable; yet stalemate is unacceptable. Thus, anyone who wishes to serve the cause of civic freedom and peace in recent years has found precious few intellectual tools that might serve his purpose.

Our book is inspired by the thought that the potential destructiveness of modern war has obviated neither the lessons of past wars, their political origins and outcomes, the general relationships between war and peace, nor the particular relationship among war, strategy, and politics. Clausewitz, in his On War, made much of the idea of the "fog of war," which beclouds those who wage it. We write about war's "unthinkable" but all too real nature so that the fog of ignorance shall not blind citizens who must make decisions about war and peace—and who must live with the consequences.

What, then, do we believe our generation—especially its young men—must know about war? First, they must be able to see through the post-Vietnam movies and slogans that make it impossible to understand how anyone could ever willingly put himself in a position to kill or be killed. An ineluctable fact is that human intercourse all too naturally produces circumstances in which reasonable people regard kill or be killed as the best option available.

War is hell. Nobody doubts that. War means death, destruction of families, cold, hunger, and the subjection to harsh authority. So why is so much of mankind at war? One answer is that peace is no picnic. The very evils we associate with war have fallen upon mankind more fully in times and places well removed from battlefields and in conditions conventionally called peace. Especially in this century, the victims of peace outnumber the victims of war.[1]

Perhaps 35 million people, of whom 25 million were civilians, have died as a direct consequence of military operations since 1900. These people have been killed by armies, navies, and air forces using the latest equipment and techniques. The soldiers who died this way suffered before their demise as well as during the final minutes. Nonetheless, they not only had a fighting chance, but their governments were also making at least some efforts to keep them comfortable. Even civilian victims were afforded some measure of protection.

During the same period, however, at least 100 million human beings have been killed by police forces or their equivalent, almost never using heavy weapons but relying on hunger, exposure, barbed wire, and forced labor to kill the bulk, executing the rest by shooting them with small arms, by rolling over them with trucks (a favorite technique in China around 1950), by gassing them, or, as in the Cambodian holocaust of 1975–79, by smashing their skulls with wooden clubs. These 100 million usually suffered for months or years before the end and perhaps suffered most of all by their help-lessness in the face of monstrous acts committed against them and their families. Those who killed these 100 million men, women, and children did not have to overcome resistance, much less armed resistance. Because the victims could not (while others would not) make war on their own behalf, the killers did their killing in peace. Regardless of whether the victims were Armenians, Jews, Tutsis, Ukrainians, Chinese, or Cambodians, the stories of these historic horrors of peace are very similar.

Our Argument

One of the primordial causes of war is fear of this kind of peace. One does not have to stand on the threshold of a gas chamber or watch one's family starve on a train to Siberia to prefer combat to the absence thereof. From time immemorial people have learned that if they did not take up arms and risk their lives in battle, quick death or mild slavery was the best fate they could expect. On the other hand, another major motive for war has been the desire of some men to gain the opportunity to slaughter other men peacefully. Men have sought battle not just for the glory and profit of victory but also to satisfy deep hatred. The tendency to think of combat strictly as a means of killing or subjugating your neighbor before he does it to you has been the rule rather than the exception in history.

Second, people do not fight only for self-preservation. They also do it out of love for some things (or people) and out of hate for others. The serious student must recognize that the popular American playground slogan "fighting never solves anything" is a historical howler. In fact, for better or for worse, the great issues regarding how men ought to live have been settled by war. Had the battle of Poitiers gone the other way, Europe would have become part of the Islamic world. Arabic rather than Latin would have been the language of courts and universities in Europe, and all subsequent history would have been about struggles very different from the ones that actually occurred. English, French, and Spanish rather than Arabic became the languages of business and culture from Manila to Bombay, from Mombasa to Dakar and Buenos Aires, because the nations of Western Europe first defeated Islam in Europe, then in Asia and Africa. Thus they secured for themselves the chance to defeat the tribes of the New World. Later, the fate of aristocracy in Europe was sealed by the Napoleonic wars, just as surely as Negro slavery was terminated by the American Civil War and Nazism by World War II. Indeed, military force is one expression of a myriad of moral, intellectual, political, and economic arrangements. But history teaches that if any given set of these factors cannot produce military victory, that set of factors, that complex of civilization, has a high chance of disappearing.

This leads us to refute a third misunderstanding; namely, that a nation's survival depends on the "ultimate" military capacity inherent in such measurable quantities as the size, health, wealth, and technical skill of its population. No doubt "potential" is always important. But, by itself, potential never wins wars. Wars are won or lost, nations live or die, primarily by the people's willingness to fight, their ability to impose discipline on themselves, and their readiness to subordinate themselves to chiefs who know what they are doing, thereby turning potential into actual force at the right place at the right time. The early Roman Republic was inferior to its enemies, especially to the Etruscans, in size, economic strength, and sophistication. Culturally, it did not exist. Yet it was rich beyond measure in the public spiritedness of all its citizens and in the military skill of its leaders. For this reason, it was able to conquer many nations which were superior to it in other ways. The late Roman Empire, by contrast, was incomparably superior to its enemies by every measurable factor. Culturally, the barbarians were just that. But when Alaric's Goths broke through the maldeployed border legions, the rabble and leading citizens of the Imperial capital did not have in them the feats of arms that their republican ancestors had performed when the barbarian chief, Brenner, and Hannibal the Carthaginian had presented even greater military challenges. So Rome died. Its wealth, which could not buy military salvation, was carted away.

Accordingly, we correct the popular view that military power is something a nation can buy—like health care or transportation. In fact, military service is less like a commodity and more like filial love. People—especially in peacetime—may be paid to go through the motions of military service. But there is not enough money in the world to cause a man to push himself purposely through the hell of war. History shows that Machiavelli was correct: mercenary armies will usually ruin a nation both when they lose and when they win. In the end, people fight for themselves.

This leads us to our fifth point: The widely held view that wars arise out of certain sets of circumstances—arms races, economic competition, crises, and so forth—resembles more the medieval view that maggots originate from filth than it does truth. In fact, when people do not fight for self-preservation they fight for causes —causes that are espoused so strongly that they overcome the natural instinct against sacrificing one's children as well as one's self. These causes of war range from the extreme of trying to establish the Kingdom of God on earth to the extreme of, in Shakespeare's words, quarreling over the length of a straw. The final refutation of those theories which describe causes of war as sub-rational is the fact that whenever men want others to fight they speak to persuade them that what they are doing is necessary and worthy. Only when this persuasion is successful will their audience espouse their cause.

Because wars are started and fought by complex human beings for complex human motives, we argue against the view of modern social science which holds that either the onset or the outcome of wars can somehow be predetermined if enough facts are fed into computers. In fact, history's clearest teaching about war is its utter unpredictability. A war that proceeds from beginning to end as its initiators planned is perhaps the rarest of phenomena. War's unpredictability results from a set of complex, interactive factors. Soldiers and equipment on both sides always perform either better or worse than planned. The ever-present stratagems, deception, and surprise, sometimes backfire. Above all, as each side reacts to threats and opportunities, they create new ones. Sometimes things go as foreseen in the military realm, but the unfolding of events changes the purposes, the personnel, and even the political character of the parties. In this "fog" of war, the winners are those who combine flexible minds with inflexible will—and who have luck on their side.

We show that, amongst all the uncertainties of war—including new weapons—the principles of military operations have not changed through the centuries. They can be summed up in General Nathan Forrest's dictum "get there the fustest with the mostest." While over the ages men have sought recipes for successful military operations, we show that there is none, and that to seek them is to invite disaster. Any and every conventional stratagem, from "taking the high ground" to "exploiting a break in the enemy lines" can make for success or for failure, depending on one's capacity to make something of it. The only rule is that there is no rule—only the pressing need to size up a constantly changing situation, while making the most imaginative use of the forces at one's command. There is, however, one exception to the rule: surprise. It can turn the weak into the strong, and conversely, can make the strong into the unchallengeable.

Another of the principles of warfare unaffected by the centuries is that the destructiveness of war depends on the intentions of the warriors rather than on the tools at their disposal. It is sobering for us in the nuclear age to remember that genocide was routine in the ancient world, and that the great slaughters of our time have been carried out with decidedly low-tech means. Moreover, whereas the first target of nuclear weapons, Hiroshima, is today a thriving city, Carthage was erased forever by fire, sword, and Roman plows followed by men spreading salt. We argue that nuclear weapons have become useful only as advances in miniaturization and delivery vehicles have made them smaller and more accurate—less indiscriminately destructive and much more lethal to their intended military targets. In other words, they are useful insofar as they can help to achieve the common-sense purpose of war: victory. In the nuclear age (or any other) only peculiarly unmilitary minds can confuse destruction with victory. It also takes a peculiarly unmilitary mind to confuse high-technology weapons with military effectiveness. We show that nuclear weapons are not scarecrows but tools, the existence of which requires modern commanders to think, move, and shoot faster than ever before. In short, modern technology gives military commanders perhaps more options than ever before to achieve decisive results with low-collateral damage.

We maintain that low-technology or low-intensity conflicts are not inherently more or less effective than their high-tech counterparts in producing victory. While it is commonplace in post-Vietnam America to think of special operations—guerrilla warfare and the like—as the invincible tool of our time, we argue that, like every other kind of operation, its usefulness depends on its coordination with other measures and, above all, on circumstances. Light, mobile, chaos-causing forces in the enemy's rear are as useful today as they were when they rode on horses. Troops specially trained for sabotage, coups de main, or rescue missions can affect the outcome of wars. The raising of native forces in enemy country is an art essentially unchanged since ancient times. But we show that, contrary to popular opinion, the success of such forces nearly always depends on what happens at the front. In other words, we insist that special operations, like nuclear weapons, infantry divisions, and the orders and arguments that form armies and direct them are *parts* of war that should not be mistaken for the whole.

Knowledge itself is only a part of war. Thus, we demystify the role of intelligence. Intelligence is the discovery of facts that may be useful in conflict. Of course, any party to any conflict that knows a great deal about the other's weaknesses and plans while hiding its own has the chance to create the most decisive event of war: surprise. But in war superior knowledge does not necessarily imply sound judgment, any more than in Greek philosophy knowledge implies virtue. In war, as in other human activities, the more competent an individual the less information he will require in order to act as he should. That is often because excellent people impose their agenda on others by taking the initiative. Weak decision makers, for their part, never seem to have enough information—perhaps because they want the situation to dictate their decisions. They often get their wish! We also point out that nations and armed forces on the defensive, wondering where and how the enemy's blows will fall, need far more intelligence than those who have the luxury of choosing where to concentrate their initiatives. In war as in other activities knowledge is but one constituent part of judgment. The analysis of intelligence—for example, the process of judging the significance of facts—must be part of the larger process of strategic judgment. That is the intellectual process that ties together the ends sought, the means at hand, and the circumstances.

Perhaps the most important connection between ends and means is moral. Contrary to what many believe, not all combatants stand on the same moral plane, and the difference in moral status depends on far more than who struck the first blow. It depends upon a combination of the relative justice of each side's quarrel and of the proportion between the goodness of the ends pursued and the harm done in their pursuit. Of course nothing ever sanctions the use of means that are unjust in themselves, such as deliberately harming innocents. Such a failure to discriminate between combatants and noncombatants is morally inexcusable. We show that while it is counterproductive to try to meld these guidelines into enforceable laws—especially ex post facto, as at the Nuremberg trials—the guidelines do help us to go beyond mere opinions about right and wrong, or at least between better and worse. We also affirm that these objective moral standards for judging wars and combatants are as valid in the nuclear age as ever before. This is because, contrary to popular opinion, modern technology permits at least as much discrimination as ever in warfare, and because the differences in the moral stature of the potential nuclear combatants is as great as any that has ever existed.

Since war (insofar as it is not madness or mere tribal conflict) is the clash of different moral standards, we agree with Clausewitz that violent means are rightly the mere servants of political considerations. Nevertheless, we maintain that any attempt to resolve definitively the natural tension between the demands of military operations and those of political authority is fraught with danger. Both sets of demands are legitimate in their own right. When, as in World War I, a General Ludendorff dictates to the ministry of the interior, the results are as bad as when, during the Vietnam War, a President Johnson picks bombing targets. On one hand, the art of politics in wartime consists of guiding military operations without in any way fouling up military logic. It is difficult to find historical examples of military failures leading to political successes. On the other hand, part of the general's art consists of keeping his military choices in the perspective of the war's purposes and of the nation's good.

By a similar token, we argue that the essence of war consists of the political decision that a given cause is worth killing and sacrificing for. The means chosen to further that cause may be unbloody. Planting information in the right places in an enemy country and fanning the subsequent flames, using agents of influence to tear down some and build up others in the enemy camp, using one's power in international markets to affect an enemy's economy— none of these measures will necessarily spill blood. Nevertheless, they can be real measures of warfare if they are pursued as such. We insist on a caveat, however: there is a misconception in contemporary America that the unbloody arts of political influence are a substitute for a lack of willingness to push military operations to victory. Nothing could be further from the truth. The effect of political warfare depends almost exclusively on the assumption by everyone involved that it is part of an open-ended commitment to victory.

Because war involves the commitment of so much, and applies so much stress to society, it is often the midwife of social change. Nevertheless, we challenge the widespread view that war necessarily brings about revolutions, or that it tends to produce more authoritarian governments. In fact, wars usually accentuate or bring to the fore features or possibilities already present in a given society. The most characteristic thing about any society is how it manages to squeeze blood and treasure out of itself. No one can tell how this will affect any given society. DeGaulle pointed out that war is the "gravedigger of decadence." On one hand, war acts like a windstorm against a tree whose roots no longer grip the earth. On the other hand, as the blood and treasure flow, they can form wholly new roots so that a new tree grows to replace the old one. One of the primary threads of our civilization resulted from European kings progressively enfranchising their societies out of a practical need to gain support for war.

Of course, the effect of any war depends to a large extent on whether a nation wins or loses. The trauma of defeat may or may not linger, but it surely comes all at once. Streets are filled with the country's own defeated soldiers who are hungry, bitter, and dispirited, and also with the winner's men, all of whom are outside the law. At best they will search out and kill or deport or restrict only a few of those associated with the losing regime. But they are free to do whatever they please, and the normal behavior of conquerors is for the worse. Then there are refugees and economic dislocations. Hunger and disease are usually there too. In this atmosphere, the never-ending struggle for primacy takes on a truly Hobbesian cast. The spectacular rebirths of West Germany and Japan under kind conquerors are the exceptions to history's rule: don't ever lose a war!

Finally, we point out that the end of war is not necessarily the kind of peace in which everyone lives happily ever after. For example, looking at the Versailles treaty of 1919, Marshal Foch declared: "This is not peace. This is an armistice for twenty years." And so it turned out to be. When a war does not pronounce final judgment on its causes, the result is a *bellus interruptus* rather than peace. Furthermore, when the winner thinks that he can secure his wishes only by killing or imprisoning the losers, as in the case of the Soviet Union and communist movements such as Cambodia's Khmer Rouge, the result is the peace of the penitentiary, or the peace of the dead. But as Machiavelli pointed out five hundred years ago, unless the enemy people are thoroughly destroyed, their children will remember their parents' fate and will wait for the winner to stumble. This is not what people usually mean by peace either. Rather, peace is a kind of satisfaction or tranquility in the order of things. What the losers will and won't be satisfied with depends in part on the winners' readiness to resume the war. But as long-term winners have always known, peace also means an order under which a given people can live in a way that more or less satisfies their essential needs. Yet no peace is permanent, and nothing so surely guarantees war as dissatisfaction with contingency and the attempt to establish perpetual peace.

In sum, war is not a nightmare. It is far more fearsomely real than that. Nor has the world outgrown it, as it has outgrown horses and buggies. Today's world is filled with more people animated by greater hatred and possessed of more means to make war than ever before. It is sobering to realize how well armed even some impoverished countries are. For example, Syria has more tanks (about 2,500) than France (about 1,000).[2] Indeed, it has about one-fourth as many as the United States. Across the Third World, from India to Cuba to Tanzania, well over a billion people live under governments that tend to be bellicose, some of which have accumulated, per capita, more guns, tanks, and airplanes than the United States and its allies. For example, Syria, with fewer than ten million people, has over 2,500 tanks, while the United States with 250 million has fewer than 12,000. The Syrians have eight times as many tanks per capita as Americans. Indeed, Syria has about as many tanks as West Germany, which has six times Syria's population. Nor is Syria unusual. South Yemen has only two million people, but 450 tanks. Meticulous comparison confirms common sense: Countries with Marxist, Islamic, or military governments devote more of their resources to war material than countries governed otherwise.[3] While not all Third World countries have more arms per capita than the United States, even those that do not have huge numbers of men under arms—Vietnam has 2.8 million. Our point is simple. There are a lot of men in the world with guns pointing the wrong way.

This mass of humanity lives in squalor and brutality that is difficult for Americans to imagine. For most of mankind, life is cheap. For example, in 1987–88 India "pacified" northern Sri Lanka at the cost of perhaps ten thousand lives. Ethiopia continues to kill its citizens by the uncounted hundreds of thousands. At least half a million have perished since 1981. Tiny Mozambique has snuffed out about 400,000 lives—about the same number killed in the Iran-Iraq war. All told, during 1987 fully twenty-five wars were raging, and the toll of human beings killed *since 1945* was some seventeen million.[4]

Furthermore, over the past generation this overarmed, under-scrupled mass of humanity has been saturated with print media, radios, and televisions that have sharpened and focused hate. The "information revolution" has done everything but pacify the hearts of men. Also, it is most important to note that when "third world" media have whipped up hatred against this or that nearby target, they have often indicted the United States as the archvillain of the situation, the party ultimately responsible for the evil that must be rooted out here and now. America's image as the best-fed nation in the history of mankind has proved to be a successful thorn for rous-ing hateful envy, as has the fact that the Americans make up about 5 percent of the world's population but consume about one-third of what the world produces. But of course since the propaganda does not mention that America produces more of value than it consumes, surely shortcomings in one's life must be due to America's super-abundance, and vice versa! As a result, there is no shortage in the world of people who lack only the opportunity to wage war against the United States. Whether or not they will get such opportunities, and what might come of them, should be a matter of reasonable concern.

Then, of course, there is the Soviet Union and its bloc of captive allies, such as East Germany, and kindred regimes like Vietnam, South Yemen, Nicaragua, and so on. The people who run these regimes rest their very legitimacy on the idea that they must some-how put an end to "bourgeois society," and especially its bastion, the United States. This is not the place to estimate Soviet power or day-to-day intentions. Suffice it to say that the power is consider-able, that it has grown steadily in relation to our own, and that the Soviet leaders, not we, will decide if and when to use it. Thus, because like the medieval Venetians, or the Swiss, or the Israelis, we are something of a small island in unfriendly seas, we should learn to think at least a bit like them about military matters.

It would indeed be ostrich-like for Americans to fail to consider what *kind* of peace we could expect in an increasingly hostile world, or what kind of war such a peace might force on us, or how we might arrest or reverse a hostile trend, and what role violence might play in our doing so. Surely we will live the kind of life that we are willing and able to fight for. This raises a host of specific questions: Who among us will fight (not just serve in peacetime armed forces, but actually bleed), and what will we as a society have to do to earn that service? What concrete threats or opportunities will we consider sufficient "causes" for which to put ourselves through the hell of war? We know it will not do to wait to bestir ourselves until enemy missiles have struck, or until invasion fleets appear off our beaches. But what *will* do? And if we do fight, whom do we kill, and why? It would be silly to follow the models of the 1960s and blindly strike out against the enemy's cities. But if not, then how do we bring the war to a close? What kind of knowledge of the enemy must we have? Good intelligence would help, but it cannot dictate what we want to accomplish or provide the means for accomplishing it. This requires material preparation, strategic planning, and moral reasoning lest we do more harm than good. Of course, the American people have available a variety of economic and political instruments of conflict. But how do we employ them so that they will have their intended effect and not, as when the United States used them to try to oust Panama's drug-dealing dictator, simply convey weakness and bring ridicule? Above all, what kind of peace are we after, and what are we willing to do to get it?

To put such realities out of mind is akin to the way in which some people deal with the fact that each of us will die: by living as if it weren't so, even though deep down we all know that we eventually must deal with it. Denial only guarantees that the unpleasant reality will find one unprepared. In this sense, war is worse than death. Our denial of death may spoil whatever life there is thereafter. Yet once death strikes us, our ability to affect events will have ceased. At least we cease being responsible. But denial of war could lead us to a hell on earth, perhaps the worst feature of which would be that we would have to continue to make choices and suffer consequences. Those who imagine that the coming of nuclear war would end all life—if not in the twinkling of an eye then in a few weeks—let themselves off too easily. In fact, perhaps the most frightening feature of "the day after" the onset of a nuclear war would be that nearly all of us would read about it in the newspaper, watch the accounts on TV, and then have to face a host of thoughts that most of us had never entertained before. We would survive to suffer the consequences of our own thoughtlessness.

It stands to reason that a people who—rightly—wants very much to live in peace reduces the chances of maintaining the peace or of quickly reestablishing it exactly in relation to its failure to understand the real difference between war and peace, how wars start, how they are conducted, how they affect society, and how they end. To conduct international politics without having a realistic, practical image of the ultimate sanction of such politics is a bit like conducting flirtations while innocent of sex and all its consequences.

By writing this book, two professors try to educate in a subject that many think obscene. We agree that the subject matter is shocking. But if citizens of a great democracy shun it, we thereby deliver control of our future to tyrants inured to it.

Peace, War, and the Unity of Mankind

Peace and war flow from contrasting desires in the hearts of men. What visions of peace in the bush can lead one to give up the peace at hand? What are the moral and political consequences of any given choice to fight or not to fight? Such questions have arisen only within Western civilization—and then only since about the year 500 B.C. Prior to the Socratics in Greece and the Prophets of Israel—and even in our day in other civilizations—human beings have lived by the tribal mentality, according to which people belonging to other tribes may be as useful as fish or cattle, but are much more dangerous. In tribal languages, the name of one's own tribe is typically the same as the word for "people." The tribe's relations to others is typically the same as with wild animals that may be captured and domesticated, perhaps eaten, and certainly defended against. For example, even though Arabs have been sophisticated by Islam for over a thousand years, their language still reflects tribal practices: the word for "black person," *iswid*, is the very word for "slave." We call this state of things war. Most of the world's peoples typically do not call it anything. That's just the way things are.

The distinction between peace and war exists fully in the West because only the West fully draws the consequences of the distinction between the human and nonhuman: namely, human equality. Tribal culture does not inculcate thoughts, habits, or scruples that might restrain behavior toward foreigners. On the contrary, war against other tribes is something of a duty owed to the gods of one's own hearth.[5]

In addition, war against other tribes served practical purposes. It provided land, goods, and slaves. The essence of tribal war is to conquer a territory and to kill or sell all those inhabitants one does not wish to use as slaves. The Spartans, for example, conquered their spot on earth from the Helots, whom they kept as slaves. Each new king of Sparta began his reign by redeclaring war on the Helots.

Only when what came to be known as Western or Judeo-Christian civilization gradually accepted that, as one formulation put it, all men are created equal did this civilization come to deem armed hostility a departure from the normal state of peace, a departure that only good reasons could render legitimate. For St. Augustine and for the entire Christian tradition that has followed, the primary purpose of government is the maintenance of peace.[6] The classic Christian title for the ruler is *Defensor Pacis*, the defender of the peace. The Christian tradition approves of war under a variety of circumstances. But it leaves no doubt that war is an aberration to be justified in detail, contrary to a standing presumption in favor of peace. Hence Western literature has always been full of people agonizing over the moral claims of waging war or making peace. Surely no traditional Chinese or Indian manual of statecraft ever agonized over the legitimacy—as opposed to the prudence—of attacking a neighboring principality or of oppressing foreigners. Thus, peace, the kind characterized by people treating each other more or less as they would like to be treated, is the peculiar and hard-won creature of Western minds.

Although that creation is chock full of ancient Jewish and Greek elements, its synthesis is very peculiarly Christian. The Christian tradition values peace so highly because peace is conducive to spiritual life. Spiritual life, in turn, is of overriding importance because of the Christian imperative of saving one's immortal soul. Because that imperative bears on every individual, temporal quarrels between groups become inherently less important, and peace becomes the primordial goal of statecraft.

This line of reasoning is shared by no other tradition. Our nearest intellectual neighbor, the Muslim tradition, though it recognizes the brotherhood of all men under God, defines peace as the state proper *only among the Umma,* the believers in Islam. Nonbelievers, by definition, live in *Dar al Harb*—literally, the place of war.[7] It is proper for Muslims to cut back this realm by the sword.

The bulk of mankind, though, lives under neither the Christian nor the Islamic tradition. China's billion were never Westernized. India's near-billion, along with the bulk of the world's former western colonies from Borneo to Zanzibar, acquired only a patina of Western elements. As Western influence recedes around the world, it is increasingly undeniable that in most of Africa, much of the Middle East, and in some of Asia, the Western slogans spoken by political leaders reflect Western culture much less than they do a barely scratched tribal ethic: the boundaries of humanity do not extend much beyond the tribes.[8] The one Western modification to this ethic widely accepted in the Third World is itself a corruption of the Western tradition: The boundaries of humanity do not extend beyond one's own *party.*

In this century we have become accustomed to thinking of total war (mass violence aimed at eliminating, enslaving, or driving out alien populations) as a modern phenomenon. It actually is a return to a practice that was routine before Greeks and Jews separately discovered that there was such a thing as mankind. Today it is all too easy to realize that, even in the West, the distinction between peace and war is fragile. But few have stopped to examine the ideas that gnaw away at the Western notion of mankind, and hence at the war/peace distinction. Five centuries ago, Machiavelli began to impress on generations of rulers, would-be rulers, and shapers of minds the image of the successful modern man, emancipated from Christian civilization. This man's mind, if not his body, is always engaged in what fashion nowadays calls a violent zero-sum game, that is, a contest for primacy in which the need to kill in order to live is ever present. When Machiavelli's paragon of modern virtue is riding in the countryside, he asks himself and his friends what they would do if this or that enemy appeared on a hill. When this modern man looks at any other man, he considers him his potential assassin, his potential victim, or the potential executioner of his enemies. Thomas Hobbes followed. Dispensing with Italian subtleties, he taught that what Machiavelli had counseled to the few was nothing but the "state of nature" in which all of us necessarily live, the state of war by all against all: *homo homini lupus*—man the natural predator of other men.

The illustrious modern thinkers who have purveyed similar views are legion. Indeed, much of the modern intellectual tradition intends to liberate man from the "Christian fairy tale" that all men are equally God's children, that human compatibility is the natural law, and that peace is the mandate of God. Thus, the primary challenge to the Western understanding of peace comes from within the Western tradition itself. Many modern Westerners have shed all spiritual concerns and have adopted mentalities—if not yet lifestyles—according to which absolutely all human intercourse is, by rigid definition, a form of war.

The most popular of these modern mentalities is Marxism, taught at every university in the Western world—usually implicitly. Karl Marx teaches that the history of human relations must be necessarily that of the exploitation of those who do not control the means of production by those who do. Friedrich Engels's *The Origins of the Family, Private Property and the State* argues that the relationship of parents and children in all societies that have ever existed—never mind the relationship between husband and wife—is necessarily one of mutual exploitation unto death. The only question that Marxists can consider about any human relationship whatever is who can manage to live off whom. Marx argues that this dialectic of oppression must culminate in rule by the proletariat. In his *Critique of the Gotha Programme*, Marx says that because the proletariat is so numerous and its demands are so many, its oppression of other classes will be so heavy and thorough that it will end all oppression by crushing the other classes out of existence, physically and in every other way.[9]

Of course Marxism is far from an anomaly on the modern Western intellectual scene. There are various species of social Darwinists, including some conservatives. They believe that fitness is the only right to survival and that they are among the fittest. Whether they believe that the inferior will sell themselves or be sold by others is less important than their acceptance of life as a struggle in which one's gain is another's loss. They therefore fall into what Abraham Lincoln called the primordial political sin, one form or another of the maxim: "You work, I'll eat." The most recent and virulent example of this was the Nazi effort to forcefully and literally harness the "lower beings" of Eastern Europe and to murder those they deemed too low even for slavery.

The modern world is also filled with social movements that, although they do not have the power to unleash holocausts, nevertheless spread the "bad news" of the incompatibility of interests, the natural unsociability of man. Whether the "cause" is supposed to be sex or vanishing natural resources, the question posited by such movements is the same: how to make certain that the "right" people ride in the lifeboat and the "wrong" people are in the water. For people who think like this, the imperatives of race, party, or even sex wholly obscure the bonds even of kinship—never mind those of mere humanity. For many of these modernists, no less than for Marxists, Shi'ites, or primitive tribesmen, the only question is how best to wage the war that is life.

Furthermore, even people who sincerely adhere to the tenets of Western civilization tend to cast them aside when they are overcome by hate and when the issue at hand seems to be more important than anything else. This also happens when long periods of war cause loss of perspective. The dynastic struggles of the Hundred Years' War, the constant strife between the Italian cities during the Renaissance, the devastation of Germany after the Reformation, and the continental war during the generation following the French Revolution are poignant reminders that even people well schooled in the distinction between war and peace, and who sincerely avow a preference for peace, can let constant war become a way of life and thus become inured to atrocity. Habit and trend are as influential on the ways of war and peace as they are in all other human affairs.

One of the passages of history that has drawn the most nods over the centuries is Thucydides' account of how the Peloponnesian War gradually changed the habits and expectations of all Greece so that violence toward both foreigners and countrymen became frequent and normal.[10] People's willingness to blur the distinction between war and peace, their willingness to wage war, and the vehemence with which they fight stem from their habits, from desires or fears, and from their intellectual landscape.

We are conscious that the Western distinction between peace and war is a minority opinion in the world, that it is accepted but misunderstood in much of the West, and that the philosophic bases of that tradition are anything but popular in Western universities. Nevertheless, we use this distinction as the basis of our discussion not just because it is a bastion of our civilization, but also because it can explain both itself and much of the political and historical landscape. For a variety of reasons, nothing else on the intellectual landscape can do that.

PART I

How Wars Start

CHAPTER

1

THE MEANING OF
WAR AND PEACE

It is not that they love peace less, but that they love
their kind of peace more.

—SAINT AUGUSTINE
City of God

PEOPLES define themselves by the kinds of peace they live and
the kinds of war they fight. The Civil War, so goes an old saw, is the
most typical event in American history. It was the event that
showed most clearly the issues that make American society what it
is. One of the issues is the conflict between liberty and equality.
Another is the battle between those who try to exclude others from
equal protection under the law—and those who rally under the
banner, "all men are created equal." What is the relationship of this
country's parts to its whole? To what extent should race, age, or lack
of power affect how people are treated? What can be bought and
sold, and what cannot? In the 1860s, just like at the time of the
constitutional convention, and just like today, these issues were
fought out in the context of commercial interest and religious fervor.

The American people have fought nine major wars lasting a total
of twenty-five years and have lived through two hundred years of
social change. Yet never were the inner seams of this national
structure so clearly on display as when they were strained to the
breaking point between 1861 and 1865, forcing people out of comfort-

able ambiguity to bet their lives on which of their country's aspects they wanted to predominate.

Two contrasting sets of views about these matters had grown up within the northern and southern parts of this country since well before the War of Independence. Each part of the country was at peace with itself about the choice it had made. Indeed, had either side lacked this internal peace or coherence, they could not have organized themselves to fight. Thus, the war was fought as if two different nations were involved. The American people can be grateful for this. Had the adversaries been interspersed, the seriousness of the issues might have produced an even more frightful slaughter. As time passed, the contrast sharpened as each side tried to prejudice the other's future to the point that Lincoln noted, "a house divided against itself cannot stand."

War as the Ultimate Election

Both the practical and the moral consequences of any war depend in substantial part on the purposes for which it is fought. So, incidentally, does the war's ferocity. Why were wars in eighteenth-century Europe such courtly affairs while at the same time battles between tribes along most of the coast of Africa were depopulating vast areas? While the Europeans were fighting to decide whose flag would fly over a particular province, the African tribes of that time were fighting over which would sell the others to Arab slave wholesalers. Why, during World War II did German (never mind Italian) units easily surrender to American units but resist Soviet units much more strenuously? Undeniably, because the character of the United States, and hence the nature of the war with the United States, were such that any reasonable German could expect better treatment from the Americans than from the Russians. The Germans knew that regardless of Hitler's global rhetoric, their war with the Soviet Union meant something substantially different from their war with the United States. By the same token, why did the fighting of the Christian crusades so resemble the jihad that spread Islam across ten time zones? Could it be that the purposes of both these sets of wars were so similar? It stands to reason that wars fought for annihilation or survival, to impose or maintain religion, to impose or avoid slavery, to conquer or lose a province, or to gain or lose markets, will differ vastly from one another.

Yet we must note that purpose and habit by themselves do not determine the meaning of war. A war's character is the result of decisions actually taken. For example, during World War II the Soviet regime never bombed German cities even though it had murdered millions of its own citizens prior to the war and did not hesitate to destroy whole classes of innocents in occupied territories (for example, the massacre of much of the Polish officer corps in the Katyn Forest). Even today the Soviet regime pays homage to millennialist ends that sanction mass slaughter, and understands peace as the crushing of other classes' existence. By contrast, the American and British regimes, habituated to nonlethal politics and built on a nonmillennialist moral base, exterminated hundreds of thousands of innocents by deliberately bombing German and Japanese cities. Why the reversal of roles? The reason seems to be that the Soviet leadership was able to exercise enough self-discipline to pursue its wholesale barbarism by a discriminating retail approach to warfare. Soviet leaders knew that, as much as they hated the Germans, Germany's defeat would be but one step toward crushing the world's bourgeoisie. In contrast, the great democracies during the war indulged themselves in talk about wiping away the absolute evil embodied in Germany and acted accordingly.

The meaning of any war depends on how and why the people who fight it act as they do and on how they end up. War is always both the violent negation of the enemy and the violent affirmation of what one's own side is all about. War and the prospect of war demand that people bet their lives and the future of their families on one side or another of allegiances, quarrels, propositions, or faiths. Often, war is the logical end of those allegiances or quarrels. Thus, it confronts people with the consequences of their commitments. It asks: Do you *really* want to bet your life on *this*? So, from society's humblest soldier to its biggest pillar, war forces men to choose the causes to which they will or will not lend themselves.

True, the bonds of group discipline are tightest in wartime. Still, there are also many more opportunities and incentives to defeat, overthrow, or change one's own regime. The enemy usually welcomes defectors. But one does not have to resort to treason if one does not fully espouse the aims of one's own side or dislikes its

leaders. Apathy is usually quite enough to ensure that the other side
will prevail. Domestic factions are usually ready to exploit the dis-
content that always accompanies wars. Furthermore, regimes are
seldom as open to change, for better or for worse, as they are during
life-and-death struggles. In sum, because wars require the active,
enthusiastic participation of large numbers of people to resolve the
most important issues with which men deal, they are the ultimate
form of election. And wars offer unusually effective ways of register-
ing one's vote.

"What if they gave a war and nobody came?" This saying, popular
among Americans who opposed this country's war against North
Vietnam between 1965 and 1975, reflects an essential fact: wars
cannot be the private quarrels of rulers. Any ruler who runs a secret
war while his opponent campaigns for support is asking to lose both
the war and his influence over a population on whom he has imposed sacrifices without meaning. Even during the European Middle
Ages—an anomalous time in history when rulers tried to fight their
own battles personally—rulers had to convince people who would
otherwise have no interest in the quarrel to fight for their cause.
They also had to convince an even wider group of people to pay for
the war. Of course, recruiting, equipping, and paying for an army
that must fight far away requires more explanation than recruiting
an army to fight at home against invaders. But even the job of getting
people to show up for a war of home defense is not a trivial one.
True, once people are put in a situation in which they must fight for
their lives, they often fight regardless of the reasons they were put
there. Yet, sometimes being in the face of the enemy will only
heighten the sense of meaninglessness and hasten the collapse.

The act of raising and paying for armies may well be the most
typical act that any regime performs. It is the act for the performance
of which any regime must call upon the deepest allegiances it has.
Only then does it find out just how deep and sincere those allegiances are. When a regime calls upon people to leave their daily
lives for certain discomfort and possible death, it must, as the contemporary saying goes, cash in its chips. Perhaps the most distinguishing feature of any regime are the bases on which it claims
military service—the chips that it cashes in, whether they be feudal
oaths, habits, hatreds old or new, hopes, fears, appealing visions, and
so on. The problem is only superficially absent in societies that put
into the field armies composed largely of slaves or people who are
there strictly because they are compelled to be there. In such cases,

the political problem merely resides among those who drive the slaves. What if the ruler "gave a war" and the cadres didn't show up—or showed up half-heartedly? Surely the most important feature of any society is how and how well it ensures that when it does give a war, the right people show up and perform in a way that will allow the society to survive and stay independent.

Perhaps the most important questions one can ask of any society are who will fight for it? How well will they fight? What will it take to call forth this allegiance? In what form will it come forth? During the Roman republic, for example, military service was one of the privileges of citizenship. Those most responsible for making their city what it was were also most responsible for fighting its battles. They eagerly paid for their own weapons. The republic not only won its wars, but in so doing strengthened its citizens' love for the city. Rome was their life. Centuries later, vast wealth and high culture could not save the seat of the Western empire when those who counted in the city of Rome did not even think of taking sword in hand against the barbarians. Their ambitions were not the empire's.

A country's war making always reflects its society. For example, in medieval France those who counted, the mounted noblemen who were the only real "constituents" of the realm, were as eager to fight for their country as any republican Roman ever was. Indeed, they were so jealous of the right to a preferred place in combat that they relegated infantry and archery to a place on the battlefield comparable in significance to their lowly place in society. Hence, the French suffered defeat after defeat by English kings, whose zeal for combat and pride in rank did not blind them to the usefulness of longbows and pikes. The "scientific" mercenary armies of eighteenth-century Europe accurately reflected the attitude of the elite, only a small number of whom retained a taste for battle. The kings and nobles of the time played in the international arena for limited stakes, with little passion. But they, their societies, and their armies were swept away by the French Revolution's call to all men to fight for a new way of life. The armies of the French Revolution engaged the entire nation in efforts perhaps even more demanding than those of republican Rome. By 1914 the whole Western world, plus Japan, had imitated them.

But by 1914, the peoples of Europe were no longer fighting to free themselves from elites who had become parasites, nor for political independence, nor for any purpose that a detached observer would find reasonable. The stakes in their conflicts were not high by historic standards. Yet the societies of Europe were organized and psy-chologically ready to feed military organizations that would make "total efforts, regardless of cost." Thus did World War I doubly deci-mate Europe's young manhood for causes that obviously could not justify the carnage. Because the stakes in World War I were ob-viously not worth the slaughter, the proposition gained currency in Western thought that war itself is senseless and that states that make war are senseless as well. Thus, World War I and its enormous aftershock, World War II, dealt blows to the raison d'être of Euro-pean states from which they have yet to fully recover.

Today, as one looks at the wealthy societies of Europe and of European descent—societies that seemingly have everything—there are no obvious answers to the questions: What reasons might move "those who count" in these societies to fight or even to make the preparations without which an eventual decision to fight would be meaningless? Do they find in their own society any meaning, noble or base, for which they would kill or be killed? It is not a sufficient answer to say that these societies now find their meaning in peace, because this begs the question: Whose peace?

Kinds of Peace

Peace is as much an election as war is. Whereas war is a kind of movement that proceeds from dissatisfaction, peace is rest that pro-ceeds from satisfaction. But satisfaction with what? The condemned man, the slave, the stymied, the man who got half a loaf, the pillar of the community, and the conqueror each may be satisfied enough not to struggle. But what are they satisfied with? There is the satisfac-tion of communion with God, the satisfaction of the pig at the trough, of purposelessness or of purpose, of building up or of tearing down, of a fulfilled vision, of acquiescence in monstrosities, or of ceasing to care. In other words, to say that peace is the absence of fighting is to try to escape the inescapable question: What is one satisfied with? And why?

St. Augustine noted that everyone wants peace, and that every-one, however dimly, understands it as a kind of order that is generally accepted. Even the members of a gang who live by killing and robbing others expect to receive orderly forbearance from one an-- other in order to enjoy the fruits of their crimes. Augustine's point is that if anyone follows the logic of this natural desire all the way, he will end up treating others as he himself would want to be treated. But Augustine is the first to admit that people will do whatever they can to shortcut the logic of peace—to cause others to acquiesce in the order that *they* want. Still, Augustine and every other perceptive thinker and statesman has realized that force alone may only bring about the peace of the dead by exterminating another people or the peace of the prison by constantly guarding unbowed enemies. To bring about anything beyond momentary acquiescence, one must also to some extent engage the affections or habits of the people with whom one wishes to live in peace.

Different people will accept peace on different terms. For example, given the Afghan people's indomitable resistance to the Soviet Union's occupation of their country, it has become commonplace to say that the Afghans would die to the last man rather than let any foreigner rule them in any way. But this is not so. The British ruled the Afghans in the nineteenth century, never totally but with much less trouble than the Soviets. The explanation is simple. The Afghans never saw the British as a threat to what they hold dearest: Islam. Whereas the Afghans saw the British occupation as a bother that most of the time was not worth resisting, they see the Soviet occupation as a mortal threat to their immortal souls. The British for a time got most of what they wanted in Afghanistan because they wanted something that the Afghans did not so much mind giving up.

The Romans, too, made clear to those on whom they would impose peace that they did not mean to change their internal customs. This helped to establish the Pax Romana, but not without violence. After all, the customs of the various Mediterranean peoples had not included paying tribute of money and men to Rome and the indignity of hosting foreign rulers on sacred soil. Hence the Pax Romana was punctuated by revolts, such as that of the Jews in A.D. 70, which resulted in the Diaspora. The Jews were the only nation who suffered dispersion and whose culture did not die.

It is easier to impose any and all conditions on peoples who lack the intense cultural identity and religious faith of the Jews and Afghans and who lack the discipline that is necessary to face hardship. Consider the primary model of peace in the modern world drawn by Thomas Hobbes. According to Hobbes's tradition each human being is inescapably interested above all in self-preservation. All other loves, hates, hopes, and fears fade away before the fear of violent death. Such people bestow to one among themselves the absolute power of life and death over each and all strictly because they fear death at each other's hands. For such people, peace means cringing surrender to the most powerful force around, regardless of its demands, so long as it promises safety from others.

Machiavelli long ago noted how easy it is to impose one's own peace on people who are accustomed to being subjects. One need only defeat the master in one battle and he will be abandoned. Then, with the former master out of the way, the people will be satisfied with a new master, almost regardless of what he does. If the people have some reservations, Machiavelli gives us Cesare Borgia as a guide to successful pacification. First, Borgia hired a henchman named Orco to sow terror in the land. Then, to draw resentment away from himself without losing the capacity to overawe, he had Orco cut in half. The bloody mess left in a public square along with the knife, he tells us, made the people both satisfied and stupefied. This is the peace, because this is the satisfaction of people whose primary preoccupation is attachment to their own skins.

Note, however, where this sort of peace can lead. The managers of both the Soviet and Nazi extermination camps kept peace among the condemned by conspicuous cruelty and by giving the impression that those who were not killed at any given time might be allowed to live. Alas, these murderous managers had little trouble in turning tomorrow's victims into today's collaborators. Thus attachment to life, untempered by anything that might lead them to risk their lives, led millions to the slaughterhouse—the peace of the dead.

But as we have seen, some peoples are not satisfied with mere life. They will not rest in peace so long as a wrong, real or imagined, remains unrighted. This can have a variety of effects, depending on the nature of the outstanding grievances. Some peoples are in the grip of causes that cannot possibly be appeased. The Anabaptists of Renaissance times could never rest in peace because the New Jerusalem of perfection would simply not come about, regardless of how many priests and burghers they slaughtered. Real peace came to Bohemia, Munster, and other places only after the Anabaptists themselves had been killed. Similarly, real Marxists will never be able to rest in peace while alive because no matter how many "enemies of the people" they kill, the "new Communist man" is not a biological or moral possibility.

Is it possible to pacify the ideologically unpacifiable other than by killing them? Historical experience shows that if one tries to put down such ideologies solely by killing, one will fail. Ideas can be conquered only by other ideas. Thus St. Dominic, in his 13th-century campaign against the Albigensian heresy in southern France combined the sword and the sermon, as well as practical demonstrations of rightly ordered clerical and civil authority. His campaign restored peace to the region because he distinguished correctly who could and could not be convinced—and killed the latter.

Those whose dissatisfaction comes chiefly from their desire to possess more in order to enjoy themselves more are in another category. Indeed, it happens that passion's grip can be loosened easily enough by raising up obstacles to its satisfaction that would be unpleasant and dangerous to overcome. This is known as deterrence. For example, readers of Shakespeare are familiar with the process by which Henry V decided to invade France. First he wanted more domain and glory. Then he checked and found that the enterprise was feasible without undue strain. Only then did he listen to a legal-moral argument. It is clear that this argument would have had a much different impact on him had he previously judged that the enterprise would be difficult. Deterrence is like a cold shower on passion. However, a note of caution is in order. Some passions are unquenchable, and there is no guarantee that any given deterrent will quench the quenchable ones. Still, deterrence is usually an aid to reason because if any person's passion could be pursued cheaply, it would be very difficult for that person to listen to reason.

But the desire to possess more, particularly to have more glory, is sometimes so powerful that deterrence is not enough, especially when able men are involved. Napoleon, for example, was no ideologue. He simply combined so much self-confidence with his insatiable appetite for glory that no difficulty loomed large enough to deter him. This is not to say that deterrence is always the friend of reason. There are, after all, the pacifist passions: self-indulgence and fear. Contemporary American writing on war is full of loose talk about how the prospect of the use of nuclear weapons deters the Soviet Union from aggression. This is undoubtedly so to some extent. But is it not true that this same prospect hampers the free world from resisting aggression even more? Because deterrence cuts both ways, much depends on a comparison of the character of both sides' leaders.

This does not mean that those who are coolheaded will hence be pacifists. In fact, dispassionate judgment sometimes argues against fear, against being deterred from war. Also, lack of passion is no guarantee against wrong or perverse judgment. For Machiavelli, Hobbes, and the tradition that follows them, reason is a mere scout for the passions, and hence predisposes people to war. But in the classical tradition from Plato to Hooker reason goes along with a preference for the right order of things, namely justice, the state of things in which everyone gets what he deserves. Thus oriented, a man is at peace with himself and potentially with others as well.

Anyone, whether a private citizen or a ruler, who has his passions under control and his priorities in order seeks only what is rightly due to each. Once that is clear, the question of what to be at peace with becomes a matter of prudence. The right order of things is not to be made on earth, and the attempt to make it so here makes not for peace but rather for permanent dissatisfaction and unending war. How far it is possible to approach the right order of things at any given time in any given place is a prudential judgment. By making such judgments, individual men and nations each make the kinds of peace of which they are worthy.

CHAPTER
2

THE CAUSES OF WAR

Why do the nations so furiously rage together?
—Psalm 2

THE elementary question has echoed down the ages. Countless wounded and bereaved, and others simply contemplating the destruction of war have cried out: "Why?" Men have speculated about the causes of war in general and of particular wars. But *what is a cause?*

The dictionary offers two strikingly different meanings of "cause." Both answer the "why" of war. A cause, says the dictionary, is that which "produces an effect, result, or consequence." But then, it says, a cause also is "a goal or principle served with dedication and zeal." Thus, causes may be those forces, factors, and events that are supposed to drive nations into conflict. But causes also are the purposes that animate nations, that their leaders choose, and that men deem worth fighting and dying for. The fifth line of the final stanza of the "Star Spangled Banner" exemplifies the latter meaning: "Then conquer we must when our cause is just."

In our times, social scientists typically explore the *first* meaning of cause and neglect the second. This approach is deterministic. Wars happen because of a confluence of *generic* factors, however defined. The fact that individuals decide to get involved seems beside the point to these social scientists, who claim to understand protagonists better than they themselves. War is supposed to happen without anyone really wanting it. After all, how could anyone want hell? So to the extent that "factors" don't explain it, it must have been an accident.

Others, however, including practitioners of statecraft, philosophers, poets, and many historians dwell on the voluntaristic meaning of "causes." This second view focuses on what actual people want out of any given war. To them wars are contests between causes, contests which, as the Greek storyteller Homer says, destroy "the glorious deeds of men," but which nevertheless men desire not only because of base motives—envy, greed, lust, revenge—but also because they offer the chance to display noble qualities—bravery, courage, prowess, judgment, and honor. Thus, the classical scholar, F. E. Adcock, tells us of Homer's *Iliad*:

> The greatest moment of Achilles is the moment when, as the Greeks
> are being driven back after the death of Patroclus, he stands unarmed
> at the Trench, and the sound of his sole voice strikes fear into the ranks
> of Troy.[1]

There is a third alternative: Until recent times, most Westerners, like the Psalmist, have thought war to be a natural, if odious, aspect of human existence, akin to other calamities and challenges such as storms, earthquakes, famines, physical afflictions, and ultimately, mortality. The Jews of the Old Testament often described the ravages of war as Yaweh's chastisement for the transgressions of the chosen people. Christians see war as merely another manifestation of free will exercised by imperfect human beings. War arises from the same inexhaustible fountain as every other man-made ill, from robbery to adultery to fraud. This third alternative is compatible with the second, but not with the first.

A fourth type of theory has become popular most recently. Influential thinkers have come to regard war as a gruesome clinical abnormality—a pathological practice to be cured rather than something with which we must live as best we can. This attitude has given rise to attempts to search for war's "root causes," even as medical scientists search for causes and cures for diseases. But note that such researchers see the root of the disease not in imperfect, imperfectible individuals, but rather in imperfect but perfectible social organizations. Hence, their focus is not on personal repentance and spiritual growth, but rather on identifying the social surgery that they believe must be done. This approach is thus compatible with the first, rather than with the second and third alternatives we have sketched.

In the United States and other Western societies today such "peace research" is a growth industry, lavishly supported by governments, foundations, and other benefactors. While some contribute funds in the hope of an ultimate cure, others wish to increase the likelihood that their favorite social surgeons will put the knife to their least favorite causes and people. Thus, this kind of peace research is a form of war, albeit war against some people's favorite "root causes" of war.

Shortly before World War I, the American steel magnate-philanthropist, Andrew Carnegie, in his will funded what was to become the first major American center for the study of the subject, the Carnegie Endowment for International Peace. So confident was he that war might some day disappear from the face of the earth that he specified that the trustees of his legacy then would shift remaining trust funds to other worthy causes. Seventy-five years later the endowment's peace work is still very active, and very sectarian.

Thus, these four sets of explanations—based on generic circumstances, human will, human imperfection, and social organization—really fall into two categories: the generic and the volitional. Let us examine them in turn.

Generic Causes of War

Searching for "generic causes" of war, we encounter a profusion of theories akin to the welter of tongues spoken by the legendary builders of the Tower of Babel. Some are inspired by not-too-hidden political agendas. For many peace theorists, those offering explanations contrary to their own are themselves warmongers upon whom war must be waged for the sake of peace.

The prototypical example of generic causality theory is Quincy Wright's monumental *Study of War*. At the heart of Wright's method for deciding whether any given war will break out is a mathematical formula that expresses what Wright contends is the relationship between the many factors involved in any nation's decision to go to war with another.[2] Wright finds the many factors that determine the decision on all levels of human existence: the biological and cultural level, the social and political level, the level of legal institutions, and the level of technology. Each factor, like each human desire, could lead to war if it is not counterbalanced by another. War comes when the balancing act fails. The formula expresses the balance, and purports to explain and perhaps predict breakdowns. It purports to be more than a simple mechanism for assigning numerical values to such factors as hostility and expectations of economic gain and loss. It attempts to use mathematical expressions, such as integrals and derivatives, to treat these phenomena in what appears to be a sophisticated method. But in the end, the formula requires the arbitrary substitution of numbers for qualities and even for imponderables, and is an obvious example of the principle, garbage in, garbage out.

All other theories proposing generic causes are in a way partial versions of the Wright formula.[3] Instead of attempting to explain definitively the onset of war by drawing together and "objectifying" all factors affecting the onset of war, they take just one or just a few of these "objective factors," whether they be race, religion, or arms competition, as *the sole* explanation. In fact, however, the factor they mention may not even be an explanation, or not a terribly important one in the minds of those who start any given war. For example, standard Marxist explanations for World War II stress the importance of German industrial cartels such as I. G. Farben.[4] But how important is such an abstract factor compared with the actual presence in the Nazi party of the master rabble-rouser, Joseph Goebbels? Given that Goebbels attributes his becoming a Nazi to his mother-in-law, is *she* to be ranked as a cause, or are mothers-in-law in general?

But while those who follow Quincy Wright may have difficulty convincing the man on the street that their "objective factors" and formulae mean anything, the U.S. military services and the CIA pay tens of millions of dollars each year for their wares. While other social scientists can only claim to provide the wisdom by which government officials may judge for themselves who is likely to fight whom over what, "objective" social scientists sell the ready-made results of complex, presumably authoritative processes.

Those social scientists who have sought the roots of war in causal theory have investigated many levels of human behavior and experience (psychology); particular human cultures (anthropology); particular political strategic orders (political science); particular economic systems; and particular arrangements and dispositions among nations and nation-states (international relations). None of this research and speculation has succeeded in predicting any war or any peace. Even when modern social science finds objective correlations between any one event or condition and the onset of war, for instance, an increase in armament levels, it cannot make the intellectual leap that separates correlation from cause. To say that the relationship between two generic events or conditions (for example, industrial expansion and social mobility) is the cause of a third event or condition is to abstract from what actually happens in particular places at particular times and from what particular individuals are trying to accomplish.

Empirical studies have indeed confirmed what common sense teaches. Some cultures are indeed inherently more peaceable than others and particular types of polities (states) are more peaceable than others. It is not irrelevant that the ratio of the military budget to the gross domestic product of communist and Islamic countries is four times that for all other kinds of countries.[5] Particular economic systems may even be inherently more peaceable than others. Karl Marx himself pointed out that capitalism shuns war because of its depressing effects on stock markets, while "oriental despotism" thrives on war. And perhaps certain particular arrangements between states, for example, fluid balances of power rather than blocs of alliances, are more conducive to peace than others. Nevertheless, knowing all this, one is still far from understanding why any given war actually occurs in the real world. Ironically, peaceable kingdoms, being nice, may tempt aggressors to devour them, while nations armed to the teeth, whether they are nice like Switzerland or nasty like Afghanistan, may live undisturbed for generations. Thus an inclination to peace is no guarantee of maintaining it. However, peaceful nations, having taken up the sword, may fight with greater vigor and perhaps with less reasonable restraint than ones known for their martial spirit. All of this uncertainty exists because the disposition to fight arises from truly important contests of purpose and will between nations in concrete circumstances. It is impossible to predict what such contests may bring about.

The final proof that cultural characteristics do not bring about war is that while a nation's culture changes only slowly, its propensity to war changes quickly. The supposedly war-prone Japanese, who carried their savage military conquest deep into China, Southeast Asia, and the Pacific Islands in the 1930s and 1940s, seem today nearly bereft of martial spirit. Yet, Japanese culture, with its emphasis on discipline and clannishness, has changed little, while Japanese genes have not changed at all. The Jews of Israel, who now command one of the world's most effective armies, contrast vividly with their immediate forebears, the many Jews of Europe who allowed themselves to be herded into boxcars en route to Auschwitz and other Nazi extermination camps. Surely Jewish genes have not changed. Rather, Jews, Japanese, and all other peoples behave as they do at any given time because they are animated by particular regimes that call forth certain human qualities and suppress others. People also behave as they do because, at any given time, they either have or do not have particular leaders who succeed in making a "cause" out of the situation in which they find themselves. For example, Moses molded the Jews into a fearsome nation through the process of delivering them from Egyptian captivity. What some see as disasters, others see as opportunities.

Does this mean that man is infinitely malleable, and that while some particular cultures, states, and other conditions corrupt him, making him into a bellicose beast, other regimes could make man good and incapable of war? After all, the credo of the United Nations Educational, Scientific, and Cultural Organization (UNESCO) is that because "wars begin in the minds of men," and because the mind is malleable, peace can be firmly and permanently planted there. This is the credo of social engineers of all kinds. By examining it, we shall see why it is mistaken.[6]

One theory on the generic causes of war, however, stands outside of this deterministic framework. The Christian realism that St. Augustine teaches in the City of God locates the source of war in the will of sinful men. Augustine thus assumes the ever-present possibility of war but seeks to diminish its frequency and savagery by teaching how to tame it. This is profoundly discouraging to peace researchers, and indeed to all determinists. For, if man is a depraved creature, fallen from grace, imperfect, naturally and unpredictably prone to belligerence and aggression, then what more can be said except that human beings must learn to live in this state from day to day as best they can, and attempt to ameliorate its effects whenever possible.

Christian realists of our times, such as the American theologian Reinhold Niebuhr, however, have questioned the logical causal relationship between war and human imperfections, whether individual or collective.[7] As they see things, by no means does it follow that all imperfect men are aggressive; nor does it follow that the aggressive behavior of nations is due to the aggressive compulsions of individuals. A nation of submissive robots may more easily be led to battle than one of aggressive individualists. The key to these possibilities lies in Plato's well-known point that a country reflects its leaders to the point that, for practical purposes, it is those leaders "writ large"—with all their virtues, passions, and shortcomings. If the leaders are aggressive, and circumstances allow them to follow their bent, others will either go along or revolt to change the regime.

Still, there is a non sequitur in any theory that grounds collective warlike behavior of nations in the aggressive attributes of individuals. Collective aggression and personal aggression are two different things. Determinists simply should not imagine that warlike leaders could impress their character on nations of sheep, and vice versa. But they do. When the young Bolshevik Stalin clandestinely visited Germany to meet with German Communists, he concluded that, inured as they were to authority, they were utterly contemptible as revolutionaries. Stalin imagined that if his German counterparts were ordered to seize a railroad station they would first meekly line up at the ticket window to buy admission passes. He could not imagine these peaceable Germans whipped up to the sort of violence that suited his tastes. But in 1941, Stalin saw orderly hordes of these obedient Germans nearly topple his regime. Had the Germans been less prone to be obedient subordinates, they might not have lent themselves so easily to Hitler's aggression.

Each generation in the liberal West has been exposed to a particular intellectual fad that has named a particular culprit for war. In eighteenth-century Europe and in the American colonies, the main malefactors were widely deemed to be monarchs and dynasts.[8] There seemed to be a superficial plausibility to their logic. The main wars of the previous centuries had been waged among the courts of England, France, Austria, Prussia, and Spain. The will of European aristocrats, so went the accusation, was unchecked by public opinion. These aristocrats' objectives were said to be irrelevant or contrary to the real needs and aspirations of the people. This being so, truly peace-loving polities would be republics, in which decisions about war and peace would be made by men who would represent the people's desire to avoid becoming cannon fodder. The authorities would have no right to make war arbitrarily. Secret diplomacy

and secret alliances and commitments would be anathema. To para-
phrase George Orwell, "Monarchies bad, Republics good." The
United States of America, born in this period, adopted a Constitution
incorporating these sentiments.

The view that war is spawned by the absence of democracy
heavily influenced the world views of English liberals and the
American Founding Fathers. Jefferson and Tom Paine, the pam-
phleteer, saw the causes of wars as ceaseless struggles by dynastic
courts over real estate in Europe waged in remote regions of the
globe.[9] Thus, "progressive" Americans came to see the principle of
the "balance of power," which evidently regulated the affairs of
European cabinets in war and peace, as a cause of war made worse
by its cruel disregard for the wishes of ordinary people. This was the
rhetorical chariot on which Woodrow Wilson carried America into
World War I. It was part of the basis for U.S. hostility to European
colonial power after World War II, and remains a factor in U.S.
foreign policy today.

Marx, for his part, taught that the true progressive engine of modern history was the class conflict between the exploiting oppressors
and the exploited oppressed—in our time, the bourgeoisie and the
proletariat. The old ruling classes would vainly use any means to
postpone their inevitable overthrow. Marx depicted this conflict as
basically a *vertical* conflict between upper and lower classes. Lenin
carried Marx's doctrine onto the horizontal level: War would also
include the clash of capitalist powers among themselves—for the
right to seize and subjugate less-developed peoples, overseas markets, and sources of new materials. This *new* dynamic process,
added to Marx's vertical conflict, was the "highest" form of bourgeois exploitation, the true manifestation of a dying ancien régime,
and the chief cause of modern war.

This kind of historical determinism is the philosophical basis of
Soviet foreign policy today, and is accepted by all socialist states in
the world, as well as by many people in the free world. Its logic is
that the only real peace, the peace of socialism, comes when all
domestic and foreign vestiges of capitalism, including vast categories
of human beings, are (to use a Stalinist expression) "liquidated." All
other forms of peace are fraudulent. In the twentieth century perhaps
as many human beings have been "liquidated" in the name of
Marxist-Leninism as have been killed in the two "conventional"
world wars.[10] Obviously, *Pravda* wrote the truth when it declared in
Brezhnev's time, "the Marxist-Leninist concept of peaceful coexistence does in no way contain the pacifist-like promotion of peace."[11]

ACCIDENTAL WAR

The epitome of the view that war is caused by something other than the will of those who start it is that it has no cause at all, that it is an accident. The misconceptions, misunderstandings, miscalculations, and technical malfunctionings of international affairs may combine to produce tragic, unwanted conflagrations in much the same way a traffic accident occurs. A visual impairment, a flaw in the road, or bad weather may cause two cars to collide. The hapless drivers who swerve into each others' paths do not intend to hit each other. Each later might be held for negligence, but no more.

Now, it is almost always true that those who deliberately take up arms are uncertain what will ensue. One might indeed argue that if both sides knew the consequences a war might not take place. But all human decisions are taken in ignorance of the future, and nations have regretted decisions not to fight as much as they have regretted decisions to go to war. Moreover, the argument for accidental war is based on the assumption that no one really wants war, but that many let themselves be put into situations where somehow they are "forced to choose" war. Perhaps another analogy is the familiar explanation that college students don't really choose drunken sex in the basement of fraternity houses—it just "happens"—much the same way, some say, paraphrasing Emerson, that World War I "happened": "Things were in the saddle." Today, those who favor arms-control agreements argue that because nuclear war might break out accidentally through some combination of technical malfunctions and human errors, "things," for example, the weapons themselves, ought to be done away with lest they displace their masters in the saddle of decision making.

Fortunately for all concerned, there are no historical case studies of accidental nuclear wars, although imaginative scenarios have been written about them. Those who today are in charge of "strategic weapons"—land-based missiles or rockets, bombers, or nuclear submarines—know all too well the dangers of a possible accident, such as a mistaken radar blip or the malfunction of a control system. Since such weapons are swift, and the time between discharge and arrival on target can be extremely short, decisions about "war or peace" for the targeted state may have to be made in a very short time, possibly minutes. Some yearn for the old days, when time spans were longer, when leaders had weeks or months to deliberate on such momentous things. Not without reason then, after the

Cuban missile crisis the nuclear superpowers highlighted the de-
fects of their communications with each other and have established
hardened, dependable systems ("hot lines") capable of handling
messages rapidly between those in ultimate command.

Nevertheless, the skeptic must ask, is it really true that there can
be truly accidental wars? If so, when have they happened in history?
As the Australian historian Geoffrey Blainey observes in *The Causes
of War*, while "political scientists have tended to accept the idea that
some wars are accidental, historians have been wary."[12] It is difficult, he says, to find a war which on investigation fits this description. This is not to say that an accidental war has never happened;
perhaps one has. We do not know of one, though, and the likelihood
of such a war being discovered in history is exceedingly remote.

Miscalculations and misperceptions are not accidents. Are misperceptions of the "other side's" actions or intentions fortuitous at
all? Blainey cites events at the onset of the Russo-Japanese War of
1904 as an example. He asks:

> Why did Japan so seriously misconstrue Russia's intentions? . . . [The
> answer] may lie in an observation made . . . by a Cambridge philoso-
> pher and literary critic, I. A. Richards. . . . all we have to do is substitute
> 'diplomatic dispatch' for 'poem': fundamentally, . . . when any person
> misreads a poem it is because, *as he is at that moment*, he wants to. The
> interpretation he puts upon the words is the most agile and the most
> active among several interpretations that are within the possibilities of
> his mind. Every interpretation is motivated by some interest, and the
> idea that appears is the sign of these interests that are its unseen
> masters.

Blainey concludes:

> It seems that an "accidental war" becomes more likely in proportion to
> the presence of other conditions making for war. Ironically, an "acci-
> dental war" is more likely if the non-accidental factors are strong.
> Translated from war to law, the concept means that a murder is more
> likely to be unintentional if the prisoner had strong intentions of com-
> mitting murder.[13]

One can carry Blainey's thoughts further. "War instigating accidents" do not occur the way traffic accidents do. In highway mis-
haps, the motorists seldom know each other, and in any event, have
had no previous personal dislike of one another. Any previous ac-

quaintance would not have contributed to the disaster. Not so among nations. "Accidental wars" rarely, if ever, occur between nations that otherwise have no reason to be enemies, to fear or to hate each other, or to see their interests as fundamentally antagonistic and unresolvable by peaceful means. Canadians today do not spend nights of terror in fear of an American strike, accidental or intentional. (Canada in any event has virtually no forces to cope with an attack from *any* quarter, were such to occur.) Thus, should a crazed Canadian pilot bomb a U.S. border post, or a crazed American pilot bomb a Canadian border post, the United States and Canada would most surely not go to war. When accidents take place, friendly nations deal with them by means other than violent reprisals, "second strikes," and the like. And this is true also of accidents between states whose *policies* are not disposed to enmity, but who are not necessarily friends.[14]

The same can also be true of great rivals who regard each other warily but do not want to fight. Note that the centuries of hostility between Russia and China have never produced a major war. Every "cause" for war (in both senses of the word) has been present, but no one has caused a war. In our time, we must note that the now almost-forgotten shootdown by Soviet aircraft of an innocent Korean airliner carrying 287 people (including a U.S. congressman) in 1983 was a classic casus belli. The U.S. had entered World War I after 128 Americans had died when Germany torpedoed the *Lusitania*. Journalist Seymour Hersh contends that the Soviets mistook the airliner for an intelligence aircraft. In fact the Soviets had both the airliner and the intelligence plane on radar at the same time. But whether the slaughter was accidental or intentional is beside the point. Even if the United States had declared the killing of the congressman an "act of war" it is highly unlikely that it would have deemed this as a "casus belli," a cause for war. That is quite simply because war between the United States and the Soviet Union would be a very big deal indeed, and would have to be caused by a complex of causes important enough to justify something that size. All of this is to say that decisions about who is and is not an enemy are intensely political—they are the very opposite of accidents. Getting into war is not like catching a cold. It is more like catching AIDS. It's not easy.

We come here upon a profound philosophical matter: the nature of enmity. As the German legal philosopher Carl Schmitt pointed out years ago in his *The Concept of the Political*, most modern Western languages, in contrast to Greek and Latin, do not distinguish between public and private enemies.[15] In Latin, however, the public enemy is *hostis*, not *inimicus*. The distinction corresponds to that among evils: *malum prohibitum*—bad because a decision has been made to prohibit it, and *malum in se*—evil in itself. In the *Republic*, Plato also sharply distinguishes the political enemy from the private one.[16] This distinction is supremely important. As Schmitt points out, Western languages fail to distinguish between the enemy who embodies evil, and the political enemy who is simply on the other side:

> The enemy in the political sense need not be hated personally, and in the private sphere only does it make sense to love one's enemy, i.e., one's adversary. . . . [The] state as an organized political entity decides for itself the friend-enemy distinction. The political [enmity] is the most extreme antagonism. For to the enemy concept belongs the ever present possibility of combat. . . . War follows from enmity. War is the existential negation of the enemy.[17]

Political enmity is anything but accidental. Nor does the fact of political enmity dictate war. What, if anything, one does to an enemy is a matter for prudence to decide.

When all is said and done it remains true, despite Blainey, that hostile powers today have a great stake in the rational control of force to achieve strategic ends. Of course, inadvertence and miscalculation are inherent both in the actual conduct of war and in tactical crisis situations where there are known enemies. But whether or not deep predisposition to enmity translates into actual warfare is for prudent statecraft to decide.

Voluntaristic Theories of War

When we inquire into the *voluntary* causes of war—into the motives of those who decide to fight—we not only examine the motives of those who fire or threaten to fire the first shot, but also of those who choose to respond. Any war is at the least a *duellum*. In August 1914, for instance, Serbia's refusal to submit to an Austrian ultimatum signified Serbia's choice to go to war rather than to remain peacefully within the Hapsburg sphere of influence. War thus entails a mutual agreement to fight. (The agreement may also be rejected by capitulation. In October 1938 democratic Czechoslovakia peacefully accepted Hitler's demands, and was widely, if briefly, praised for its reasonableness by the leaders of "peace loving" democracies.)

When we investigate the variety of purposes that war has served in history, and the variety of purposes for which men have chosen to fight, we enter the realm of the *political*. If we believe Clausewitz was correct in saying that war is "a continuation of politics by an admixture of other means," then purpose is the very essence of war. Purpose is manifest in benign and malevolent guises far too numerous to catalogue: despoliation, enrichment, and conquest; revenge, and retribution; establishing or unifying nations and empires; instituting a just order of things for one nation or among all nations; subjugating and punishing evil; carrying civilization and secular or religious faiths to other peoples and places; and, of course, the defense of the realm against foreign and domestic enemies.

It is true that leaders often feel driven by forces beyond their control and despairingly succumb to "necessity." Yet even in the direst of circumstances, and regardless of how awful the alternatives, leaders are still responsible for choosing one course over another. In October 1938, when Czechoslovakia's civilian leaders peacefully capitulated to Hitler, they did so knowing that the option of a lonely defensive war advocated by high military advisers would likely have led to defeat and violent occupation. The Czech generals knew as well as the civilians that Czechoslovakia's Western friends had abandoned her. But they believed that if they fought, they would force the West to intervene. The civilian leaders did not want to take that chance and believed that their only choice was between a war followed by Nazi occupation or Nazi occupation without a war. They chose the latter in the hope that it would be milder. In retrospect, they made the wrong choice.

The choice of surrender is as deliberate as the choice of war. In September 1918, as the fortunes of war turned against Imperial Germany, the high command controlled by General Ludendorff convinced the kaiser to surrender while Allied armies were still far from German soil. But in 1945, with most of Germany already occupied and all her cities in shambles, Hitler continued to execute as traitors people suspected of harboring thoughts of peace. Obviously, circumstances in and of themselves dictate neither war nor peace.

Nor do circumstances dictate the degree of commitment to a particular war. For example, from 1915 to 1918 the Italian army conducted a successful offensive war on terrain that strongly favored the Austrian defenders. This mountainous front moved by miles while the French, British, and German armies, fighting on terrain that favored offensive operations, moved their front by yards. By contrast, between 1940 and 1943 the Italian army proved generally unfit for even easy operations, despite the far greater regimentation of Italian society introduced by fascism. Clearly, the regimentation and military orientation of fascism were not enough to overcome the Italian people's lack of enthusiasm for sharing Germany's cause in World War II.

The same point may be seen from a different angle if we look at how the behavior of Soviet troops changed during the year following the German invasion in 1941. At first Soviet troops surrendered by the hundreds of thousands, as millions of Ukrainians, Baltic peoples, other minorities, and even Russians, welcomed the Germans as liberators from Communism. Clearly, neither the Russian army nor the populace would fight for the Communist cause against Germany. But both the Soviet army and the Soviet people learned rather quickly and brutally that the invader was not so much Germany as it was Nazism, from which they could expect only death and slavery. Suddenly the cause was no longer a regime, but life itself. At the same time, Stalin realized that although the Russian people would not defend Communism, they would fight for Holy Mother Russia. Given different causes, the Russian people fought heroically. Thus, also, one does not wonder that in 1861 an American public accustomed to biblical injunctions to fight for right, and led by Abraham Lincoln, should have fought even its own brothers for the abstract ideals of the Union and against slavery, while singing "The Battle Hymn of the Republic." Nor is it surprising that in the 1970s another American polity, accustomed to the *Playboy* philosophy, and led by presidents of somewhat ambiguous moral standing who repeatedly and emphatically refused to identify the enemy, label him evil, and call for his defeat should have stood by and watched the peoples of Southeast Asia—on behalf of whose freedom it had made a halfhearted commitment—sink wholly into slavery.

War is a test of, among other things, how much and how wisely peoples love the things for which their regimes stand. For example, World War II quickly told the leaders of Italian fascism how little the people's attendance at their rallies meant. By contrast, during the Falklands-Malvinas War of 1982, the Argentine people showed perhaps even greater adherence to the objective of securing those worthless islands than the military government had expected—all out of genuine patriotism. It turned out that the people loved the islands more than they loved their government. But popular dedication could not make up for the Argentine military government's diplomatic miscalculation that Britain would not fight and for the Argentine military's incompetence in the fight. In both of these cases, though for different reasons, the regimes flunked the test of war. Because the people did not love the principles on which the regimes stood enough to suffer and lose with those regimes, they withdrew their allegiance and the regimes died. Indeed the people took just revenge on them for their miscalculations. The Argentine generals wound up in jail, and Mussolini ended up hanging from a meathook outside a Milan gas station.

Anyone who counsels his fellow citizens to make war—or to stop fighting, or to try to avoid a war—bears heavy responsibility both for judging what will be gained or lost by the decision and for divining what the outcome of the conflict will be. The first task requires the highest test of prudence; the second seems to be beyond human power. Thucydides named fear as the most frequent reason why people decide to fight, fear of growing enemy power, fear for one's fate in a situation that seems to be worsening, or even fear lest a long-sought prize should escape from one's hand. But surely fear is as likely a reason for staying out of war, fear that one's own nation is not up to the task, that the rewards will not be worth the effort, or that the war will foster alliances, unleash energies, or justify attitudes that could prove ruinous. Thus, it seems that Thucydides' point is that regardless of where it leads, any calculation made under the shadow of war is necessarily fearful and less likely to yield the fruits of dispassionate reflections than it might.

Rare indeed is a testimony like that of Winston Churchill about that night in May 1940, when World War II ceased to be a "phony war." Having watched his country riven and weakened by the desire not to look the looming Nazi danger in the face, he slept peacefully because he was relieved that the issue was now unmistakably clear and so was the bloody task ahead.[18] Such calm can only come from profound confidence, if not in one's own nation (in 1939–40, Churchill was surely *not* confident of a good outcome), then in one's own judgment that the course chosen is the best under the circumstances.

This sort of firmness in judgment rarely comes from accurately, almost geometrically calculating the results of the many vectors affecting the situation. Neither the direction nor the force of each vector is precisely knowable. But the most important and the most variable of variables is the moral evaluation that the combatants make of one another. So, firmness in judgment can only come from an evaluation of the moral stakes. For example, in June 1940, the dominant faction of French politics represented by General Weygand and Marshal Pétain calculated the correlation of military forces competently and thus reasonably surrendered to what they wrongly thought was the equivalent of Wilhelmine Germany. Churchill could count German superiority as well as the French generals. Hence his peace of mind in his determination to fight to the death was not based on a different calculation of the correlation of forces. Rather, it was based on a moral evaluation of Nazi Germany entirely different from Pétain's. Due to these differing moral evaluations, a decision that was unreasonable for Pétain was inescapable for Churchill. Thus did the balance of Churchill's fears calmly weigh on the side of an outcome he could not plan in 1939–40.

Thus, the *volitional* approach, emphasizing purpose, shows that the causes of war are far more easily understood by concrete occurrences of history rather than by general, theoretical explanations of war. The future is unknowable precisely because it depends on decisions that free human beings have not yet made.

Past Causes

We conclude from all this that the only investigation of the causes of war that is intellectually respectable is that of the unique origins and causes and nature of *particular* past wars. The lessons of past wars, if used with caution, can help illuminate contemporary crises, though often they are used merely to score debating points. The ordinary human mind understands the past better than it understands the present, which is filled with uncertainty. The future, with all its surprises, is unknowable. The obvious danger in applying the lessons of past wars to present or future wars is that we tend to deceive ourselves with our favorite images from the past. As some generals busily prepare to fight the last war, civilians succumb to the all too human temptation to *prevent* the last war: "No more Vietnams!"; "No more Sarajevos!"; "No more Munichs!"

The philosopher Santayana once said that those who "fail to learn from the past are condemned to repeat it." Unfortunately, Santayana did not specify *which* past or whose version of the past. In the 1930s, particular "lessons" drawn from the way in which America was allegedly drawn into World War I provided ammunition for isolationists who did not wish a repetition of the same scenario. The result was a series of so-called Neutrality Acts prohibiting measures to aid the Western democracies' resistance to Nazi Germany: Never again! Immediately after World War II, many American minds were powerfully influenced by remembrances of how U.S. passivity to Axis aggression in the 1930s—from Manchuria to Czechoslovakia —contributed to the national catastrophe of 1941. So in 1950, when Communist armies invaded South Korea, President Truman's mind automatically turned to the tragic sequence in the 1930s of unresisted totalitarian aggression in Asia and Europe. He swiftly posted American military forces to Korea with full, if tacit, support from his cabinet, Congress, and the American public, which also "remembered"—never again! The U.S. commitment to Vietnam flowed from this lesson. But the United States lost that war. So, ever since Vietnam, vivid recollections of the particular ways in which the United States "allowed itself" to become incrementally involved in it have played a powerful role in debates about whether the United States ought to be involved in Africa and even in Central America: Never again!

There is a perennial debate among "consumers" of the lessons of recent past wars, between those who see in armaments and military commitments the source of war; and those who see, in armed deterrence, the prime condition of peace. How many concrete "lessons of the past" illuminate or possibly resolve this debate?

The issue of the causes of World War I is still much alive today in academic circles. Many Western scholars in the interwar decades of the 1920s and 1930s agreed that the war was caused by two great and ominous processes. The first was the polarization of Europe into two opposing alliance systems, the Triple Alliance (Germany, Austria-Hungary, Italy) and the Triple Entente (Great Britain, France, Russia). Before the 1880s, the great powers had lived in a fluid balance of power alignments within a concert of Europe more or less unchanged since Napoleon had been vanquished in 1815. Ideological conflict such as we now know had no significant place in the European diplomacy of that period. Yet by 1914, on the eve of World War I, the great powers squared off in opposing armed camps, accused each other of being the harbingers of the end of culture and civilization, and formed alliances set on hair-triggers that might go off anytime. Small flare ups thus gained the potential for starting a huge conflagration, which is exactly what happened at Sarajevo in July 1914.

The second reason most commonly postulated for bringing on World War I was a supposedly dizzying arms race between the two European alliances. For both offensive and defensive reasons, the two armed camps allegedly kept stockpiling armaments and expanding their armies; for no reason other than bringing on war. Most destabilizing was the German-initiated arms race in that era's version of world strategic weaponry: the dreadnought battleship. After 1899 Germany and Britain spent vast sums on their battleship-building because the Germans were determined to match the British, and the British were equally determined to stay ahead. This ended up terrifying Britain into closer ties with the Franco-Russian alliance, helping to ensure that the next war would be a world war. Thus Europe devoted more and more of its resources to building military power. It was expensive, and in 1914, it turned out to be destructive.

The specter of bloc polarization, arms races, mutual misunderstandings, and of a "war nobody wanted" shaped liberal interwar (1919–39) thinking. Hence, alliances and attempts to balance power were seen as dangerous in and of themselves. Instead the order of the day was isolationism disguised as universal collective security, through the League of Nations.

Yet there is good reason to challenge the basic view that "nobody" wanted World War I. Major historians today again point the finger at Imperial Germany for deliberately aiming to dominate Europe and to challenge decisively British sea power; for deliberately egging Austria on to war with Serbia; and for using Russian troop mobilization as a pretext for armed aggression against France. The "myth of Sarajevo," that war broke out accidentally, that an action-reaction chain of events caught statesmen up in a maelstrom beyond their control, does not correspond to the true sequence of historical causation, in which deliberate choices for war were made *in Berlin*.[19] The kaiser wanted war, and the other nations of Europe consented to it. Moreover, no one can read the newspapers or letters written in the first year of that war without being impressed by the alacrity, dedication, and even the joy with which every nation of Europe threw itself into that meat grinder. If any proof be needed, note that the socialist parties of Europe, for whom pacifism was holy writ, wholeheartedly threw it away and became their respective countries' biggest war boosters. The two significant exceptions in 1915 were named Benito Mussolini and V. I. Lenin.

But the causes of World War II do not resemble the supposed causes of World War I. How, then, can we generalize about the causes of modern wars? Whether one believes in the significance of culture, or of arms races, or of economics, one cannot deny that the origins of World War II lay in an international situation utterly different from the one that preceded World War I. Not only were arms races and competing alliance systems absent in the 1930s, but it even appears that had such systems existed, they might have averted World War II. The same things that supposedly caused World War I might well have made World War II unnecessary or impossible had they again been present in the 1930s. It seems, then, that in wholly different circumstances and for different reasons the same thing happened. Some people thought they could gain by war, and they persuaded nations to follow.

As in the years before World War I, in the years before World War II, Germany engaged in a massive arms buildup. But unlike the period from 1904 to 1914, German rearmament in the 1930s drew no response from the Western democracies—mired in the Great Depression and political instability—until the end of the decade when it was already too late. The 1930s arms race was a one-sided, unreciprocated affair in which Western liberals tried to placate Adolf Hitler by showing him that he would not need all the weapons he was acquiring because they themselves would not arm. But while reciprocal military buildup might have sobered Hitler, the democracies' restraint made Hitler's buildup much more cost-effective at the margin. Restraint thus fostered madness and gave the madman disproportionate force.

In the immediate years before World War II, no alliance system opposed the growing German threat. Even though an early anti-Hitler consensus might well have deterred his adventurism, the Western democracies—England, France, and the United States—failed to link up among themselves and present a common front out of a general revulsion of what was supposed to have happened in 1914. Stalin, who held no illusions about 1914, made frantic overtures to the West from 1936 until 1938, trying to form an anti-Hitler alliance. Stalin's accommodation with Hitler in 1939 came only after he decided the West would never come around. The United States was totally aloof from European balance-of-power politics in the 1930s, thus exacerbating the illusion of Western weakness that encouraged Hitler. When Hitler started the war in 1939, he had sound reasons to believe that the British and French would not come to the aid of Poland.

After World War II, the liberal-democratic West extracted one important moral lesson from the 1930s: Appeasement is no way to treat an aggressor bent on world dominion. Appeasement, it was widely believed after 1945, only whets the appetite of the aggressor while revealing to him the weakness and irresolution of the appeaser. The League of Nations had failed to take appropriate action when Japan invaded Manchuria in 1931, when Italy invaded Ethiopia in 1935, and when Germany reoccupied the Rhineland in 1936. To Western liberals, the lesson to be drawn from this failure is the importance of deterrence for protecting peace. Most people today still agree that military strength, backed by the credible will to use it, is the guarantor of world peace.

But since the late 1960s, the "lessons of Vietnam" have cut directly against that conclusion and thus have revived the "lessons of World War I." The specter of "the war nobody wanted" in 1914 parallels the agenda of many of today's American peace researchers: to wit, that the world is on the brink of the "war that nobody wants" in the 1990s, and that we should once again turn to the two extremes of isolationism and collective security. But how can one dismiss the lessons of World War II? If taken literally, all of these contradictory lessons serve better to confuse than to guide the decisions of statesmen.[20]

Aggression as a Cause of War

Whatever the ultimate causes of war, the willful setting in motion of violence, actually loosing the dogs of war, striking the first blow—in a word, aggression—is what Aristotle might have called a proximate and efficient cause of war. Its image is formidable. Armies smash across borders. Ships, planes, or missiles sweep down to strike vital targets with premeditated fury. The party that suffers aggression has his cause handed to him—if he can stand it, given that the first fruit of aggression is often that most precious strategic good: surprise.

The nature of surprise is best appreciated when we see that the aggressor holds the key advantage of the *initiative*, with the added advantages of the "Three Ds"—duplicity, deception, and disinformation. In this respect, the Japanese attack on Pearl Harbor did not wholly surprise. The tradition of Japanese surprise tactics was well-known in naval and military circles. The "sneak attack" on Russian-held Port Arthur had given Japan a strategic running start in the Russo-Japanese War of 1904–05. Japan's general intention to attack was a well-known political fact, and this fact had been sharpened by the decoding of Japanese messages. Although it was not a strategic surprise, Pearl Harbor was a tactical surprise because the United States did not know when, where, and how Japan would attack. The information the United States possessed in the first week of December 1941 was sufficient for American leaders to decide that the war had started and that the United States should go on the offensive. But they did not consider this course of action. Yet the information was not detailed enough to be useful for defensive purposes. On 8 December 1941, Roosevelt made the best of a bad situation by turning the U.S. losses at Pearl Harbor into a battle cry, a date that would live "in infamy."

Such is the normal peacetime popular attitude to "sneak attack" (sometimes called "unprovoked aggression") that many people instinctively sympathize with the victim, and condemn the aggressor out of hand. In 1914, when Imperial Germany launched its Schlieffen attack into hapless, neutral Belgium, "world opinion" rallied impotently around "poor little Belgium." In 1939, when the Red Army launched its "winter war" against Finland, "world opinion" rallied impotently around "brave little Finland," as it did around Afghanistan after the Red Army invaded it. In any event, sympathy is of little value if it is not backed by positive support, or if the victim quickly succumbs to the shock of surprise.

Even when faced with imminent aggression, wise statesmen sometimes have *allowed* an aggressor to strike first while realizing the risks of such strategic passivity. They have done this to demonstrate their yearning for peace and their unwarlike demeanor to their own public, to allies, and to onlookers. They have thought it worthwhile to pay a price to show unambiguously who fired the first shot—*who began it!* This was the case during the last days of peace before the German attack on Belgium and France in 1914. France commanded its forces to withdraw 30 kilometers from the German border to brand the attacking Imperial German troops as aggressors and invaders. In 1941, fully aware of the likelihood of Japanese aggression, the Roosevelt administration took no measures and drafted no plans to preemptively beat off imminent attack. In 1973, Israeli authorities, seeing the shadow of imminent Syrian-Egyptian attack, chose for *political* reasons to await it and to accept the risks of receiving the blow. To act preemptively would have cost Israel its precious image as a beleaguered, imperiled nation among its friends abroad, particularly in America. Thus, when Hitler finally struck in August 1939 (as Churchill had often warned would happen), Churchill complimented the peaceful instincts and aims of the Chamberlain government whose appeasement policies he had previously opposed as harbingers of war: "In this solemn hour it is a consolation to recall and to dwell upon our repeated efforts for peace." These efforts for peace, he said, had been "ill-starred," but they also had been faithful and sincere. "That," he said, "is of the highest moral value."[21]

Yet a decision to face the first blow of aggression in order to prove one's peaceful intentions risks destruction. If the first blow is bad enough, one's own people may not be aroused at all, but cowed into submission instead. It is especially fateful and perilous if by passivity and by signalling his own dedication to peace the potential victim expects clemency or forbearance from his enemy. In most cases, the moral comfort that comes from being the victim of aggression is purchased at an exorbitant price.

Moreover, while "firing the first shot" seems to mean quite a bit, its true moral significance is much less. "Firing the first shot" is not conclusive proof of the aggressor's culpability. What if a potential victim of attack comes to know what is in store for him and preempts his attacker? Is he then the aggressor and the cause of the war or merely someone who does the best he can with a situation he did not choose? Why should he not have attacked first? Is it right to condemn to death untold numbers of one's fellow citizens by deciding to take the blow lying down? What a price of immorality to pay for the privilege of feeling morally blameless!

Still, as in the case of France in 1914, America in 1941, Israel in

1973, and so on, modern democracies have made a calculated decision, based not upon morality but rather upon raison d'état, to take the first blow. Modern democracies rarely have been aggressors in the strict sense that they have planned and carried out armed attacks on other countries with which they have been at peace. Even if, as Benjamin Franklin aphorized, "distrust and caution are the parents of security," democratic peoples tend to suspect leaders who are the first to strike even against foes whose aggressive intentions and plans are well known. Democratic leaders know this all too well. For example, had Roosevelt and his advisers secretly planned, and carried out, the preemptive surprise blow, the ensuing public uproar might have been politically fatal to his administration and, possibly, to the nation's destiny. No doubt, Roosevelt's decision was also influenced by the cold calculation that anything that Japan could dish out would not cripple America. Roosevelt balanced these two concrete facts in a reasonable way. But Japan did more harm than expected!

It is one thing to await attack, confident that the blows can be repelled or that they will not inflict strategically fatal consequences. It is quite another to risk everything. This was why on the evening of Pearl Harbor a profound sense of relief pervaded the White House because the blow had been taken, the long months of uncertainty were over, the aggressor had struck![22] Perversely, the attack proved that nobody was about to defeat mighty America. Roosevelt in 1941 might well have echoed the sentiments Lincoln expressed in 1838: "All the armies of the world with a Bonaparte at their head and disposing of all the treasure of the earth, our own excepted, could not by force make a track on the Blue Ridge or take a drink from the Ohio in a trial of a thousand years."[23] As things turned out, after Pearl Harbor the somber premonitions of Admiral Yamamoto—"we have awakened a sleeping giant and filled him with a terrible resolve"—came true to a degree, perhaps even beyond his imagination, for the giant rose indeed. America, savagely divided only days before between interventionists and isolationists, became one. (Scarcely weeks before, the U.S. Congress nearly had voted to abolish military conscription!) Only one member of Congress voted on December 8 against the declaration of war that followed the attack.

Other nations, however, are not so geographically well endowed as America. Britain's margin of safety in 1939 was much smaller than America's. Nevertheless, after Hitler's attack, Churchill was satisfied that being the victim of aggression was not so bad overall. Over the radio he told his people: "The storm of war may blow and the lands may be lashed with the fury of its gales, but in our hearts this Sunday morning there is peace. Our hands may be active, but our consciences are at rest."[24] But whereas Britain's margin of safety, largely consisting of the English Channel and the Royal Air Force, gave its people the luxury of such feelings, the people of Poland had no such luxury. As Churchill spoke, they were being bombed, shot, and herded into concentration camps. Their consciences were clean. They were united and very brave. They had a cause. But it was a lost cause.

So we must conclude that whether or not aggression provides the victim with a cause and the political benefits that flow therefrom depends entirely on circumstances. A sudden display of unexpected enemy power, to the degree that it is successful, can do more than break material resistance. It also tends to deprive political leaders of legitimacy, especially if they are perceived as having either provoked the attack or as having failed to prepare for it, or both. For example, the military blow that fell on France in 1940 discredited a whole political system and set its chief exponents against one another.[25] The world's sympathy did not help much. Neither has the world's sympathy for their causes meant much to the peoples of Hungary, Czechoslovakia, and Poland when in 1956, and again in 1968 and 1981, the Soviet Union overwhelmed them with its own army and proxy forces. Causes must be embodied by leaders—and so the Soviets killed or jailed them. And although, as Poland shows, the mere survival of a cause is not entirely dependent on the hope of military success, that hope really helps.

What about aggression in the nuclear age? As we shall see in chapter 7, modern technology has increased the importance of the opening phase of war. Today, by means of accurate nuclear-tipped ballistic missiles one side may begin by destroying the other side's capacity for rational military operations. Unless and until a nation can either hide its own stock of accurate nuclear-tipped ballistic missiles and other key military assets (ships, armored divisions, and so on), or until it can "shoot down" the missiles that might be sent against them, that nation will be forced to decide whether to be the aggressor or the sure loser. Modern technology has not negated the importance of geography. Aggression can still have a greater effect on a country like Poland, with no natural barriers to separate it from powerful neighbors, than on countries like the United States or, for that matter, South Africa, which are far removed from serious concentrations of enemy foot soldiers. Nevertheless, because modern long-range ballistic missiles potentially put every fixed, known military installation in the world within "artillery range," it is possible for acts of aggression to reduce seriously the ability even of the United States to conduct a war. Hence, because aggression now seems to be more militarily advantageous than ever before, it may be more of a "cause" of war than it ever had been in the past.

Of course, in our time, as always, aggression does not have to consist of spectacular acts. From time immemorial there have existed ways of prejudicing the outcome of a war without ever unfurling a banner and marching across a frontier. Political subversion, which includes acts ranging from planting rumors, cultivating secret allies, sabotaging key installations, and assassinating key leaders, can prejudice the outcome of a war just as much as strikes by ballistic missiles. For example, when Soviet troops invaded Afghanistan in 1979 their way had been cleared by—among other events—Soviet advisers to the Afghan army who had taken the rotors out of the engines of the military vehicles, and sympathizers in the Afghan Communist party who staged a coup against the country's president. The Afghan government never offered any resistance. The Soviets managed to cause the Afghan war in a manner that made it impossible for the Afghan government to have a cause. The Afghan people's cause against the Soviets had to arise from two nongovernmental sources: xenophobia and Islam.

As a surrogate for open military aggression, covert, or indirect aggression may more economically attain the political ends of war. It resembles direct aggression in that it aims to cripple the will and the political integrity of an adversary. Yet it surrounds those aims with fogs of ambiguity and disinformation. Was the unsuccessful assassination attempt against Pope John Paul II a surreptitious Soviet contrivance (via Bulgarian and Turkish proxies) to kill a formidable spiritual leader in order to cow Polish resistance to Soviet rule? Strong evidence to this effect was presented by Italian prosecutors in the recent trial of Bulgarian agents in Rome. Judicial confirmation of such a plot was not forthcoming—perhaps for wise political reasons: to publicly establish Soviet-Bulgarian responsibility for the planned murder of a great Christian leader might have endangered the delicate state of East-West relations.[26]

Conclusion

We are no closer to finding the philosopher's stone about war's causes than was the Psalmist. Nevertheless, some concluding thoughts are in order.

First, generic-determinist theories of war's causes, while interesting philosophically, have no practical, predictive value in providing indicators of present dangers and future wars. Some highly generalized ones which proffer stereotypes of particular cultures and political orders may have some value but are susceptible to exploitation by propagandists with hidden agendas.

Second, voluntarist theories, stressing that most if not all wars are deliberately caused and waged over important causes, are more instructive if only because they focus inquiry on real people and their agendas. They show that wars are intentional and serious undertakings, not accidents or frivolous ventures. Further, historical examples of "chosen wars" help us to understand how future ones may be deterred, fought, or won. By the same token, however, selective lessons from the past may be dangerously misapplied to contemporary situations of choice. "Honest history" in all its breadth and comprehensiveness offers many and often contradictory lessons.

This is not all bad. Knowing these contradictions should compel us to inquire into the strategic characteristics of present conflicts. Historical analogies, as warnings, as solace, and as practical advice can be powerful stimuli to policies; like prescription drugs they may help to cure, but they also can be deadly when taken in excess or as a remedy for the wrong affliction. Above all, causal analogies may be useless in the contexts of truly surprising events that admit of no known or apparent precedent. In circumstances of novelty and uncertainty where no guideposts exist, strategic thought about purposive action must take over. The very notion that the world is run by the contrasting wills of men leaves us on our own, but sober.

PART II

How Wars Are Fought

CHAPTER
3

THE FOG OF WARS

The movement of events is often as wayward and
incomprehensible as the course of human thought.
—PERICLES OF ATHENS

War is carried on in the dark.
—ARCHIDAMUS OF SPARTA

NOT THE LEAST of war's daunting aspects is its unpredictability.
No one knows how any given battle will come out, what shape the
war will take, who will win it, or what its consequences will be for
winners and losers.

Anyone who has ever been in battle has experienced its confusion. The battle is not always to the strong, because individuals
under stress at any given moment prove either better or worse at
seeing through the mess, at rallying efforts at key points, and at
changing expectations about what will happen next. King Charles
VII of Sweden and Napoleon are famous among military professionals both for winning battles against superior forces by their
"eye," which saw the correct time and place to apply maximum
efforts, and for their talent in leading enemies to divide their forces.
But at Waterloo, Blucher, the Prussian general, did not fall for Napoleon's divisive ploy, and Napoleon's "eye"—by which the Imperial Guard charged the Scottish infantry—was foiled by an unseen,
low-lying road across the Guard's path that tripped hundreds of
horses.

The uncontrollable chaos of battle is but one example of a larger truth: life (and death) is what happens to you while you are making other plans. This confusion was never better described than in Tolstoy's *War and Peace*. Tolstoy borrowed his description from the French reactionary philosopher-diplomat, Joseph de Maistre.

De Maistre was no pacifist, yet he shared with many pacifists a contempt for those war "commanders" who pretend to be in charge of the direction of combat in battles and wars, a view reflected in Tolstoy's contemptuous portrayal of Napoleon. *No one* in the heat of battle can ever fully know what is happening, much less can one fine-tune events. Thus, strictly speaking, military science is impossible. Tolstoy was inspired by this paragraph from de Maistre's *St. Petersburg Nights:*

> Many speak of battles without knowing what they are like; above all, one is prone to consider them as points on the map, whereas they cover two or three leagues of countryside; people say gravely: How come you do not know what happened in that fight, since you were there? But one could often say precisely the contrary. He who is on the right, does he know what is happening on the left? Does he even know what is going on two steps away from him? I easily conjure up one of those horrid scenes: in a vast terrain covered by the wherewithal of carnage, and which the feet of men and horses are tearing apart; in the middle of fire and of billows of smoke; dumbstruck, carried away by the shock of firearms and of military instruments, by voices that command, scream, or flicker out; surrounded by the dead, by the dying, and by mutilated corpses; possessed in turn by fear, by hope, by rage, by five or six different crazy passions, what does man become? What does he see? What does he know after a few hours? What power has he over himself and over others? Among this crowd of warriors who have fought all day, afterward there is not even one, not even the general, who knows the winner. You do not need me to tell you of modern battles, of famous battles whose memory will never perish; battles which have changed the face of Europe, and which were lost only because this or that man believed they were; so that supposing all circumstances to be equal, and not one more drop of blood shed on one side than on the other, another general would have had the *Te Deum* sung on his side, and would have forced history to say everything to the contrary of what it will say.[1]

Tolstoy wrote from experience—the Russian defeat of Napoleon had not sprung from superior military or political genius. Neither Napoleon nor his Russian opponent, Kutussov, had won at Borodino, the principal battle of the Franco-Russian War of 1812. The Russian victory came from Russia's unwillingness to accept defeat, and from a primordial determination to continue fighting. This determination might not have paid off. But pay off it did, because Napoleon made the unforeseeable mistake of staying in Moscow too late into the autumn. Thus, Tolstoy concludes, victory and defeat are not to be understood as consequences of rationally managed physical and political engagements; rather, they are the consequences of profoundly moral-psychological conditions.

Tolstoy's conclusion is valid, yet the "fog of war" does not negate the value of capable commanders. As Clausewitz recognized, the fog of war is a profoundly important aspect of reality which, though it cannot be wholly eliminated, the commander must anticipate and struggle with rather than submit to.

It is true that many battles, once begun, "run themselves" while the commanders are passive witnesses to the carnage. As the historian Bruce Catton has written of the Civil War battle at Antietam (1862) which the Union army narrowly won at immense cost:

> Masterpiece of art it assuredly was not: rather, a dreary succession of missed opportunities. Not once had the commanding general put out his hand to pull his battle plan together to undo the mistakes of his subordinates. The battle had been left to fight itself, and the general was a spectator. . . .[2]

But Antietam is not a simple refutation of Clausewitz's contention that military leaders must try to control the chaos of battle, nor is it a simple confirmation of Tolstoy's and de Maistre's contention that such chaos is uncontrollable. Rather, the events at Antietam were an instance of *deformation* and collapse of strategic principles in the heat of war. The general in charge, McClellan, was soon to be replaced by Grant, who though not up to the standards of Stonewall Jackson, never mind Napoleon, controlled events better and produced more decisive victories.

Because societies and regimes react more unpredictably to war than armies react to battle, wars are even "foggier" than battles. A regime, like the Turkish Empire in the eighteenth century, might look wealthy and invincible, but may have filled positions of authority with losers, fit only for impressing one another. Another regime, like the American Confederacy of 1861–65, might be led by the ablest of men and yet prove to be totally handicapped by its lack of central command for marshalling resources. Moreover, a weapon that initially appears to be decisive might not be if the enemy develops countermeasures under the lash of war. This is what happened to the German submarine fleet in World War II. By a similar token, in that war the United States and Britain literally wasted enormous resources in strategic bombing because of a belief in its effectiveness that was based on nothing but a priori conjecture. But in a wholly unexpected sense, strategic bombing did not turn out to be a waste at all. It channeled so much technical, managerial, and financial help to the U.S. aircraft industry that it has dominated the world's civil aviation market ever since the war.[3]

The fog that surrounds the outcomes of war has always tempted people to spin theories about what lies on the other side. Yet reality is always a surprise. For example, this century's wars have played havoc with the predictions of its most notable ideology, Marxism. Contrary to Marxist expectations, none of the wars of the twentieth century consummated a revolution in the advanced capitalist nations. Nor did the wars increase capitalism's dependence on underdeveloped colonies. Marxist-Leninists might claim that the colonies were able to turn World War II into a revolution that forced Great Britain, France, Belgium, the Netherlands, and Italy to grant them independence. Yet the facts tell another story. In the case of Britain, the key commitment to Indian independence had been made between 1919 and 1936 for reasons wholly moral-psychological. France, for its part, gave its colonies the bum's rush beginning in 1958, long after it had surpassed prewar economic levels. Moreover, while Marxist doctrine had predicted that decolonization would be followed by the collapse of capitalist economies, the very opposite happened: Instead of becoming impoverished, decolonized Europe enjoyed the biggest and fastest rise in prosperity it had ever known.

The fog of war is thickest for those least willing or able to impose their will on events, and it is most transparent for those most able to affect the conditions in which they operate. For example, many American military planners responsible for the central front in Europe, conscious of the Warsaw Pact's roughly 3 to 1 superiority in materiel and 1.5 to 1 superiority in manpower,[4] find solace in the well-known fact that, by and large, the non-Soviet troops in the Warsaw Pact armies facing NATO deeply hate anything Russian or Communist. Perhaps, the Americans muse, these troops would not follow Soviet orders to march against the West. How could the Soviets be sure of their loyalty? And so the Americans sit back on a cushion of uncertainty. But the Soviets, facing that same uncertainty, work to shape it. Like Livy's Romans and Machiavelli's prince, the Soviets try to engineer circumstances to force people who hate them to fight on their side. They continuously point out to their captive allies that the West has no plans to change the line of demarcation in Europe and that, whatever happens in the future, Polish, Hungarian, and Czech troops along with their families will remain in the Soviet sphere of influence. The Soviets also develop special units within East European armies whose members have special ties of personal interest to the Soviet Union, and they make sure that these units have special responsibility for policing the others. They also plan to deploy East European units so that if they were to retreat they would come under the West's fire—and under Soviet fire too. Of course, the Soviets cannot see the future any more clearly than Americans can see it, any more than those living by a river can foretell how high it will rise at the height of the next rains. But in this instance the Soviets' actions are like building dikes to channel a possible flood, while American military planners hope for fair weather.

What Makes the Fog?

The fog of war is the result of the unpredictable interaction of incalculable human factors. "No one," Clausewitz wrote, "starts a war—or rather, no one in his senses ought to do so—without first being clear in his mind what he intends to achieve by that war and how he intends to conduct it."[5] This is because one's own intentions and plans are all one can be sure of.

No one can fully know the other side's intentions. Either side's capabilities are a matter of opinion. What will actually happen, that is, how long the war will last and what will become of it, no one should pretend to know. One reason for this is that, in wartime, as Clausewitz put it, "the will is directed at an animate object that reacts." To put the matter differently, wars are contests between active wills. The expression "the dice of Mars" suggests the uncertainties of fortune even when, at the onset, the dice seem to be loaded one way or another. This "uncertainty principle" applies particularly to wars among great powers.[6]

A second reason no one can predict the nature of a war is that those who choose to start a given war usually take great pains to conceal their intentions from their enemies or to misrepresent their plans, capabilities, and deployments. As warfare unfolds, it tends to becloud its own ebb and flow. Years later, military historians may learn things about great battles which never dawned on astute and observant commanders at the time. By then the information is useless, except for didactic purposes in war colleges.[7] For good reasons, military establishments set great store in maintaining a precious system of "C³"—command, control, and communication—but when this fails or fails to perform effectively, battle tends to become blind and anarchic.[8] That is when subordinate commanders, on their own in some corner of the battlefield make the difference by performing better or worse than expected, by seizing opportunities, or by panicking.

A third reason is that no one can foretell which side will more quickly change its own ways to minimize the other side's strengths. For example, in the first battle of the Anglo-Zulu War of 1879 some fifteen hundred rifle-armed British soldiers were killed by perhaps twice their number of spear-carrying Zulus. But on July 4, in the final battle at Ulundi, although the Zulus had some rifles, their twenty-thousand-man army was destroyed while killing only twelve British soldiers.[9] Machine guns broke the formidable, disciplined Zulu lines. British cavalry then ran down the scattered warriors. The British had learned simply that hand-to-hand fighting with disciplined lines of Zulus was not a good idea and found the weapons to deal with them, while the Zulus failed to abandon the style of warfare that had given them so much success against opponents both black and white, in favor of the only style that might have defeated the British in the long run, guerrilla war.

But the principal reason why major wars are unpredictable is that their scope, duration, intensity, and purposes depend to some extent on how hard each side tries and on the degree to which the war engages the nation's energies and ingenuity. For example, observers of the Napoleonic Wars were startled by the unexpected military and political consequences of a revolutionary principle—the "nation in arms." Since then, societies have poured more of their bodies and souls into war than Clausewitz ever imagined. Not surprisingly, those who have managed to marshal more of their strength have had an advantage, not the least of which has been surprising their enemies with unexpected power.

The relationship between the latent power of nations and their forces-in-being is inherently unclear. With advantages of hindsight, we know that great errors can be made, in advance, in over- or underestimating both the military potential of adversaries and the belligerence of peaceful peoples once aroused.

Consider, for instance, the state of American war preparedness and morale before and after Pearl Harbor. Before the Japanese attack, American army conscripts were being trained with broomsticks in lieu of rifles and America's gross national product was about $100 billion. Three years later, the U.S. "arsenal of democracy" was producing more war materiel than all other belligerents combined, and the U.S. military budget *alone* was near $100 billion. A peaceful people had become the "arsenal of democracy." Static analyses of human phenomena are bad analyses.

Similarly, in the 1850s few could have imagined either the vast human and material resources that the American North and South would soon mobilize for war or the continental scope of the military operations that would ensue. Anyone who tried to predict this war's intensity by keeping track of military buildups would have gotten it all wrong. Neither side had prepared materially either to wage or deter the Civil War. But the thirty-year political buildup to that war sufficed to make it the nineteenth century's bloodiest. So unexpected was the war's fury that Washington's fashionable ladies drove out under parasols to view the first encounter between Union and Confederate forces at Manassas (or Bull Run). They came back screaming, some covered with the blood of the wounded in their carriages. North and South were soon mobilizing in ways they had never imagined.

In August 1914, European military experts were well prepared for mobilization. However, their war plans were based on expectations which, although reasonable, turned out to be wrong. Most experts thought the European war would be brief. And why not? The experience of a whole century's continental European wars had been that the decision would come in a few weeks or months. The Schleswig-Holstein campaign of 1864, the Austro-Prussian War of 1866, the Franco-Prussian War of 1870, and the Balkan wars of the late nineteenth and early twentieth centuries were all short; in each the strategic decision came quickly, and peace returned. In 1914, many believed all of the factors that made for quick decisions had increased in importance. Road and rail transport had improved, facilitating the bold and swift movements of armies. Besides, everyone knew that the sheer cost of modern war would exhaust the belligerents' treasuries. The specter of fiscal bankruptcy would quickly drive everyone to the peace table. The experts' facts were correct. The costs, and the disproportion between costs and stakes, *should have* driven all sides to the peace table—and fast. Instead, aroused peoples backed mindless military leaders while the wonders of modern transport merely fed blood and treasure into fixed fronts that consumed them.

Why are some wars bigger and others smaller, some more and others less violent than expected? Our contemporary jargon would suggest that we are considering "escalation"—as if there were a ladder of size and intensity that nations can dispassionately choose to mount or to dismount. We, however, argue that each of the factors contributing to a greater or lesser "totality" of war—for instance, political commitment, popular enthusiasm and hatred, economic mobilization, military strategy, weapons employed, competence of commanders, and the number of nations involved—is subject to change in unpredictable ways. The individuals involved are not dispassionate technicians in white coats, nor are they blind representatives of impersonal forces. The nature and outcome of wars are unpredictable precisely because they are determined by a complex of emotional, high-pressure decisions.

The combinations and permutations of these decisions is infinitely variable. For all factors to combine to produce self-immolating intensity in the same conflict is absurdly improbable. There is no reason to expect that escalation in intensity and scope are inevitable. In the real world, they can combine in quite asymmetrical ways. A nightmarish fear of truly total war may paralyze the will to deter or limit it. Timely applications of force—"the stitch in time"—may actually *avert* larger conflicts, just as such a stitch may *aggravate* other forces, passions, and purposes.

Consider the well-known propensity of those who feel that they are facing superior forces to call in allies. Whether or not this turns out to be unwise (for example, the Greeks invited Roman dominion this way), it always widens the war. During the American Civil War, for example, the South ardently sought help from Britain and France, and almost got it. In fact, during the war France seized control of Mexico. If the European powers had acted more boldly, the size of the war and its repercussions throughout the world would have grown significantly. That is why Lincoln, knowing that nations almost never embrace losing causes, sought big victories quickly.

Indeed, as Britain and France were on the brink of recognizing the Confederacy, news came that the Battle of Antietam had stalled and the Battle of Gettysburg had dashed the South's chances of success. Britain and France stayed out. Eighty years later, however, Adolf Hitler bet mistakenly that "lightning war" against Poland would present Britain and France with a moot cause. He was right that the two democracies would not lift a finger for Poland. But instead, they concluded that Hitler was an unappeasable danger to themselves and went to war on their own behalf.

How much will a war mean to those who wage it? Clearly personalist dictators such as Nicaragua's Anastasio Somoza or Cuba's Fulgencio Batista, who were committed above all to pleasant living and whose Swiss bank accounts were full—and whose followers were in similar positions—could hardly have been expected to slug it out very vigorously with insurgents whose leaders had no life—and no livelihood—but the international Communist movement. Yet two Guatemalan dictators, Lucas Garcia and Rios Montt, a primitive and a preacher respectively, fought and won a war against Communist guerrillas and apparently never opened Swiss bank accounts.[10]

Obviously, people's commitment to a war changes during the war. Despite almost daily declarations about how the Vietnam War was a test of America's credibility, Presidents Johnson and Nixon never took the war seriously enough to declare it formally, and thus effectively diminished their own and their country's political commitment even while pouring in more money and troops. Watching their enemy's political weakness strengthened North Vietnam and its allies far more than American bombs and bullets could weaken them. We will never know how North Vietnam's commitment would have fared if the United States had not engaged so many troops but had declared war instead.

Although it is generally true that success breeds commitment, and defeat the opposite, success can also bring on insouciance. For example, the awe-inspiring early successes of Hitler's blitzkrieg partly explain the Third Reich's failure to mobilize the German economy. German confidence in swift total victory meant that German troops on the Eastern front in 1941 were logistically ill-equipped for Russia's none-too-secret weapon, winter. Even in the darkest months of Russia's agonies in 1942, Soviet factories' tank production vastly exceeded lethargic German output. As Albert Speer later admitted in his memoirs, German total mobilization was not seriously attempted until 1943.[11] By then, the American, British, and Soviet war economies had been fully mobilized for years. German women were not conscripted for factory work until well after the siege of Stalingrad in 1942–43. While American women were becoming "Rosie The Riveter," the German wartime hausfrau typically kept the home fires burning.

The mobilization of technology also depends on the level of the belligerents' commitment. Albert Speer, for example, recounts how the famed German physicist Werner Heisenberg was asked by Hitler's government to investigate the technical feasibility of the atom bomb. But Heisenberg was not enthusiastic about the Nazis winning the war.[12] So his truthful report intentionally emphasized the enormity of what would have to be done instead of laying out an appealing plan for doing what was admittedly a large job. Meanwhile in America, scientists—many of them Jews or refugees from Hitler's Europe—had every incentive to be positively ingenious and to get the atom bomb built as quickly as possible. By a similar token, in the 1980s the American technical community was split on the question of whether antiballistic missile defenses are feasible. Naturally, those who, like Edward Teller, had a history of opposition to the Soviet Union, tended to describe the task of building antimissile defenses in ways that invited effort. Others, like Val Fitch and Sidney Drell, both presidents of the American Physical Society who had a history of leftist activism, described the task in ways that discouraged effort.[13]

The principal reason for the fog of war is that so much depends on human purpose, and human purpose is so variable.

Piercing the Fog

The Greeks consulted oracles. The Romans tried to read the entrails of sacrificed chickens. The tradition of staging "war games" for both training and prediction has no known beginning. Soothsayers, magicians, and charlatans of every kind have long purported to tell rulers how the next war would come out—for a price. In our time this hoary habit wears the "uniform of the day": the computer scientist's white coat. Today's soothsayers are at least as expensive as their forebears. In 1988, the Pentagon announced a one billion-dollar project for a computer facility whose sole job would be to 'run' various simulations of battles between hypothetical Soviet ballistic missiles and hypothetical American antimissile defenses.[14] This is only the showiest of the dozen major simulation centers within the U.S. military establishment that mathematically model the performance of everything from components of individual weapons to tactics and procedures and entire wars. Since the early 1960s, computer simulation, which is part of a larger intellectual and bureaucratic process called "systems analysis," has largely replaced "command judgment" as the basis for most major decisions in the U.S. military.

Advocates of this approach to decision making claim that it removes uncertainty from choice by objectifying and testing the consequences. But the best it can do is to discover the consequences of the assumptions inherent in the test scheme. Does a given tank or a laser perform adequately? That depends on what one assumes is the "hardness" of its target and on how one assumes the target would be operated. Much would also depend on how one defines adequate performance. Systems analysis can come up with entirely different judgments depending on the assumptions with which it starts. At best its results are tautologies recognized as such. Its appeal, however, lies in its bureaucratic effects. By buttressing their choices, or their deferral of choices, with studies that seem objectively to pierce the fog of the future, military bureaucrats exercise power while keeping the option of claiming that they are not responsible for eventual failures because they acted "by the numbers." Another example of this is the practice of the U.S. Joint Chiefs of Staff to hold high-level war games in which they themselves are both the "blue team" and the judges of the outcome. Not surprisingly, whenever the games are held like this the "blue team" never loses. The Chiefs could give themselves A's without going through the process. But then their judgment would not look so authoritative.

The results of systems analysis can be shocking examples of what the ancient Greeks called hubris. For example, in 1964 Secretary of Defense Robert McNamara claimed that his newly established Program Analysis and Evaluation Department had figured out the precise numbers of 105-mm towed howitzers and 4.2-inch mortars that the Pentagon would need for the next war, that the United States had 270 percent of the former and 290 percent of the latter, and that it was going to sell the remainder![15] While it makes sense to judge that the number of cannon (or anything else) may be too high or too low or about right, it is utter nonsense to live by precise predictions of wartime needs. Although it is sensible to try to thin the fog of war by formulating as good an idea as one can of what may lie beyond, the worst thing one can do is to hypostatize assumptions about how this or that weapon or tactic will work and then treat these assumptions as if they were reality. As Stalin used to remind his generals and intelligence officers, to live by one's own assumptions is to fall into self-made traps.[16]

One reason why systems analysis has become so popular in our time is that one important aspect of war in the period circa 1965–90 is rather easily predictable. Given the assumption that no defenses exist against long-range ballistic missiles, and given a certain number of missiles of known reliability, warheads with known explosive yields and targets of known location and vulnerability, predicting the results of missile strikes is a matter of mere arithmetic. But note: Long before 1990 it became clear that antimissile defense was a growing reality (if only in the Soviet Union) and that the increasing mobility of strategic targets had deprived the simple yield-on-target calculus of much of its utility. Furthermore, even the limited applicability of systems analysis to predicting ICBM warfare does not extend to predicting other types of warfare.

Yet it is true that, here and there, the fog can fleetingly be pierced to some extent. Having knowledge of the enemy's strength and plans and given time, it is possible to rehearse attacks. The Japanese pilots who attacked Pearl Harbor in 1941 practiced by looking at a scale model of the area from the angles at which they would be approaching it. The Israeli soldiers who attacked the Ugandan soldiers and terrorists at Entebbe Airport in 1976 practiced in a mock-up of the airport hastily thrown together according to its original Israeli designs. Almost everything went as planned. In 1971, however, a group of American special forces built a mock-up of a North Vietnamese prisoner of war camp so accurately that even the hinges on the cages opened the right way. They rehearsed a rescue mission to perfection, only to find that by the time they struck, the American prisoners had been moved.[17]

Rehearsal is wonderful, but it costs time. Besides, it is terribly dependent on good intelligence and flawless security. To the extent that the intelligence is flawed, rehearsals prepare the troops for the wrong fight. And if the enemy learns the details of one's rehearsal, he can prepare a surprise that will be all the more devastating because the attacking forces will be going through a rigid drill. That is why there is never any excuse for rehearsed operation not having a "plan B." Alas, rehearsal is far more useful for attack than for defense because it is easier to plan one's own attack than to predict the enemy's.

All attempts to pierce the fog must be based on knowledge of the enemy. Knowledge of the enemy *before* the war starts is difficult enough to gain because of the enemy's concealment and deception. But such knowledge is not to be confused with knowledge of the enemy's actual performance. That can only be gained the hard way. One major battle may confirm or nullify previous impressions and give rise to wholly new impressions. One strategic victory or defeat can change the reputations of victors and vanquished alike. Military historians now recount how Western analysts at the time of Hitler's attack on Russia in June 1941 mistakenly predicted a speedy collapse of the Red Army in a matter of weeks.[18] By the same token, General Howe, commanding British troops in Boston in 1776, believed that a whiff of grapeshot would tame the colonial's rabble-in-arms at Bunker Hill. A catalog of such underestimates in history would be as long as a catalog of adversary overestimates. The outcome of battle confirms or refutes estimates, just as the proof of a pudding is in its eating. Such uncertainties are no monopoly of the military; they are present in other contests—in sports, in democratic electoral politics, and in the stock market.

Nations have been built on one great victory that gave heart for others. Similarly, the loss of one battle can begin to unravel the psychological and military fiber of empires. For example, the British surrender to the Japanese of their great Asian naval fortress, Singapore, in early 1942 echoed throughout Asia. Here was the mightiest European empire bested in battle by an Asian nation! This startling event inspired in non-Western nationalist leaders a hitherto chimeric vision of independence, even though Japanese victory made them all far less independent than they had been before. Although the Japanese Empire was eventually broken by the might of another Western power, America, scarcely more than a decade after the British surrender at Singapore the British, French, and Dutch empires in South and Southeast Asia all had collapsed, giving way to turbulent, independent regimes.

How then is the fog of war to be pierced? Only by the willful actions of leaders, since it results from turbulent human emotions; it can only be pierced (to the extent to which piercing it is possible) by the assertion of human qualities that master those emotions.

Machiavelli's portrait of Cesare Borgia contains an account of one of the most competent jobs of hedging against uncertainty ever performed. Borgia stuck to the basics. Build the best and most reliable armed forces you can, and place your allies into positions from which it would be arguably suicidal for them to desert. Win battles which encourage your side and which raise the enemy's incentive to negotiate. Strike the decisive blow when it is least expected. Never assume that anyone will forbear doing all the harm of which he is capable or that the next step into the fog will not be your most difficult. Never rely on the gratuitous help of others. Make sure that in every move your reach is equal to your grasp, and think several moves ahead. Above all, keep your eye on the objective.[19]

Victory

Since no one can see through the fog of war and so many things are beyond one's control, anyone entering the fog is best advised to look at all the things he can see and control from the perspective of the only reliable compass: the idea of victory—the attainment of the goal for which he is fighting.

Victory is the natural purpose of war, in the sense that produce is the natural purpose of farming. It means the imposition of one's will upon the other.

Historically victory has meant putting the enemy's military forces in a position from which they are unable to resist further pressure. Victory does not mean the annihilation of enemy forces or that further prosecution of the war would be without cost to the victor. But it does mean that the vanquished recognize that the military situation would become increasingly worse, without hope of reversal. Also, for those in a hopeless military position actually to consider themselves vanquished, they must believe that the enemy is willing, even eager, to continue the war unless its demands are met. Otherwise, the situation is not hopeless at all.

This generation of American statesmen, who believe that victory is an archaic concept and that military power must be carefully graduated to send signals for securing specific objectives, have been proven wrong both in Korea and in Vietnam. In Vietnam, Ho Chi

Minh and Le Duc Tho learned through the drastic limitation of the power applied against them that U.S. presidents meant what they said about being disinterested in victory. In December 1972, President Nixon's actions appeared to imply another mindset. Nixon mined North Vietnam's harbors and bombed the country in a way that seriously portended the destruction of the North Vietnamese communist regime. But this change in action did not cancel the overriding fact that Nixon was no more interested in victory than he or his predecessors had ever been. Thus, when the "Christmas bombing" led North Vietnam to ask for an armistice and the Paris Agreement of 1973, all the conditions for an American victory were met—except one. Because the North Vietnamese knew that the Americans would not prosecute the war in order to gain the concessions embodied in the Paris Agreements, they also knew that those agreements did not force North Vietnam to choose between abandoning its war aims and seeing its regime destroyed. On the contrary, in the absence of U.S. resolve, the agreements meant that North Vietnam's victory and America's defeat were at hand. Although in achieving victory it is not often necessary to destroy completely the enemy's armed forces, never mind the enemy's society, it is a sine qua non of victory that the defeated party believe that such destruction would follow. In other words, the amount of military power that must be applied to consummate a victory is inversely proportional to the "winner's" reputation for ferocity, and, of course, directly proportional to how onerous the winner's demands are.

The ultimate weapon for sealing victory is the foot soldier, whose bayonet against the enemy's belly can compel obedience and thus perform what some American political scientists believe to be the quintessential political act—determining who gets what, when, and how.

Not even the bayonet, however, is omnipotent in this regard. History is full of examples of peoples whose armies were defeated and who nevertheless repelled resisting bayonets and police truncheons through paramilitary means. Nevertheless, history teaches that resistance movements, no matter how inspired, almost always fail unless they somehow combine their activities with a war waged against their oppressor by a third power. Unless they have such close coordination, or unless the enemy is somehow morally incapacitated, resistance movements lead to executions and deportations.

Just as there is an art to winning wars and maximizing gains, there is also an art to losing and minimizing the consequences of defeat. The trick, for the defeated, is somehow to avoid occupation. "In defeat, defiance," counseled Winston Churchill. That can be done very well—if one avoids occupation. The defeated party must retain enough military power and fighting spirit to limit the winner's demands, or perhaps even to limit the winner's gains to the ones he was able to seize on the battlefield. This, of course, is what Britain managed to accomplish in the early days of World War II. It suffered a huge loss in France and was also compelled to withdraw from Norway. The Soviet Union similarly suffered enormous defeats and retreats. But because Churchill and, to a lesser extent, Stalin were prudent enough to cut their losses in losing battles, they were able to save sufficient forces to defy the winner. There should be no illusion. By June 1940, Hitler had won the war. In 1940, Britain spurned German peace offers that could only be described as generous, and was able to build on what remained, ultimately to seal its victory by occupying Germany.

It is interesting to note that as German troops were pushed onto the defensive beginning in 1943, traditional German commanders drew conclusions similar to those Churchill had drawn three years before: Conserve troops, retreat, and fortify so as to be able to defy the enemy to obtain either a not-too-onerous peace or time in which to prepare new offensives. But the Nazi regime would have nothing to do with such prudence. It could not deal with the unknown by continuously adjusting the balance between its millenialist political objectives and military strategy. Students and practitioners of the military craft must constantly realize that such irrationality and incompetence can and do exist. But the basis of the craft must be balancing the length of one's reach and the strength of one's grasp.

The war councils must constantly consider the questions that every fighting man as well as every father, mother, wife, and sweetheart constantly asks: When do we win? How will this attack or this defense help end the war and get us the things for which we are fighting? However thick the fog of war may be, those vital questions are always crystal clear.

CHAPTER
4

THE POLITICAL
CONDITIONS OF
BATTLE

Stiffen the sinews, summon up the blood,
Disguise fair nature with hard-favored rage;
Then lend the eye a terrible aspect . . .
Now set the teeth and stretch the nostrils wide,
Hold hard the breath, and bend up every spirit
To his full height.
—SHAKESPEARE
King Henry V. 3.3

SINCE NAVIGATING through the fog of war is the most politically willful of activities, we begin our discussion of military operations with some observations on the practical political questions that every belligerent nation must resolve: Who will fight? Who will lead? How? What will the basic plan be? Nations tend to change their answers to these basic questions as they move through wars.

Who Will Fight?

Who will pay the blood-tax? Will the armed forces be composed of men for whom arms are a family tradition—a self-perpetuating military caste—or of men for whom the armed forces are merely a reasonably well paid career? Or will the armed forces be drawn principally from society at large so that men serve only for a short time and without much pay? If so, will all able-bodied men serve, or only some? If some are exempted from the blood-tax, how will they be chosen? Will men be enticed into the armed forces with pay and benefits, or will they be drafted?

In Western civilization, where the Oriental tradition of slave armies never took root, military service has always been regarded either as something that goes with citizenship or as something that the ruler manages to purchase on behalf of the polity (in which case the citizen as taxpayer is merely obliged to help pay the bill for the military). Arguments in favor of these two contrasting approaches shed light on primordial questions about the nature of citizenship.

Purchasing military service is an old practice. Thucydides tells of commanders in the Peloponnesian War augmenting their forces by going to towns near their lines of march to engage bowmen or stone-slingers. Athens used its treasure to lure foreign and domestic rowers to its *triremes*, the battleships of the day. During the Renaissance, Switzerland was known throughout Europe as the exporter of its prime commodity: fine pikemen. A vestige of this tradition remains today in the Swiss Guards, who police the Vatican and serve as bodyguards of the Pope. Today also, Pakistanis serve for pay in the armed forces of Saudi Arabia. France permits foreigners to serve in its Foreign Legion, which, however, is not so much a means of purchasing foreigners' services as it is a vestige of the time when foreigners chose to fight for the supranational ideals of the French Revolution. Britain still today allows persons from northern India to enlist in its Gurkha regiments; they fought ferociously in the Falklands War. But that is a vestige of the time when Britain fielded the vast army of an empire that included the Indian subcontinent, Arabia, black and white Africa, Canada, and Australia.

The Turkish Empire once employed yet another kind of soldier— the janissary. These young men had been taken from their homes as children and raised to be elite troops. Well fed, trained, and equipped, loyal to the sultan alone, the janissaries stiffened armies throughout various parts of the empire, guarded the sultan, and served as shock troops. Similarly forcible abductions of native children for long-term service have been carried out by Cubans in Angola and the Soviets in Afghanistan.

The art of recruiting and managing armies from subject countries was fully developed by Rome and described by Livy. Since about

1950, the chief practitioner of this art has been the Soviet Union. The imperial power usually places its own imperial officers in key positions in the subject countries' armies. For example, after World War II, the Soviet Union appointed its own Marshal Rokossovski as Poland's minister of defense. He was a Russian general in a Polish uniform.

The imperial power must insure that the subject countries' leading officers, and certain special units enjoying special privileges and equipment, are more loyal to the empire than to their own people. Above all, the imperial power must see to it that when subject armies are mobilized, their soldiers know that if they revolt, the empire intends to kill them and to devastate their homes and families. Subject armies may hate the empire with all their hearts. But if their lines of command and communication are controlled by the empire, and if they are far from home—sandwiched perhaps between the empire's troops to their rear and facing in front enemy forces that regard them as part and parcel of the empire—they are most likely to do the empire's work. Thus it was with Rome; thus it is with the Soviet Union today.

Armies may also be purchased wholesale by forming alliances. Nowadays, as in the past, this is the primary means of purchasing armies abroad. Perhaps the best example of a modern mercenary alliance was Mussolini's participation in Hitler's war against Britain and France in 1940. This case illustrates one of the two possible outcomes of such a purchase: Because the purchased armies of Italy had no interest in the fight, they performed miserably. This forced Hitler to take troops he could not spare from the Russian front to reinforce fronts in Greece and Italy that would not have existed in the first place had he not brought Italy into the war. Thus, much of the time "bought" armies are dangerous because they tend to lose.

But if foreign-bought armies win, they may be even more dangerous to the purchaser than when they lose. In 1494 the Pope brought the king of France into Italy to help him in a quarrel with Milan and Venice. France's King Charles won, but France was not finally expelled from Italy until 1870! During World War II, many Americans and some Englishmen argued that it was clever to spare Western lives and efforts and to allow the Soviet armies to bleed in order to defeat the *Wehrmacht* in Eastern Europe. In a sense, the West bought Soviet services on the Eastern front by leaving that front to Stalin. The Soviets did indeed pay a heavy price for Eastern Europe, but having paid it, they were not about to give up their prize simply because the Atlantic Charter's democratic principles would have obliged them to permit Poles, Hungarians, Czechs, Rumanians, Germans, and Bulgarians to choose their own governments and to align themselves with the West.

Purchasing allies in hope of avoiding war is perhaps the riskiest and most self-deceptive means of increasing one's forces. As Machiavelli has pointed out, one's own countrymen (never mind foreigners) are all too ready to promise fidelity in battles that seem improbable or are in the indefinite future. But as prospects of death and privation take shape, allies tend to remember that the purpose of their adherence in the first place was to *avoid* fighting. Hence, they tend to urge accommodation with the enemy—at the price of real military power—as a condition for maintaining the alliance.

In the 1930s both Britain and France found that their alliance weakened rather than improved their ability to deal with Hitler's growing menace. Neither country would act without the other, and each found in the other's reticence an excuse for its own. Each also saw in the other's armed forces a reason not to increase its own. France desperately wanted British troops on its soil, not so much for what they could do against Germany but as an assurance of a political commitment, which by itself, she hoped, would keep war from starting, or from becoming serious. Britain agreed to send troops for precisely the reasons the French wanted them, but with insufficient thought about what would actually happen if the Germans attacked seriously. The British Expeditionary Force was thus hostage to a certain political design that served to lull both Britain and France into complacency.

When Germany attacked in May 1940, it quickly became clear that both countries would have been better off had they fully committed themselves to their own defense rather than trusting in their own and in their allies' half-commitments. Today many Europeans want U.S. troops stationed in Germany not so much for what they could do to stop a Soviet invasion, but rather as a token of an American political commitment. The United States keeps troops in Europe for that very reason and gives little thought to what it would do if the Soviets were to launch a large-scale attack. It is very possible that any alliance that reinforces its members' tendency not to think about fighting does more harm than good.

The practice of purchasing the military services of one's own citizens developed in the West during the Renaissance, when kings could no longer count on noblemen to bring along to battle a sufficient number of infantry and bowmen who would serve them out of feudal loyalty. The rise of cities free from feudal obligations provided pools of manpower. Since no one in the premodern, Christian West believed that secular authorities had the right to *compel* military service, money became the mother's milk of armies. Money had been important in Thucydides' time. But now it became nearly everything. The armies of King Louis XIV and of the Duke of Marlborough that fought for control over the valleys of the Rhine and upper Danube at the beginning of the eighteenth century were made up of an aristocratic core of officers; professional, long-service non-commissioned officers; and fighting men hired for the duration of the campaign. The only change in this pattern up to the French Revolution is that the European officer corps became somewhat less aristocratic as kings commissioned more commoners as officers, and these officers tended more and more to draw their livelihood and status from their royal commissions. The French Revolution gave impetus to this trend even in the countries that remained monarchies. The best example is Prussia, where titles of nobility came to be the result of rank *earned* by performance. The Napoleonic wars ushered in the age of secular ideology, and hence spawned the drafting of simple soldiers.

After 1815, however, even France—which under both the revolution and Bonaparte was a "nation-in-arms"—returned to the previous practice of enlisting soldiers through financial incentives. This was widely decried by the political left as a bourgeois body blow to both patriotism and national power. In the 1830s, France introduced a novel combination of compulsion and incentive: selective service. Theoretically, every young Frenchman was obliged to lend his person to his country's glory. Theoretically, everyone, regardless of class, would share the same soup and barracks. This pleased the French imperialist left. But France did not have any use for, and could not afford, the huge army that would have resulted from universal service. France's wars for the foreseeable future would not be in Europe but in Africa and Asia. Short-term draftees would not do for those campaigns. So men were drafted for as long as eight years, and were paid reasonably well. This produced a small, professional army. Since bourgeois families would not tolerate having their sons randomly taken for such big slices of life, the law permitted anyone to satisfy his military obligation by hiring someone to fill his place in the military, a practice also followed by the U.S. federal government during the Civil War. Of course, this system produced reservists both few and old. Consequently, the system worked only until France had to fight a European power, Prussia, in 1871. Prussia had also used selective service, but the Prussian system's enlistments were shorter, its base was wider, and it produced a bigger base of reservists for mobilization. After its defeat by Prussia, and with the return of the left under the reestablished Republic, France returned to universal military service, which produced the huge army of World War I. In the modern world, all major armed forces use universal service all the time, or plan to do so in wartime.

The practical question of how to arrange peacetime forces depends both on how the society regards itself and on how it thinks of the wars it might have to fight. Nowadays, for instance, Britain maintains a small armed force made up of long-term enlistees enticed by pay, many of whom make a career of the military. While its reserve forces are small, Britain is committed by the North Atlantic Treaty Organization, and by virtue of its ties to its former colonies, potentially to fighting a world war. The rest of Western Europe nominally has the same commitment only in case the Soviet Union were to try to conquer Europe or North America. But the rest of Western Europe theoretically has established a universal military obligation even in peacetime, even though only a small percentage of the potential draftees are taken. This may be due less to serious consideration of what it would take actually to help fight a world war than to the judgment that the draft fosters integration among the various social classes and a sense of civic responsibility. The Communist countries, for their part, have universal military service and draft just about all who are fit. That is both because Leninist doctrine sees nations playing the role of classes in the great struggle that is life and because Leninist practice requires as much regimentation of society as can be managed.

Until World War II, the United States followed the British tradition of a small, relatively well-paid, long-service, standing armed force that could be augmented by wartime conscription. But the United States faced the problem of reserves very differently from the rest of the world. America's frontier origins, reflected in its federal system, had provided it with state militias—the National Guard. The United States, unlike the rest of the world (save Switzerland and, to some extent, the other English-speaking pioneer societies of Canada, Australia, and South Africa), had no lack of civic responsibility. After World War II, as Americans found world-wide responsibilities thrust upon them, they have debated how best to raise the large forces required to meet these responsibilities. The waning of frontier habits and the declining vigor of state and local governments (due to the rise of a huge federal bureaucracy), as well as the rise of divisive ideological and racial conflicts led many Americans to conclude that the draft was necessary for social as well as for military reasons. But the United States did not want to bear the social and economic burden of very large armed forces that would result from drafting most eighteen- to twenty-year-olds.

The postwar solution, selective service, relied on local draft boards to select the best qualified young men from a cross section of the population. Between 1954 and 1964, the system worked roughly as intended: A cross-section of rich and poor, black and white, unschooled and graduates alike were either drafted or, with their draft boards breathing down their necks, enlisted as privates or "volunteered" for officer training. True, young men who continued their education or were obliged to take care of families could defer their responsibilities. But few who pursued Ph.D. studies until they were too old for the military, or who started families, did so to escape the draft. The Vietnam War changed all that. Then, draft avoidance through deferment became so widespread it largely exempted the upper middle class from military service. When this happened, the draft became a cause of national disunity rather than unity. So, after a brief (1969–72) experiment with selective service by lottery—with sharply curtailed deferments—the Nixon administration abandoned the military draft altogether.

The chief argument for doing away with the draft was a combination of classical liberalism ("no innocent person should be deprived of liberty unless the nation's requirements are so dire as to demand that everyone be so deprived for a short period"), pragmatism ("by offering the right pay we can recruit the forces we need quite efficiently"), and finally, whistling in the dark ("military service should be performed out of patriotism, not coercion, and the U.S. is full of patriots"). The fact that many of those who urged the "volunteer army" most strongly were the ones least likely to volunteer pointed to the main reason why politicians felt pressure to end the draft. Perhaps the most influential portion of the U.S. public, the upper-middle class, wanted to "drop out" of the obligation to support the U.S. armed forces with their bodies and the bodies of their loved ones. Significantly, most people in this group did not object to America's playing an active role in the world. Indeed, except for a few extreme leftists, most thought that an active foreign policy and powerful armed forces were necessary and did not object to paying lots of taxes to support them. But they no longer wanted these things badly enough to commit themselves or people they cared about. They may not have thought of international affairs as a spectator sport, but they wanted no part for themselves in any of the rough stuff.

Republican presidents Richard Nixon and Ronald Reagan and Democrat Jimmy Carter have turned the political question—who shall pay the blood-tax?—into one of market economics: Have the armed forces been attracting enough qualified people so that they can accomplish their mission?

Yet the political implications of the American "all volunteer force" are obvious. About one-fourth of its numbers are black (some two and a half times the percentage of blacks in the population). Ten percent are women. Most important, practically none are from this country's upper and upper-middle socioeconomic groups. The families of those who make national policy have effectively "dropped out" of the institution that enforces such policy, and the families of those who pay the blood-tax have only a theoretical connection with the policymakers—people with vastly different tastes and habits. So far there has been no debate in the United States about how realistically and effectively national policy can be made by leaders who do not personally feel its possible military consequences. Nor, despite a spate of movies about the Vietnam War that touch this theme tangentially, has there been debate over how, in a crisis, the social classes who pay the blood-tax are likely to accept directions from those who lead but do not bleed.

For example, there is widespread agreement among American leaders that some three hundred thousand U.S. troops and over one million military dependents should be stationed in Europe, regardless of NATO's inability to protect them against attack from superior Warsaw Pact forces. The nation's leaders agree, none too loudly, that the true role of American troops in Europe is that of hostages—to reassure America's European allies that a Soviet invasion of Europe would involve the United States in a way that no one wishes to specify. But it is not clear that U.S. leaders would so commit U.S. troops if the commitment involved their own families. Nor is it clear that the social classes who supply America's military forces understand the sacrificial role these troops are intended to play.

A far-fetched argument can be made that the public would consciously sanction such a role because that is what the troops were hired to do. But the U.S. public certainly would not sanction such a policy if it involved draftees. As for the "all volunteer force," note that the average American lets his child join on the basis of the government's claim that the armed forces are a "great place to start," where the kid could "be all that you can be." Neither the recruiting pitches, military posture statements, congressional debates, nor the president in his State of the Union addresses mentions that the job of these troops would be to serve as hostages, that they would not be equipped to defeat a Soviet invasion of Europe, and that if it came, the best they could hope for would be to become prisoners of war.

Moreover, if war came to Europe, would such troops themselves obey the call to perform the role of sacrificial hostages? How would their families react? How would white, affluent, "quiche-eating" U.S. leaders answer the charge that they were sacrificing America's poor and black? Nothing so debilitates a nation in war as the perception that the blood-tax is being assessed unfairly. Indeed, that is the stuff of revolution.

Contemporary America also offers perhaps the most extreme answer ever given in history to the question "Should women fight?" The standard answer throughout history has been "No!" Except in Western civilization, this protective attitude toward women has not been due to tenderness. Most men at most times have rudely exploited the weaker sex more or less as slaves, and for precisely the same reason as masters exploit slaves, because they could get away with doing it (note Aristotle's definition of the barbarian as one who equates women with slaves). In all civilizations but our own the life expectancy of women has been lower than that of men. What is the reason, then, why men have kept the bloody business of battle to themselves? Is it possible that they have wanted to exclude women from something they considered glorious? This is unlikely because men have kept women out of combat even in times of direst necessity, when auxiliary corps of women fighters might have made the difference between victory and defeat. Yet in all but a few odd cases, more prominent in books than in reality, men who otherwise routinely used women for the roughest, meanest labor have chosen not to use them in battle.

The reasons are twofold. First, the natural attraction between men and women is so strong that if it is allowed to be present on the battlefield, commanders can be certain that it will distract fighters from a task to which they must give their undivided attention. Also, because that natural affection gives rise to special attention by some individuals to others, it is sure to detract from the loyalty that fighters must give to their unit. Second, and even more powerful, is the realization that a society's women are the living assurance that no matter what happens, the society will survive. An army of men may be destroyed one year, and twenty years later the sons born to the dead men's wives and sisters could reverse the result. A war may decimate a society's men. But so long as the women are not touched, the demographic catastrophe will last only one or two generations. For example, if in World War I France had lost 1.5 million young *women* rather than young men, its loss would not have been made up in a generation, but would actually have become worse before improving. The separation of women from combat thus is rooted in mankind's basic instincts for survival.

But the question of the role of women in war has become pressing in our time because modern war involves all of society, and because equality of the sexes has become one of the principal tenets of modern conventional wisdom. All modern countries have encouraged women to work in war-equipment industries and to replace men mobilized for military service. The Soviet Union in World War II even conscripted female labor. The Nazis, initially averse to women in work places, used female as well as male forced laborers after 1943 when the war took a turn for the worse. The armed forces of all modern countries, especially in wartime, make use of women in staff functions far from combat and in medical functions immediately behind the lines. Israel trains women's units to protect their homes and farms while the men are at the front.

The United States, however, has made a historically unique attempt to fully integrate women into the armed forces while still barring them from combat. It has done this out of a combination of the push of egalitarian ideology and of the pull of necessity—the shortage of qualified male "volunteers" in the armed forces. In the United States, women enter military service through the same avenues as men (enlistment followed by basic training, officer candidate schools, reserve officer training corps at colleges, and service academies). Like men, women trainees shoot rifles, crawl through the mud, fight hand-to-hand, and so on. However, they are not asked to do this as much or as vigorously as men. Furthermore, by law they are assigned to jobs that require none of those things. One often hears that the integration of women has gone very well, and that the U.S. armed forces function perhaps better with women than they have without them. This is true. But it is surely due to the fact that the U.S. armed forces in peacetime are almost indistinguishable from civilian society in their daily duties. The average working day of the average member of the U.S. armed forces is not so different from that of his or her civilian friends. In wartime, however, all military forces are vastly different from *any* civilian society. They work around the clock in makeshift conditions; they kill and get killed. So today, because women make up such a substantial part of U.S. forces and above all because they hold so many kinds of jobs (ranging from piloting transport aircraft to processing battlefield intelligence), their involvement in future battles is certain. The number of women likely to be thus killed will be far too small to make a demographic impact, but more than enough to cause both a disruption in U.S. forces and arouse bitter recrimination over having hired women to do duties that men would not compel one another to perform.

Who Will Lead?

War brings military considerations into the everyday business of government. By its nature, that business is nonmilitary, even if the man running it happens to be a general. However, the moment that any government, whether headed by a civilian or a military man, makes the decision to go to war, it must wrestle with the fact that the art of government in wartime has both a political and a military dimension. Its primary task is to balance both dimensions. General Ludendorff, Germany's dictator in World War I, and President Franklin D. Roosevelt, who led the United States through World War II, were equally wrong to say, in Ludendorff's words, "Overall, politics must serve the war." The art of wartime leadership is not to destroy the natural tension between political and military requirements, but to synthesize it.

The fluid connection between the actual conduct of battles and the political aims of war may be seen in the American Civil War. Clausewitz's maxim regarding the supremacy of the political aim in war in no way implies that war aims are unalterably fixed once war begins. Rather it implies that the politicians in command must be

sensitive to the course of battle. Battlefield necessity may actually
work to modify, lower, or dramatically elevate the political objectives of war. So, although Gettysburg, not Antietam, proved to be the
true military turning point in the American Civil War, the news of
Antietam led Lincoln to make a major change in political strategy.
No longer was the war to have as its sole, overriding purpose the
mere restoration of the Union. Only weeks after Antietam, his
Emancipation Proclamation declared that Negro slaves in seces-
sionist states from then on would be free from bondage. Lincoln
knew this wartime act could have a practical effect upon the course
of battle—for one thing, winning over the loyalty of Negroes to the
Union war effort. Nearly 180,000 of them quickly donned the Union
blue uniform. But the proclamation also elevated Union war aims to
a morally higher plateau than had the goal of recapturing wayward
Southern states. It soon became regarded as a milestone in the long
history of human rights. Later, in 1863, Lincoln thus described the
intimate connection between the moral and the material exigencies
of combat: "The emancipation policy, and the use of colored troops,
constitute the heaviest blow yet dealt to the rebellion."[1] In hindsight, the moral force of Lincoln's subsequent Gettysburg address
and its moving affirmation of human freedom can scarcely be imagined had it not been preceded by the Emancipation Proclamation.

Once such political thresholds, such Rubicons, have been crossed,
there is no going back. As the Civil War drew to a close, Lincoln was
reminded that he had issued the Proclamation solely on his authority as commander in chief of the armed forces during wartime.
When the war ended, the argument went, so too would his authority
to deprive slaveowners of their property. Unless and until the Constitution could be modified, Lincoln would have to reimpose slavery. But Lincoln rejected this reasoning. The war and his peculiar
war-measure, the Proclamation, had already changed the Constitution. The text would have to catch up with reality somehow. At any
rate, he himself would not reenslave anybody for any reason what-
soever. If Congress passed a law to the contrary, it would have to find
someone else to enforce it. Here was political leadership conscious of
the civil effects of military measures.

But political and military elements do not always combine so
harmoniously. The quest for battlefield victory may overwhelm the
political leadership, which then abdicates and stares impotently at
the storms of war. Conversely, ignorant or imprudent civilians may

saddle the generals with political-strategic objectives that they for professional reasons come to view as impossible.

For example, in the First World War, the German generals froze German statecraft into accepting a rigid prewar strategy dictating an automatic two-front war against both France and Russia. Moreover, the Schlieffen plan's insistence that the French army be outflanked on the Western front through Belgium ensured that yet another country, Britain, its channel coast then threatened, would enter the war against Germany. When the war broke out, the political leadership in Berlin further capitulated to the generals' definitions of the necessities of war. By 1917, Germany had come under the military dictatorship of General Erich Ludendorff, and his extreme dictates for battle and victory were accepted even by the kaiser himself, subordinating all other political possibilities. A catastrophe ensued.

Twenty years later, Germany went to the other extreme, civilian super-supremacy, and suffered an even worse catastrophe. From what we now know, from 1938 onward many if not most high-ranking Junker generals were genuinely alarmed by Hitler's war plans. In 1938 some of them engaged in desperate and treasonous actions during the Munich negotiations, planning to arrest Hitler while secretly urging the British government, then under Prime Minister Chamberlain, not to appease but to resist Hitler's political ultimata.[2]

When Hitler in 1941 ordered the German *Wehrmacht* into his war on the Eastern front against the Soviet Union, the generals' professional military aim—defeating the Red Army—quickly came into fundamental conflict with Hitler's political aim, of destroying Slavic culture in all of Eastern Europe and Russia. The generals cited the battlefield necessity of continuing to be welcomed by Ukrainians and Great Russians as liberators from Stalin's tyrannous rule. But the civilians would have none of this. So, behind the *Wehrmacht* came Hitler's political army, the SS, which soon rallied most (but not all) Russians behind Stalin. Hitler stubbornly clung to his absolute political aim of a new racial order even after he recognized that he was suffering defeat on the battlefield.

Excessive civilian control is as harmful in democracies as it is in dictatorships. During the War of 1812, when President James Madison as commander in chief took personal charge of army units defending the nation's capital, the White House was captured and burned.

Even when political-military relations are going smoothly, political leaders' preoccupation with military matters may unconsciously subordinate the higher, political goals of war to immediate battlefield concerns. For example, the Roosevelt administration in World War II came to regard the political and military objectives as aimed directly and exclusively toward "winning of the war" and punishing the enemy. This pushed *all other* political considerations out of sight, and out of mind. FDR remarked that "Dr. Win-the-War" had replaced "Dr. New Deal." This singlemindedness had some good side effects. Roosevelt, somewhat like Stalin (but wholly unlike Hitler), suspended his controversial domestic social programs for the duration of the war. By 1945 it would have been impossible even for Roosevelt to reimpose the dead hand of New Deal economics upon a bullishly antisocialist America.

Alas, that was only half the story. In his direction of the war, Roosevelt also forbade military commanders to divert resources from the goal of defeating the Axis powers to shape the postwar world. Thus his administration resolutely opposed any battlefield actions that could have checked the relentless advance of Soviet political-military might in Europe. American troops were forbidden from liberating Prague and Berlin. They were even ordered to retreat from portions of Germany that they had already occupied. The legacy of that (successful) resolution was the Soviet subjugation of half of Europe to a totalitarian system as severe as the Nazi system that American armies were destroying on the battlefield. Thus, because Roosevelt took his eye off the ball that counted most, American men unwittingly died to help create a Soviet threat to America far bigger than the German threat they were in the process of destroying.

Excessive involvement by political leaders in actual operations may also usurp the necessary functions of the field commander, introducing confusion and complications. The advent of sophisticated and reliable communications has increased civilian leaders' temptations to meddle. In the *Mayaguez* incident of 1975, in which Khmer Rouge Cambodians seized an American freighter, President Ford and Secretary of State Henry Kissinger micromanaged the recapture of the vessel from the White House situation room, using satellite photos and radio to monitor and command the assault to the point of conversing directly with the pilots. One Marine commander on the spot reportedly became so confused by conflicting orders that he finally "just turned the radio off."[3]

Who, then, should decide what? There is only one sound principle: authority must be proportionate to responsibility. The person in
charge of planning any given operation must also be the one responsible for making it succeed. When this principle is violated and
several people have something to say about what is done but nobody
is in charge, only luck can avoid disaster.

Perhaps the best example of diffusion, indeed confusion, of command was the U.S. operation to rescue diplomatic personnel being
held hostage in Iran in 1980. The complex operation was planned by
the Office of the Joint Chiefs of Staff. Service chiefs and senior generals settled questions about the composition of the force. Other
generals settled questions of timing. The plan was then assigned to
an Army colonel to execute. The plan was not his. Indeed it was not
anyone's. If he found fault with the training and equipment of the
people assigned to him, he could not change them or ask a single
responsible individual to change them. To change anything before
the beginning of the operation would be a time-consuming political
process far above his pay grade. Moreover, communications were so
good that he could be in contact with all of his many superiors
throughout the operation. All could offer suggestions or make criti-
cisms. But none would be responsible. Of course, neither would he.
So the hostage rescue force flew its prescribed path though a blind-
ing dust storm was raging, going neither left nor right, above it, or
landing to let it blow over. It lost helicopters to dust and confusion,
and argued across half the world about whether to go on. The commandos were so unused to working with one another that they
crashed into each other.[4] But everyone got medals.

Leadership: Making Things Happen

Anyone who thinks of command as the mere flow of orders from
higher to lower ranks is likely to fail as a leader and to weaken even
the authority that mere rank has given him.

Any military unit that merely fulfills the letter of its orders will
fail even more surely than a company whose unionized employees
"work to rule." Human organizations function if their members

believe in what they are doing and don't just go through the motions. Anyone who has ever been in the military has noticed that ships or battalions, sometimes whole divisions or armies, reflect the personality and competence of their commanding officer. The troops are generally good judges of the character and competence of their commanding officers. They quickly answer such questions as: "What's driving him?" "What's he after?" "Does he give a damn about us?" "Does he know what he's doing?" "Can he get us out of this scrape?" Above all, troops know *what* their commander is serious about. Is it the mission? Is it medals? Is it show? The troops can spot a phony. Usually, the commander gets out of his troops what he shows the troops *he* is really after.

No operation is likely to succeed if the people who are supposed to make it work don't want it to, or if they are discouraged, disconsolate, morally defeated, sullen, uncooperative, inattentive, or lazy. In war more than in most human contests, success goes to those who want it, who keep their heads up and look for ways of winning, and who work hard and hopefully. But war is not inherently appetizing work. How, then, to keep up essential morale?

General Douglas MacArthur once summed up the requirements for morale as follows:

> The unfailing formula for production of morale is patriotism, self-respect, discipline, and self-confidence within a military unit, joined with fair treatment and merited appreciation from without. . . . It will quickly wither and die if soldiers come to believe themselves the victims of indifference or injustice on the part of their government, or of ignorance, personal ambition or ineptitude on the part of their military leaders.[5]

In World War II, General Patton expressed one age-old recipe—convince one's soldiers that they ought to fear the enemy less than they fear their own commander. Hannibal, Livy tells us, kept his army on its toes by exemplary displays of "inhuman cruelty" toward his troops. Although there are many ways of keeping up discipline no one has ever been able to dispense with at least some fearsome examples of what happens to slackers. The Soviet Union, for example, deploys KGB troops *behind* its regular forces, with orders to kill anyone who is not moving up with sufficient alacrity. Discipline is also affected by the combination of danger that the troops sense and the hope they have of surmounting that danger by doing their jobs well. For example, Hannibal's armies stayed together in part because he had taken them deep into enemy country. Thus, his soldiers knew that desertion would surely have meant death or slavery. Their only hope of survival lay in following orders, and Hannibal gave daily proof that he knew what he was doing. This is the basic insight that led Hernán Cortés to burn his ships upon landing on the shores of Mexico so that his troops would know that they had only two choices: conquer the Aztec empire or die, and that he was the only one who had a plan.

Morale also involves being nice to troops who do their jobs. No human being will be generous with his work or his life if he feels unappreciated. It is remarkable how much of themselves people will give in return for being made to feel appreciated by the great. It is worth noting that in December 1981 before ordering its ZOMO special troops to crush the Solidarity trade union, the Polish government issued those troops that rare treat: chocolate bars. Perhaps Poland's General Jaruzelsky was trying to imitate Napoleon, who used to issue brandy, "eau de vie" (the water of life), on the eve of battle.

Wise commanders always tell their troops the importance of what they are doing, and how the folks at home are counting on them. Alas, they usually overdo it, engendering cynicism. A few words frequently have a greater effect than a long speech. Thus de Gaulle's message to the first Free French division (the first major French unit to beat the Germans since the debacle of 1940) upon its successful delaying action at Bir-Hakeim on 10 July 1942: "General Koenig! Know and tell your troops that all France is looking at you and that you are her pride."[6] When apparently sincere discussions of the importance of the current campaign are accompanied by material signs of appreciation, the invigorating effect is visible. The opposite is unmistakable. In 1916–17 soldiers on the Western front not only lived miserably but saw that their likely deaths would surely be meaningless. Hence morale dropped, and armies were kept together only by exemplary executions.

Of course, morale also depends on habits of loyalty. British and German units in World War II each had been accustomed to being together for a long time. Thus, their members kept up high standards of performance even during demoralizing times in order not to let one another down. The Japanese, for their part, maintained fighting morale apparently because it was inconceivable for them to do anything else.

Morale also depends on faith in leaders and on hope of victory. If the two disappear, soldiers tend to believe they have been sold out and throw away their weapons. Surprise is so devastating to armies in part because it destroys the men's confidence in their leaders. This is what happened to much of the French army in 1940. The German advance was so unlike what their leaders had led them to expect that the army drew the (correct) conclusion that their leaders had no idea of what they were doing and no convincing answers to the question, What's next? Surprise can wreck the morale of nations as well as of armies. When a whole political establishment weds itself to the proposition of "peace in our time" and then war comes, that establishment loses credibility. It is impossible for people identified with a discredited policy to lead a nation in the opposite direction. In practice, hope must be personified by credible people.

Another case in point is the morale of U.S. forces in Vietnam. Contrary to the movies on the subject, U.S. forces had no morale problems until well into 1969, when it became unmistakable that the United States was not going to try to win the war and was going to turn it over to the South Vietnamese as quickly as possible. That is when the drugs, the insubordination, and the practice of just going through the motions took over. Indeed, the decision to stop building up and start building down turned domestic opposition to the war from a fringe position that had lost out within the Democratic party, which then had lost the election of 1968, into something with obvious legitimacy. It is true that Americans in Vietnam lived very comfortably. But the answers to their natural questions: "What am I doing here? Am I on the right side? Do my leaders know where they are taking me? What will people say and do if I slack off?" were so historically unsatisfactory that it is a wonder morale was as high as it was.

In the end, leadership consists of providing and of personifying (as Churchill did) good answers to the questions that move people. The leader must exude the impression that he knows where he is going and knows how to get there. He must convince that the goal, once reached, will be worthwhile, and that those who stick with him will be taken care of. He must give constant proof of all these things. Regardless of how good he is at charming or cajoling, events must prove him right. Christopher Columbus calmed his men by lying about the distance they had traveled each day, lest the magnitude of their separation from home overwhelm them. And Columbus was a charmer. Nevertheless, he was on the verge of falling victim to mutiny when land came into view on 12 October 1492. In World War I, Germany's spring 1918 offensive ground to a halt because the troops had been told too many times that the next assault would be the last. In contrast, troops follow all too blindly those leaders with a reputation for success, or who can evoke wonderful vistas of what lies beyond the horizon. Shakespeare gives us an example in Henry V's speech before the Battle of Agincourt of one kind of leadership —the promise that participation in *this* enterprise is ennobling. But Dante, in the eighth *bolgia* of the eighth ring of hell (reserved for deceivers) shows us Ulysses' punishment for using the gift of leadership to take men where they should not go. As every soldier knows, there are some leaders whom men will eagerly follow to hell itself, and others who are not trusted to show the way to the latrine.

Strategy: Where to Go, and How

Strategy is a fancy word for a road map for getting from here to there, from the situation at hand to the situation one wishes to attain. Strategy is the very opposite of abstract thinking. It is the intellectual connection between the things one wants to achieve, the means at hand, and the circumstances. It is a mistake to give the name "strategy" to a set of particular attitudes, prejudices, or wishes. Thus, anti-communism is not a strategy, nor is a penchant for, say, controlling the sea. For that matter, John Kennedy's "strategy" of building a "wall of freedom" around Cuba, and the U.S. government's "strategy" between 1947 and about 1969 of "containment" of the Soviet Union were wishes, not strategies, because they did not envisage chains of specific acts that would produce specific results leading to the desired outcome.

To be a strategy a plan does not have to succeed. It just has to consist of components that have been thought through reasonably well, and to have a reasonable chance of success. The Schlieffen plan for the invasion of France in World War I, for example, failed because of flawed execution and because of General Joffre's especially spirited counterattack. But it was arguably a reasonable plan for employing Germany's resources to defeat France. The finest contemporary examples of successful strategy are General MacArthur's island-hopping campaign in the Pacific in 1942–45 and North Vietnam's political-military rout of the United States in 1965–73.

To make war strategy, on any level of command, is to answer five sets of questions. First, what do I really want out of this situation? What will rid me of my fears or satisfy my needs so that I will be able to rest in peace or go on to something else? Have I thought things through well enough to be satisfied that the thing I'm after is neither a mirage nor the lid to Pandora's box? Second, Whom or what do I have to kill, destroy, besiege, intimidate, or constrain to get what I want? Once I have done these things will I have achieved what I want? In other words, at what point do I win? Third, what can my enemy do to keep me from killing, destroying, or constraining as I must? What forces does he have and how best could he use them to his own advantage? Fourth, what forces are available to me to defeat the best opposition that my enemy can throw at me, and how can I use them? Can I entice more forces to my side? Can I entice any away from his? Can I deal with an expansion of the war? What military options are available to me and to my enemy at any given time? Fifth, am I willing to do what is necessary in good time to win? Do I have a realistic estimate of the costs? Is the whole thing worth the trouble?

To clarify one's ends is not easy—mostly because of the common human tendency to want to have one's cake while eating it too. Thus, for example, the United States in the 1980s joined in a war against Nicaragua's Communist regime with the obviously contradictory goals of overthrowing it and reaching a modus vivendi with it. In addition, and, as happened to the United States in World War II, the hatred that war engendered can narrow the goals of the war to simple destruction of the enemy regime, and crowds out consideration of what is to happen after the fighting is over.

The acme of mindlessness, however, is to enter a war as the United States did in Lebanon between 1982 and 1984 for the purpose of stopping the fighting. This begs all the questions. What kind of peace do we want to see? Who stands in the way of peace? What actions of ours will remove the obstacles to peace? Mindlessly inserted into Lebanon, United States Marines were used for target practice by various factions in the war. Since the United States had not designated a political enemy, and the Marines lacked the power to search out their tormentors, as a police force in control of a country would, they continued to die without fighting back until they were withdrawn.

Sometimes the problem is indecision about the scope of the conflict. In 1950, General MacArthur and his superiors in Washington agreed that the North Korean army was the enemy, and that the objective was to defeat it militarily. Thus, Washington agreed with MacArthur's plan to outflank the enemy troops via the amphibious landing at Inchon. Both Washington and MacArthur realized that there was a chance that victory over North Korea would bring China or the Soviet Union into the war. But while MacArthur did not mind this possibility, and was willing to use the full power of the United States to defeat what he believed was the real enemy, Washington abhorred it and was unwilling to treat either China or the Soviet Union as the enemy. Hence, in 1950 the United States pursued the defeat of North Korea without having thought through whether it would be willing to deal with the consequences of victory.

In the operations of war, intentions don't count as much as calculations. Thus, the United States killed thousands of people in South Vietnam whose deaths made absolutely no difference to the outcome of the war, while sparing the few dozen in North Vietnam whose deaths would have ended the war. By a similar token, Israel went to war three times in one generation without any idea of what it would have to do to win what Israel really wants—its enemies' recognition of its right to exist. All three Israeli actions have been desperate struggles to stave off disaster. Thus, although it thrashed its enemies each time, it is no surprise that Israel failed to win its objective. In contrast, Bismarck calculated that Austria was the chief obstacle to the unification of Germany under Prussia, and that if Austria were defeated in the field, its links with Bavaria and the Rhenish protectorates would snap. In fact, after Prussia beat Austria in 1866, it found no further obstacles to gaining its objective.

Churchill once cautioned British military strategists that sometimes it is necessary to take the enemy into account. The enemy will have his own strategy and his own means of carrying it out. During the American Civil War, for example, it was all very well for the Union Army to take the thousand-mile route along the Mississippi to cut the Confederacy in two during 1863. But in the meantime Robert

E. Lee had taken his Army of Northern Virginia deep into Pennsyl-
vania. Had Lee won at Gettysburg, which he almost did, a march of
150 miles would have allowed him to cut the Union in two. The
Union would have regretted the overconfidence that led to dispersing its forces. By the same token, as the United States was landing in
the Philippines in 1944, it realized that the Japanese navy would
make a major effort to wreck the landings, and prepared to meet it.
But the United States did not realize that the Japanese would make
two powerful thrusts at the landings.[7]

The strategist would always like to know what the enemy plans to
do. But he seldom does. So he has no choice but to put himself in the
enemy's shoes and to figure out what the enemy's best shot would
be. This exercise tests the strategist's intellectual honesty, his willingness to see the challenge as neither more nor less daunting than it
is. Overestimating the enemy is often as fatal as underestimating
him. Thus, for example, in 1948 and again in 1961 when East German and Soviet soldiers blocked roads to Berlin and in the city as
well, the United States respected the barriers because it feared that
these moves were backed by Soviet resolve to start World War III.

What do I have to do to avoid or defeat the best shot that the
enemy is realistically going to throw at me and to destroy his ability
to resist me? Realism is necessary not only in estimating forces
available to either side, but also about the element of time. Britain
and France, for example, grossly neglected this element in September 1939. Both had just declared war on Germany in retaliation
for its attack on Poland. Both knew that Germany had left only
skeletal defenses in the West, but that after Poland was crushed, no
later than mid-November, those defenses would be back up to
strength. The British and French knew that they had clear superiority, but that it would last for only a short time. Thereafter, it would
take years for Britain and France to match the power Germany had
built up. So, the allies could choose to pay a small bill immediately,
or a huge one later. Their choice to wait in the hope that the war that
had just begun would somehow not be for real was irresponsible.

The effect of the forces one has available also depends on the
tempo of operations. The German advance into France in 1940 was
so devastating because its speed left no time for recovery. But the
tempo of the American bombing in North Vietnam was so slow that
it allowed the enemy to recover from each operation. There is no
case in history of a war won through the piecemeal commitment of
resources. Victory comes when the enemy's will to fight is broken by

a specific defeat. The whole point of strategy is to figure out what that defeat would be and to inflict it.

Finally, strategy consists of a commitment to do whatever is necessary to make the plan work. This does not imply that once a plan is made it should be followed inflexibly. But it does imply the realization that to fight "on the cheap" either materially or politically is to court disaster.

CHAPTER
5

MATERIAL CONDITIONS
OF BATTLE

He maketh the rain to fall on the just and the
unjust.

—Matthew 5:45

W HOEVER FIGHTS, whoever leads, and whatever his strategy,
any combatant must slug it out within the variable limitations imposed by nature and materiel. There is no magic in war. Assuming
one is meeting the political conditions necessary for success in battle, the only trick one can muster is to match one's objectives and
capabilities to the environment in which one must operate: to avoid
destruction by the weather, to match one's tactics to one's weapons,
and not to let men and equipment be consumed without good
results.

Weather and Terrain

Weather is perhaps the most obvious illustration of the proposition
that nature is but the neutral backdrop for military operations, and
that its various features may be considered helpful or harmful, even

decisively so, according to the wisdom, technology, and energy with which commanders adjust their plans to those features. Many have noted, for example, that both Napoleon's and Hitler's soldiers were defeated in part by Russia's cold weather. But surely cold itself did not defeat them, because Russian flesh freezes at the same temperature as European flesh. Rather, the Europeans were simply not prepared to live and fight in the cold. In December 1941, for example, as the German authorities were requisitioning civilians' fur coats to send to the Moscow front, Russian troops were arriving from Siberia in what the German generals enviously described as "superb winter clothing." In fact, given Russia's predominantly flat, wet topography and lack of good roads, cold weather actually facilitates the movement of armies overland if they are suitably equipped. The Germans did not enter Russia intending to winter there.[1] When winter came, they were prepared neither for winter nor for cutting their losses; hence, their scramble for fur coats to tide them over.

Extremes of weather may intervene in battles. But they seldom change the fundamental balance of forces. At a certain point, however, preparations become so elaborate and troops consume so much attention keeping the cold from freezing them and incapacitating equipment that fighting ability ceases to exist. Thus, places that are too far north or south simply do not become the scene of military operations, except when they are as strategically located as the North Cape, where the Soviet Union and Norway may someday fight for sole control of the gateway to the North Atlantic.

Conventional wisdom holds that the German counteroffensive in the Ardennes in December 1944 was wrecked by the onset of clear skies on December 23, allowing the numerically superior American air force to enter as a factor in the Battle of the Bulge. The skies in fact had been cloudy since before the start of the battle on the 16th, during which the Germans had been able to act as if the American monopoly of the aerial "high ground" did not exist.[2] During that period it was almost as if the airplane had not been invented or Germany had not frittered away its air force during the previous four years. But it was unreasonable for the German high command to expect this variable environmental factor to long obscure what had become a decisive deficiency in their forces. General Von Rundstedt could not command permanent cloud cover.

Still, weather can be usefully taken into account for tactical purposes. A major ground offensive, meant to advance over long distances and to hold territory, would not be launched when the earth is expected to be soaked. Such offensives require much in the way of supplies, and mud slows or altogether halts the movement of heavy transport. In Angola in the 1980s, for example, the Soviet Union's heavily armed Cuban and Angolan proxies time their annual offensives against Jonas Savimbi's bush headquarters to coincide with the onset of the Southern Hemisphere's dry season. By contrast, lightly armed forces fighting against heavily armed ones prefer wet weather because mud hampers small groups of men and mules far less than it hampers heavy transport. Moreover, small groups of lightly armed troops can use bad weather as a screen behind which to sneak up on the enemy. George Washington did this when he led his men across the Delaware River in December 1776 for a surprise attack on a stronger British garrison in Trenton, New Jersey. So the rainy season favors the guerrilla, while good weather favors the regulars. When both sides rely on heavy weapons and transport, both wait for good weather before fighting. Thus, in the early spring of 1943, both the German and Soviet high commands made no secret that the plains near Kursk would be the site of a major tank battle, but both waited for the ground to dry out first.

Permanent good weather (as in the desert) imposes certain requirements on those who operate in it. Because desert distances are long and supplies nonexistent, the desert makes unusual demands on logistics. Desert forces need plenty of water, food, and especially fuel. In 1941 and early 1942, when Rommel's Afrika Korps was well supplied, the superior tactical talent of German and Italian officers manifested itself in quick, daring moves, and the British came to call Rommel "The Desert Fox." But during 1942 the British navy won control of the Mediterranean and prevented adequate supplies from reaching the Afrika Korps. With his soldiers hungry, on foot, and without air cover, Rommel could not be nearly so foxy.

Another factor in desert warfare is that neither vegetation nor weather provide hiding places. Hence, an army's safety and its ability to surprise enemies can only result from seeing the enemy first and/or being able to move faster. In the old days sharp eyes and fast horses made the difference. Nowadays air and satellite reconnaissance, strike aircraft, and motorized land forces do the job. In 1987, for example, Libyan tank forces were defeated by Chadian machine guns and antitank rockets mounted on trucks. This modern-day desert light cavalry was able to lay a good ambush thanks to information provided by U.S. satellite reconnaissance.

Because there is normally nowhere to hide in the desert, air superiority, both as regards reconnaissance and combat, has become very important. On the other hand, the same unobstructed view that makes airplanes so fearsome also makes them vulnerable to surface-to-air missiles. Indeed, in the Sinai Desert in 1973 Egypt made the best showing of any Arab country against Israel by keeping its ground forces under the umbrella of high-altitude and low-altitude surface-to-air missiles. So long as it did so the Israeli air force spent itself against these well-prepared defenses with little effect. But when the Egyptians foolishly departed from this plan, and moved out from their umbrella, the Israeli tank-plane combination chewed them up.

The fact that aircraft are so vulnerable to surface-to-air missiles in "big sky" country means that only the fastest and finest aircraft are suitable for desert fighting. Helicopters, because they are slow, cannot fly within line of sight of the enemy for long lest they be shot down.

Finally, the openness of the desert means that more shots of every kind will find their mark there than elsewhere. So, desert battles tend to be quick, violent, and to consume huge amounts of material quickly. The desert is tough on soldiers, too. Human beings cannot function normally for more than an hour at a time in tanks under the desert sun. Once the enemy is in view, however, the pace of desert operations makes rest impossible. Thus, in the Arab-Israeli wars a large part of Israel's advantage lay in the ability of its troops to function with minimal rest.

Jungle fighting is very different. Hiding is easy, and overland movement is painfully slow, even during relatively dry times. Lines of sight are short. All of this means that tanks are virtually useless, and the speed of aircraft means little or is even a liability. By contrast, helicopters are wonderful for moving people from jungle clearing to jungle clearing. But it is also easy to sit under a canopy of trees with a machine gun or a crude antiaircraft missile, wait for a helicopter to come over, and shoot it down before its occupants know what is happening. While firing out of a jungle is easy, firing either bullets or bombs into a jungle is not terribly productive since the thick vegetation tends to absorb bullets and bomb fragments.

This means that whereas deserts are fit for quick offensive warfare, jungles are better suited for protracted defensive campaigns. While desert ambushes are unusual, especially in an age of air reconnaissance, jungle ambushes are the rule. Nor do forces waging offensives in the jungles have a good option of "starving out" their opponents by cutting off their supply lines, because, in general, neither food nor water are lacking in jungles. To be sure, jungles are full of other discomforts, but none are as pressing as thirst in the desert or arctic cold. This means that jungle fighting is inherently slow, and that the battle must be carried by many small, lightly armed groups who slug it out almost hand to hand.

High Ground

Nature imposes a rule of thumb: Take the high ground. The rule proceeds from the immutable fact that it is more difficult to walk up a ridge or shoot an arrow upward than it is to stand on a ridge throwing rocks down. The invention of firearms, which shoot as well up as they do down, did not change this law except that the longer range of firearms made valuable the conquest of heights that had been useless before. Even the invention of nuclear weapons has not negated the value of mountains as natural fortresses, as anyone knows who is familiar with Switzerland's plan to use tunnels in mountains as sheltered runways for its combat aircraft. Thus, until very recently, mountain peoples, however armed, could count on confronting invaders with the fact that as invading forces moved up, straining men and machines, retreating defenders could be "covered" by their fellows stationed higher. These defenders would be fresh and relatively well supplied. As the battle continued to move up, the attackers would weaken and the defenders would grow stronger. This is how Afghan tribes resisted both Genghis Khan's Mongols and the British army.

But changing technology has affected the military usefulness of high ground. Generally, high ground is still useful if one possesses the technology to exploit it, but it will not make up for a lack of technology or military skill. Since 1979, for example, the Soviet army's helicopters have significantly reduced the mountains' value to the Afghans. Helicopters simply climb faster than humans, and can deposit attacking troops above the highest layer of defenders, as well as astride the defenders' routes of supply and retreat. Of course, helicopters are not immune to the logic of mountain warfare: Mountains provide excellent vantage points from which to see helicopters and to shoot them down—*provided* one has the missiles with which to do the job. Thus in 1986, as the Afghans began to receive serious missiles with which to fight Soviet helicopters, they recovered some of the advantages that nature had given them but that the huge disparity between their technology and that of their Soviet enemies had taken away.

The Synthetic High Ground

Let us now briefly consider the question of the "high ground" as it regards the air and outer space.

Until the mid-nineteenth century, armies would battle for possession of high ground in part because it offered the only means of observing their enemies. Beginning in the American Civil War, however, armies began to use tethered, hot-air balloons to lift observers over enemy positions. No sooner did the first balloon come within the range of enemy guns than it was treated just like what it was: an enemy outpost on a nearby hill. The battle for control of the synthetic "high ground" had begun. How important has this contest been?

During World War I, the amount of machine-gun fire and explosive ordnance delivered by aircraft was negligible in comparison with the mountains of ordnance fired from the ground. Aircraft did not determine the outcome of any major battle. The airplane was used primarily as an observation platform. Yet, for the privilege of observing, and also for the sheer desire to win mastery of the sky, flyers in airplanes of wood, canvas, and wire fought like the knights of old.

During the Spanish civil war, almost twenty years later, airplanes that could carry a ton of bombs became truly useful for purposes other than observation. Airplanes became a kind of very long-range, very flexible artillery. Dive-bombers became especially useful for clearing the way for fast-moving forces far faster and more accurately than artillery could. Airplanes could also disrupt enemy artillery before it ever came into the range of battle. This tank-plane combination proved to be the queen of World War II battles. The modern airplane potentially placed enemy forces in a predicament similar to the one they would have to face had they been located just under a cliff, from the edge of which enemy forces are dropping bombs. Given the growing ability of airplanes to carry bombs, a force unable to control the "high ground" above itself stood little chance. This became especially obvious in naval warfare during the battle of Midway—the first naval battle in history in which none of the ships of the opposing sides ever saw one another. Aircraft did all the fighting.

Aircraft have also improved in their ability to carry out their original function: reconnaissance. Miniaturized, high-resolution cameras, infrared detection equipment, side-looking radar imagery equipment, electronic intercept recorders, and radiation detectors have made it possible for modern aircraft, respectively, to record tiny objects on the ground, to notice whether an airplane is fueled or a car has been driven lately (by the amount of heat it gives off), to see large objects through clouds, to listen to conversations, or to determine if there are nuclear weapons in the vicinity.

Does this mean that the airplane is the decisive weapon? Only sometimes. After all, the battle for control of the high ground can also be waged successfully from below. Ground-based radars that "see" aircraft against the sky and modern interceptor missiles directed by modern computers can impose frightful attrition upon intruders. If the defender also employs radars carried by high-flying aircraft that can distinguish low fliers against the ground and can direct its own missiles to intercept them, then even the finest modern aircraft can be made ineffective as offensive weapons—unless the way is cleared for them by bombs falling from an even higher ground: outer space.

Long-range ballistic missiles are essentially very long-range artillery, whose projectiles arch up through and then fall out of outer space. In order for such missiles to be useful at all, however, the location of their targets must be known precisely, as must the effect of their fire: was the target destroyed, or not? Where else should we shoot? In the 1980s these questions have become more important as missiles, as well as other strategic assets, have become mobile. The answer to these questions—indeed, the key to the continued military usefulness of ballistic missiles—lies in matching the mobility of targets with ever more extensive coverage by cameras and electronic sensors based on satellites in orbit. Whoever controls this high ground can theoretically keep his enemy under constant surveillance, while preventing his enemy from knowing where to shoot. From this highest ground one can theoretically also close outer space to the enemy's ballistic missiles or to rockets carrying the enemy's satellites into orbit.

The basic techniques that enable a nation to fight for control of the high ground of space are the very same that enable a country to launch satellites. A rocket can either place a satellite at a point in space or it can carry a bomb to destroy a satellite that is already there. Sending one satellite to rendezvous with another may involve either resupplying that satellite or destroying it.

As we will see below, the very techniques that have allowed mankind to place satellites in orbit, and that allow satellites to point cameras and antennae precisely at points on the ground and at each another, also allow them to destroy each other or to destroy ballistic missiles flying through space. In this function, too, altitude makes a difference. Geometry says that if a satellite is in orbit 300 miles above the earth, its line of sight will be unobstructed by the earth's horizon for about 1,600 miles in any direction. But if that satellite is traveling 800 miles above the earth, its line of sight will be unobstructed for to some 2,500 miles.[3] Satellites at these altitudes can see ballistic missiles. But can they do anything about them?

At the outset of the space age the means for making use of satellites for antimissile purposes were lacking. In 1962, American scientists learned how to make one object in orbit rendezvous with another. Theoretically, this constituted the capability to destroy enemy satellites. Yet satellites in high orbits still did not have the means to do such maneuvers fast enough to destroy ballistic missiles. Even if such a satellite had carried an interceptor rocket able to add, say, 6 kilometers per second (13,600 miles per hour) to its orbital velocity, that interceptor rocket would not have been able to catch up to the missile before its telltale engines cut off and it became very difficult to see. Satellites in low orbits could catch up with a ballistic missile providing they were close enough to begin with. But to ensure that a defensive satellite would be close enough to any given missile path, it was clear that there would have to be many hundreds of defensive satellites. Since the art of propulsion has not changed radically in twenty-five years, there is little advantage in establishing defensive stations in orbits above two hundred miles, so long as one thinks in terms of intercepting missiles with interceptor rockets. One will have to "trade off" the rockets' relatively low speed, and hence their short effective range, by basing them on a high number of orbital stations.

When it became possible to design laser and particle-beam weapons whose beams travel at or near the speed of light, it became obvious that the height of the orbits in which defensive stations could be placed would depend only on the maximum range at which these weapons could deliver a fatal dose of energy upon a missile. Whereas a rocket can destroy a missile from perhaps two hundred miles away, a contemporary laser can do it from two thousand miles. Hence, today's lasers could usefully be stationed perhaps eight hundred miles high. Instead of hundreds of satellites, dozens would do. The more powerful and accurate lasers become, the more suitable they will be for higher orbits, and therefore the fewer will be required to cover the areas from which missiles might be launched. But with lasers, as with rockets, there is a trade off between having fewer, more powerful models, and greater numbers of less powerful ones.

Higher orbits also confer upon the satellites located there the relative safety of fortresses on high ground: Rockets, just like infantrymen, take longer time and require more energy to get to higher elevations. Whereas the world's biggest rockets (Soviet ones) can deliver up to 400,000 pounds to low-earth orbit in one shot, the biggest payloads delivered to geosynchronous orbits (22,300 miles high) weigh only some 10,000 pounds. Moreover, whereas the journey to low-earth orbit takes a few minutes, the trip to geosynchronous orbit takes hours. That means that the higher a satellite is, the more energy it takes to attack it and the longer the missile attacking the satellite will be exposed to being hit from above. Also, just like a defender on a mountain crag, the higher the "ground" that the satellite holds, the more difficult it will be for sensors on the ground to see it, and for ground-based beam weapons to shoot at it accurately.

None of this is to say that whoever holds the highest orbits will prevail in space any more than that whoever holds the highest ridges will prevail on the ground. In space as on the ground, the numbers of combatants, the quality of their equipment, and the tactics with which they are employed have more to do with the outcome than the altitude at which they are deployed.

Transportation and Logistics

Even when armies moved by muscle power, their comparative abilities to transport themselves and their goods made a difference. The Roman legions were superior to their enemies for, among other reasons, the excellent discipline and organization that enabled them to carry what they needed to survive and fight in relatively good health. This discipline extended to such matters as preventing troops from rushing to drink from rivers. While other armies would drink muddy water, the Romans carried small wooden bridges to allow the drawing of clean drinking water from the main current of streams. Roman discipline also allowed the legion to make and break camps quickly. Hence, the Romans moved more high-quality human muscle power faster. No one would argue that this did not contribute to their success. Still, no one can argue that mere logistics were decisive. After all, the Roman legions of the fifth century A.D. enjoyed as much logistical superiority over the barbarians as had their predecessors 500 years earlier. But by the fifth century, the Romans had become inferior in other respects. Logistics, then, is but one factor among many.

Beginning with the Austro-Prussian War of 1866, in which the mobilization and concentration of armies was done primarily by railroad, a period began in which many have held logistics to be the essence of warfare. The reason for this belief is easy to grasp. If boarded quickly, a single train can move an army division 200 miles in an afternoon. By arranging the efficient employment of rolling stock, as well as the loading and unloading of units, an army can be mobilized and placed in a strategically advantageous position before the enemy can react. But even in the Austro-Prussian war the railroad stratagem did not work as intended. The armies were moved with historically unprecedented speed, all right, but they moved blindly. The generals had banked so much on the latest technologies that their plans for bringing their forces to battle were based on elaborate networks of train watchers, who would instantly transmit their intelligence by telegraph. However, cavalry units from both sides took Luddite joy in pulling down the telegraph poles along railroad lines, thus leaving both armies to blunder blindly into each other. In this sense, the decisive battle of Königgratz was like a giant freeway pile-up on a foggy day.

The mechanistic emphasis on railroad timetables resurfaced during World War I, when the art of war seemed to have been reduced to the grim calculus of how many pounds of artillery shells could be made to fall on each square yard of the enemy's front lines, and the planning of battles consisted almost exclusively of concentrating more and more men and explosives on sections of the front in murderous efforts to force a breakthrough "at all costs." Yet the decisive breakthrough at Amiens in August 1918 came not so much because of superior logistics but because a new tool, the tank, allowed troops to cross the "no man's land" between opposing trenches and dislodge the machine guns that had held the Western front immobile for three bloody years.

In World War II, the United States performed logistical wonders such as the world had never imagined. It built 100 aircraft carriers, 285,000 aircraft, and millions of vehicles. It laid pipelines under the English Channel to fuel the fighting in France. It sent bombers to the South Pacific to land on runways that would be completed only as the planes were in the air. Medicines and blood products stayed refrigerated all the way from the laboratories in the United States to remote corners of jungle or desert. New roads connected China with the Bay of Bengal and Alaska with the main body of North America. Never had soldiers been so superbly equipped, so well fed, and so healthy as Americans in World War II. Nevertheless, German soldiers continued to exact about a three-to-one casualty ratio against Americans until the closing months of the war. Surely, without logistical superiority, it would have been worse.

Vietnam surely dispelled the illusion regarding the benefits of logistical superiority. There is no truth to the widespread supposition that the Communists fought with field-made or captured weapons. Indeed their southern front was supplied by containerized trucks rolling on a four-lane highway from the Cambodian port of Sihanoukville (now Kompong som) to the Parrot's Beak area of South Vietnam, while the northern front was supplied by a good network of truck roads called the Ho Chi Minh Trail. Nevertheless, not even the shadow of a comparison is possible between how well the Communists and the United States and South Vietnamese troops were supplied until 1973. Americans in Vietnam lived and fought in physical comfort unimaginable even by their fathers in World War II.

Any wounded American could count on being in a state-of-the-art hospital within minutes of being hit.

America's firepower in Vietnam was overwhelming. An American infantry lieutenant recalls once mentioning on the radio that a sniper had fired on his platoon from a treeline ahead, at which time he was offered assistance by three different kinds of American gunships in the area. Poor sniper! Suffice it to say that the United States dropped three times more tons of bombs on tiny Vietnam than in all of World War II.[4] Had those bombs and bullets been spread *at random*, they might have had a greater military effect. Instead, the bulk was expended on a computerized "target list" that was drawn up in Washington and that was well known to the North Vietnamese army, which of course used these American bomb dumps as accurate guides where *not* to put men, trucks, etc., as well as for installing antiaircraft equipment. The United States simply wasted its logistical superiority. After the United States' departure in 1973, the logistical balance—especially with regard to ammunition—shifted in favor of North Vietnam, which knew how to use it.

Terrain

Terrain is predictable. Assuming that both sides know it equally well, drawing particular advantage from it depends on the opposing commanders' imagination. Consider, for example, an armed force confronted by an enemy-held city on its line of advance. Buildings, basements, sewers, culverts, and terraced hills are ideal places for defenders to hide. Rooting an enemy army out of a city is perhaps the dirtiest and most time consuming of all military operations. It is also dangerous. If the enemy has reserves elsewhere, he can wait until his opponent is embroiled in house-to-house fighting, and then call them in with disastrous effect. The Germans found this out at Stalingrad in 1942–43, where the Soviets cut off their retreat while they were bogged down in house-to-house fighting. Twenty-two divisions, comprising 230,000 men, ceased to exist, and only 90,000 of the men survived to suffer the fate of prisoners of war in Russia.[5]

The traditional military recipe for cities calls for either bypassing them or for laying siege. Bypassing cities is preferable because it avoids tough fighting, preserves the city's wealth intact so that it can be plundered in the future, and allows an army to seek a quick decision elsewhere. But what if a decision can be reached only by attacking the city? This was the case with regard to Berlin at the end of World War II. Then there is no choice. What if the enemy uses the city to shelter forces so large that it would be imprudent to bypass them? Thus, in 1944 the Germans strongly garrisoned Warsaw and dared the Red Army to come in. The Red Army then used the best possible stratagem under the circumstances—the use of allies who are already *within* the city. It called on the strong Polish underground in Warsaw to revolt openly against the Germans so that the Germans, occupied with their rear, could not make efficient use of the urban terrain when the Red Army advanced.

But the Soviets went beyond this reasonable military measure. As the Polish underground rose, the Red Army stopped. For three weeks the Red Army watched as the German garrison and the Polish underground bled one another. Only after nearly all the Polish fighters—the natural leaders of Polish society—were dead, did the Red Army enter Warsaw. The house-to-house fighting was easier than it would have been had the Polish underground not fought, but harder than it would have been if the Red Army had joined the fight while the underground remained alive. But on the other hand, after taking Warsaw this way, the Soviets did not have to deal with a lot of independent-minded and armed Poles.

Wilderness poses problems different from the ones posed by cities, but just as great. Suppose for a moment that an army from the Northern Hemisphere were to try to invade South Africa. Unless that army tried to come ashore through an amphibious operation it would have to come either from Namibian or Mozambican ports or from points even farther away. Imagine the sheer effort that would go into supplying the food, fuel, spare parts, medical supplies, bridging equipment, and other provisions that perhaps half a million fighting men would need, depending on which route they took, in order to cross the Namib desert, Limpopo or Zambesi rivers, or the Great Rift Valley, travelling over a thousand miles through desert and semi-desert country or perhaps coastal swamps, and surely some rugged mountains without good roads or with no roads at all! As road-building crews worked and as the supply lines lengthened South African light forces could harass them. Who would want to bet on the condition of the attacking force when it reached Johannesburg? The awaiting defenders would be fresh, healthy, and covered by nearby airfields. Any equipment that broke down could be fixed close by. Any wounded defender would be minutes from a hospital. But for the attackers any wounded soldiers or disabled vehicles would most likely be lost. In short, any army that tried to attack South Africa overland would face problems worse than those that the British encountered in their war against the American colonies in 1776–81.

In the 1980s the classic attempt to attack through wilderness was that of Soviet- and Cuban-led Angolan forces based in northwest Angola against the forces of Jonas Savimbi, headquartered in the southwest corner of that semi-arid country. Prior to 1985, the attacking forces, consisting almost exclusively of motorized infantry, had been stopped by guerrilla attacks against their supply lines. In 1985, however, the Soviets and Cubans included tanks in their attacking force, and covered their advance with aircraft and helicopters. Savimbi's forces were finally able to defeat the attackers only 100 miles from their headquarters because the attackers lost many tanks in transit and could not provide decisive air cover operating from fields as much as 500 miles away. In 1986 and 1987, the wilderness became an even better shield for Savimbi when his forces received American Stinger shoulder-fired missiles with which to defend themselves against the best wilderness-shrinking devices ever invented, namely airplanes.

So, in sum, wilderness is excellent cover for light troops, but it is terribly hard on regular forces. For that reason wilderness is excellent for guerrilla war, whether defensive or offensive. It is also good for defensive conventional conflict.

Rivers and canals are also generally good lines for defense. At the outset of World War II, Winston Churchill hoped that "the broad, deep, swift-flowing Rhine" could easily be garrisoned as an effective barrier against the German army. The Rhine, even more than most rivers, is indeed difficult to cross against opposition. On any river, even if the attacker's artillery can keep the opposite bank clear of defenders, the defenders' artillery can sit far back from the bank and smash pontoon bridges as they are being built. On the Rhine, however, the fast current makes it even more difficult than normal to build pontoon bridges, even without opposition. Generally, river crossings succeed when the attacker moves quickly to places that are not heavily defended. This is precisely how the Germans crossed the Rhine delta in May 1940—and how the allies re-crossed it upstream in 1944.

Once a crossing is secured, the river is no longer much of an obstacle. It becomes significant again only if the attacker is forced to retreat quickly. Then, equipment gets abandoned because it can't be moved across the river fast enough, and troops must swim for their lives. This is what happened in January 1813 when the remainder of Napoleon's Grande Armée escaped from Russia to Prussia across the Berezina River. Over one-third of the fleeing mass did not make it across a hastily built bridge near Studienka. In 1973, the Egyptian army that had surprisingly dashed across the Suez Canal to attack the Israeli army found itself unable to get back across as fast because Egypt lost control of the airspace over the canal to Israel. Thus Egyptian forces were trapped.

Because crossing even small rivers is never a trivial matter for an army, it is generally good military practice to plan the movement of troops so that they cross any river just once, rather than marching along the river's course. It is foolish to inhibit maneuvers by operating with a river alongside, and foolhardy to fight with it directly behind. Doing so threatens to turn any setback into a disaster. Nevertheless, in the Second Punic War, Hannibal broke this rule of thumb, and defeated Rome's best armies by marching down the Tiber River Valley. He risked much, but gained the prize of surprise.

Technology

When the Spanish Armada approached the English fleet in 1588 it was superior in every way but one: The English ships had deep keels. Thus, they could tack more easily than could the Spanish ships. Whereas the Spanish ships could not sail in directions far from the axis of the wind, the English ships could maneuver much more freely. That is why the Spanish ships were unable to bear down on the English ships, and why the English were able to pick off the Spanish at will, so weakening the armada that its survivors fled. Superior technology applied by a knowledgeable commander made a decisive difference.

But superior technology by itself is no guarantee of superior weapons. For example, gallows humor in the U.S. Navy at the time of the battle of Midway (1942) had it that its weapons were either experimental or obsolete. The American Torpedo bombers were so outdated that casualties were near 100 percent! The navy simply had not acted as if war in 1942 was a real possibility. So, although the United States had the finest aircraft technology in the world, Japan had the Zero, the best fighter in the air over the Pacific in 1942. Nevertheless, the United States, not Japan, won the battle of Midway because of superior intelligence and because American airplanes were lucky enough to find Japanese carriers while their planes were refueling on deck.

Sometimes inferior weapons can defeat superior ones if cleverly used. By the late 1930s and certainly after Pearl Harbor, "everyone" knew that battleships were sitting ducks for airplanes. But the United States simply filled up deck space on battleships with anti-aircraft guns that could literally put a wall of shrapnel around the ship. The result? On a particularly good day, the USS *South Dakota* shot down *thirty-five* Japanese aircraft.

Weapons technology is pointless if it is not used to actually build weapons and if these weapons are not deployed. For example, in the 1960s the United States developed the technology for producing highly accurate ballistic missiles—and indeed curiously sold a key part of this technology to the Soviet Union in 1972. But not until December 1986 did the United States deploy its first ballistic missile, the MX, with the combination of accuracy and explosive power adequate to destroy other missiles on the ground. Meanwhile, the Soviet Union had begun deploying its version of the MX, known as the SS-18, in 1976. Of course, the MX is a more technically advanced weapon than the SS-18. But the two weapons perform essentially the same task, *and* the SS-18 was deployed not only earlier, but in 308 copies rather than the MX's 50! In sum, during the 1970s and 1980s, while the United States continued to develop militarily applicable technology at a vertiginous pace, the pace at which it embodied new technology in major deployed-missile systems slowed from an average of five to an average of fifteen years.[6] This hiatus gave the Soviet Union the chance to acquire American technology and introduce it into its own weapons before the United States did. Perhaps the starkest example of this imbalance is the Soviet Union's incorporation of optical-guidance technology stolen from the American Strategic Defense Initiative program into its operational SH-11 antimis-

sile interceptor. While the United States was deliberating whether
to deploy or even research antimissile defenses, the Soviet Union
was building them, in part with stolen American technology.

Possession of superior weapons does not guarantee that they will
be used wisely. For example, in 1987 the U.S. frigate *Stark*, on patrol
in the Persian Gulf, was equipped with a self-defense Gatling gun
(the Phalanx) able to literally and automatically put a wall of bullets
between the ship and an attacking cruise missile. But when an Iraqi
cruise missile approached the ship, the Phalanx system had not
been turned on.

Perhaps the most striking example of wasted technical superiority
is the U.S. Navy's announced plan, the Maritime Strategy, to send
aircraft carrier battle groups into the Norwegian Sea at the outset of
any war with the Soviet Union without first destroying the
hundreds of Soviet airfields within range of the Norwegian Sea.[7]
Now, U.S. aircraft carriers have the indubitable technical capacity
to dominate the air over the ocean, *but only in places out of reach of
massive land-based air power.* The rule, "Thou shalt not bring sea-
based air power within range of superior land-based air power," is
more valid in the age of jet aircraft than ever before. American
carriers are infinitely superior to their Soviet counterparts. In mid-
ocean, or close to friendly coasts they are invincible defensive
weapons. But using them in an offensive against the teeth of land-
based air power is likely to nullify their advantages.

Finally, it is essential to remember that the effect on battles of
superior technology—indeed of any innovation—is strictly limited
in time. After 1588, no serious navy ordered sailing warships without deep keels. If Spain's Golden Century had not ended, a second
armada fifty years later would likely have succeeded. In our century, the major European powers did not understand the impact that
the machine gun would have on ground combat until 1916. But once
they did, they all started to use tanks. The effectiveness of tanks, of
course, depends on who constructs better guns, sighting devices,
armor, and antitank missiles. Much also depends on the tactics with
which tanks are used. By the same token, the effectiveness of aircraft centers on the constant technological competition for better
speed, maneuverability, and the ability of on-board radar systems to
"see" and "lock-on" to faraway targets by overlooking clutter from
ground reflections and from electronic countermeasures.

Today's decisive innovation becomes tomorrow's standard, and is
sure to be obsolete sometime thereafter. No one can know how long

novelty will last. Only one thing is sure: There is no such thing as an ultimate weapon. Thus, time is perhaps the most crucial element in technical innovation. *The longer an idea takes to reach the battlefield as hardware, the shorter will be its period of usefulness.* Moreover, the contemporary American practice of delaying innovations in order to make them even better, more reliable, and able to defeat countermeasures that do not yet exist is doubly foolish because it deprives operating forces of new technology until it is no longer new. In military technology, seeking the best is the enemy of choosing the good.

But the race for technical supremacy should not be misconstrued. In the war between Israel and Syria over Lebanon in 1982, the box score was eighty-one Syrian fighters destroyed and zero for Israel. This does not mean that Israel's American equipment overwhelmed Syria's Soviet equipment, but that the Israelis used what they had incomparably better than did the Syrians.

Attrition

Contrary to boasts, hardly any army fights "to the last man." Nor do competent commanders point vaguely in the direction of the enemy and simply order: "Kill." Battles, much less wars, are seldom won by inflicting indiscriminate attrition. Nevertheless, attrition of trained people and key supplies (or even just fatigue) can deprive an armed force of what it needs to go on.

For example, in the 1973 Yom Kippur War, Israel won the battle for the Golan Heights simply by imposing dreadful attrition on Syria's tanks. Israel's technique was simple. Its tank commanders had noted every boulder and depression that could provide cover for a tank, had plotted routes of withdrawal from shelter to shelter, and had assigned small groups of tanks to cover each other's retreats. When the numerically superior Syrian tanks rushed in, the Israelis made them pay for every rock and hollow. Before the battle had reached the precipice leading down into Israel proper, the Syrian tank force had been much reduced, and Israel, now enjoying numerical superiority, was free to move forward.

In 1940, during the Battle of Britain, trained pilots were the crucial element. Airplanes could be manufactured more easily than experienced pilots could be trained. Hence it was of enormous significance that the battle was conducted over British soil or over the English Channel, where the Royal navy ruled. Whereas every downed German pilot (regardless of his physical condition) was lost to Germany, German aviators actually had to kill British pilots before they would be lost to Britain. Because of the importance of trained pilots, Winston Churchill had implored the faltering French government in Tours to turn over to Britain the four hundred-odd German pilots that France had captured during its losing struggle of May–June 1940.[8] Britain would go so far as to excuse France's acceptance of an armistice if only it would turn over these pilots. The fate of 100,000 ordinary troops would not have meant so much to the outcome of the war as did the fate of those 400 pilots.

Since equipment has become more important in war, so has the attrition of equipment. Since the primary mission of aircraft is to achieve mastery of the sky, the chief target of aircraft must be other aircraft. Using aircraft for any other purpose requires a good reason, for instance, killing soldiers or destroying tanks on a particular battlefield if it will achieve a goal more important than air superiority. One classic example of a misuse of airpower was Goering's mad commitment to use the Luftwaffe to supply the German Sixth Army encircled at Stalingrad. The Luftwaffe lost so many planes and pilots that it was never a major factor in the war again.

All operations of war entail losses on both sides. These are foreseeable, though rarely calculable. Hence, commanders must ask themselves whether the attrition they are imposing on the enemy will be worth the attrition that their own forces will suffer. But—and this is the crux—the importance of the attrition on either side can be measured only in terms of the effect that it has on either side's ability to achieve its strategic goals. It will not do to count bodies on either side, because each set of bodies can mean something entirely different to its side's plans.

In our century, there has all too frequently existed an awesome contrast in the value that the respective belligerents place upon the lives of their troops in battle. The huge "human waves" of Chinese Communist "volunteers" who poured against United Nations' firepower were viewed with incredulity by the U.N. defenders. Communist casualties in the Korean War were four times as great as those of American, South Korean, and U.N. forces—1,600,000 to

437,000. (In all, only 37,000 American soldiers perished in the war
—scarcely three times the number of Union soldiers who perished
in the one-day Battle of Antietam!) Similar ghastly asymmetries
were observed on the eastern front in World Wars I and II in engagements between German and Russian forces, in the Vietnam
War, and in the recent Iran-Iraq War. In such instances a cynic
might distinguish between "capital intensive" and "labor intensive"
fighting forces. Thus, a belligerent with small regard for human life
is far less sensitive to taking casualties than one accustomed to
cherish life highly—a factor that surely must enter into strategic
calculations. The American practice of "body-counting" enemy casualties in the Vietnam War was mindless in innocently assuming
that these deaths had a bearing on North Vietnamese capabilities
and willpower.

The weight of burdens, up to some unknowable point, is relative,
as anyone knows who has ever gazed at the statue in front of Boys
Town, Nebraska: One boy carrying another over the inscription, "He
ain't heavy. He's my brother." What some consider burdens, for
example, digging ditches, others consider good sense and the chance
to build good morale. Nor will it do to try to calculate the economic
costs of each side's losses or efforts. Not only do peoples put different
values on things, but more important, *military goods are valuable
not for the materials and labor that go into them, but for the strategic
gains that can be got out of using them. No one in wartime has ever
been struck by a piece of gross national product.*

CHAPTER
6

WINNING THE BATTLE: LAND, SEA, AND AIR

Just win, baby.

—AL DAVIS
owner, Los Angeles Raiders

WHEN ARMIES MARCH and navies sail, what makes the difference between victory and defeat? From time to time throughout history, usually after a war in which a major victory or defeat occurred—especially if it was unexpected—military writers rush to explain that the "laws of war" ordain a certain formula for success. But the only answer consistent with history is that the success of military operations depends largely on how creatively commanders impose their will on a particular set of circumstances. A prescription for success in one set of circumstances can lead to disaster in another.

The wisest commentators on the operations of war, from Livy and Machiavelli to Napoleon and contemporary Soviet writers such as V. D. Sokolovskii and N. V. Ogarkov, have stressed the contingent nature of warfare: the supreme need to adapt whatever human and material means are at hand to avoid or defeat the enemy's peculiar strengths while exploiting the enemy's vulnerabilities at any given time whether on the ground, at sea, or in the air.

Decision on the Ground

From time immemorial, most battles on the ground have been decided when one side succeeded, by force, maneuver, or both, in placing enough force to the side or the rear of the enemy to disorganize him. Again and again Thucydides tells of various battle alignments in the Peloponnesian War: heavy infantry in the center or on the flanks, archers and stone-slingers on one side or to the other, and cavalry on the line or in reserve. The battle would be decided when one part of the line routed those opposite it, made a breakthrough or a flanking movement, and then wheeled right or left, thus bringing overwhelming force to bear on a line that now had to fight in several directions at once. The decisive break could be caused by anything: the shock of cavalry, a hail of stones or arrows, or the patient chopping of swords and spears. At that point, either the defeated side would retreat and close ranks again, leaving the field in good order, or there would be a rout.

The development of ever more powerful firearms has changed the means for causing breakthroughs. As late as 1914—almost 600 years after the introduction of gunpowder in the West and despite the experience of the Franco-Prussian War, in which only 10 percent of the casualties were caused by bayonets, swords, and lances—the so-called white arms—the field manual of the French army counted on the power of the bayonet thrust to break enemy lines: "There is no individual act of preliminary preparation of the attack by the artillery. Artillery and infantry operate together." But the wholesale slaughter of attacking infantry by dug-in defenders soon taught everyone that, in Marshal Henri Pétain's words, "fire kills." Since then, armies have relied on some kind of bombardment to break a path for both infantry and armor. Over the years, this bombardment has drastically increased in intensity, has struck ever deeper behind the front, and has shortened considerably. Thus during the Verdun offensive of August 1916, 3,360 artillery rounds were fired every hour, on every kilometer of front, ten hours a day for a week. In 1944, however, as the Soviet Army prepared for the Vistula-Oder attack, its artillery fired for only twenty-five minutes—but at the rate of 60,000 shells per kilometer of front, per hour![1] The shock opened the breach. By the end of World War I, the amplitude of offensives had increased so much that in order to facilitate the movement of forces exploiting a breakthrough, the bombardment had to extend beyond artillery range. Thus, some 1,500 airplanes took part in the preparation for the "breakthrough" at Amiens in 1918. During the Second World War, fleets of bombers ranged far beyond fronts to strike both fortifications and enemy reserves. The lesson seems to be that "breakthrough bombardments" are increasingly violent and concentrated in time, and that they tend to extend ever farther into the enemy's rear.

Today, as always, the attacker has the enormous advantage of concentrating his fire on the point of attack and on the routes that his infantry and armor will follow to exploit the breakthrough. The idea is the same as it was in Thucydides' time: roll up the flanks, destroy the enemy's supplies, and cut off the dug-in defenders. But modern firepower has changed the role that infantry and armor play in ground offensives. Now more than ever they follow a line of action already traced, if not predetermined, by the high-power salvos that cleared the way, well or badly, for them. Today ballistic missiles armed with nuclear or chemical warheads are replacing airplanes and to some extent artillery as the battering rams, the great prejudgers of ground combat. This does not mean that in modern ground combat the defense stands no chance. Dug-in infantry and armor, backed by strong reserves, have an enormous advantage over attacking forces that expose themselves, but only to the extent that the defenders can protect themselves against the long-range battering rams.

Wise commanders of units both large and small have always kept perhaps one-third of their ready forces away from the front as battlefield reserves. This serves the needs of both offense and defense. The reserves can be rushed into a sector where the enemy is about to break through or into a sector where one's own forces are breaking through. The reserves can help prevent a rout on one's own side or cause one for the enemy. All great battlefield commanders (Napoleon at Austerlitz and Marlborough at Blenheim come to mind) have been masters at feeling the pulse of battle and deciding just when and where to engage the reserve forces for the supreme effort.

The absence of strong, highly mobile reserves—from the platoon level to that of an empire—must be counted as one of the most fatal errors in warfare. Rome was sacked in A.D. 410 because once the barbarians had broken through the border legions, the reserve forces under Romulus Augustulus were simply too weak. Rome would not have been taken if this last Roman emperor of the West had had under his direct command even a small fraction of the legions still intact on the far-flung borders of the empire. Reserves are especially important in modern combat. In May 1940, when German troops had broken through French lines on a narrow two-mile front at Sedan, Winston Churchill asked the French government, "Where is the maneuver mass?" French generals looked at the floor as their leader said, "Aucune"—there wasn't any.[2] Moreover, because the Germans who had broken through were riding tanks and trucks, it was out of the question for French forces on the front to pull back fast enough to constitute a mobile army to give battle to the intruder. The French were doomed.

The importance of mobile reserves does not diminish the importance of fortifications. The Maginot Line, for example, has been unjustly maligned. Like all fortifications it was supposed to economize troops at the front precisely so that they could be used as mobile reserves. After all, if any enemy has to work to get through a fortified line, or to go around it, he presents an inviting target to "linebacking" reserves. Unfortunately, the French chose to look at the Maginot Line not as a strategic tool but as an excuse to economize overall.

Some learned a lesson from this disaster, while others did not. In the late summer of 1940, Britain, while preparing for a possible German invasion, deployed a thin cordon of troops along the coast, but kept the bulk of its home forces as a mobile reserve "on which everything would depend." However, when the shoe was on the other foot and Hitler was preparing to meet the Allied invasion of the continent, he repeated the mistakes that the French had made in 1940. He created a brilliant spider's web of fortifications. But, as Churchill noted, "he forgot the spider."[3] There was no "maneuver mass" to smash the Allies as they broke out of the Normandy beachheads in August 1944.

The NATO alliance, for its part, is preparing a defense of West Germany that seems to violate every rule of ground combat. American, British, and West German troops are spread out against the inter-German border, while Benelux and French contingents are layered behind. There is no mobile reserve, and indeed there are no nuclear mine fields on the German border because of a twin political commitment to "forward defense," that is, to limiting the fighting to the border and to making the fighting as nondisruptive as possible.

In addition, of course, NATO forces are outnumbered in tanks by three to one, in artillery by five to one, and in infantry-fighting vehicles by five to one.[4] The likelihood of a successful preclusive defense is zero. There are no plans for "elastic" defense, that is, rapid withdrawal in the face of attack followed by sharp counterattacks when the force of the attack is spent. Instead of plans for the likely eventuality of a Soviet breakthrough there are vague words about the possible use of nuclear weapons.[5]

Yet since combat in Europe would take place in the context of the worldwide U.S.–Soviet military balance, any thought of using nuclear weapons against the Soviets anywhere must take into account the fact that since the mid-1970s, the Soviet Union has had the capacity to inflict more damage on the United States than the United States could inflict on the Soviet Union. How can one think of trying to avoid defeat on one level of warfare by inviting certain defeat on another, far more destructive level? Modern conditions do not invalidate common sense about military matters. They strengthen it.

Amphibious Operations

Landing and fighting on a hostile shore multiplies the difficulties of naval and ground operations. First, one must defeat or evade the enemy's ships. Then one must fight the waves, tides, sand, and Murphy's Law to get men and equipment on shore. If the beach is defended, ship-based aircraft and guns have the tough job of overwhelming land-based aircraft and guns. Then the invader must do it all over again and again to keep his troops supplied. On top of these difficulties are the pains of ground combat.

The advantage of amphibious operations is that they allow an attacker to move whole forces by sea at around fifteen miles per hour and land them wherever he chooses. They almost guarantee tactical surprise. Attacking forces can be concentrated at the point of attack very quickly to outflank or bypass or circle behind a defending force.

The first requirement of amphibious warfare is naval superiority. It is impossible to deal with nature and shore defenses while fighting a naval battle. So if the attacking navy has not yet eliminated its opponent, it must be prepared to screen the landing area. In World War II, Hitler did not invade Britain because he did not have a navy capable of challenging Britain's. He counted on being able to cripple the Royal Navy and control the channel with the Luftwaffe, but first it had to cripple the Royal Air Force. This is what the Battle of Britain was about. When the RAF beat the Luftwaffe, the Royal Navy was assured control of the channel and Britain was safe from invasion. The Germans could have sneaked a few shiploads of men across the channel, but such operations would have been inconsequential. An amphibious invasion requires at least a naval screen, and Britain, not Germany, was in a position to provide it.

The United States Navy fought the battle of Leyte Gulf precisely to cover the invasion of the Philippines. The battle was fought in two separate parts. Had the Japanese commander of the essentially victorious northern fleet continued toward Leyte despite the damage to his fleet, he would have been able to cut through the invasion fleet and wreck the main U.S. landings. But he mistakenly supposed that he would be met by the other half of the U.S. fleet, and chose not to hazard Japan's few remaining capital ships. By contrast, with the exception of a few submarines, when the Allies invaded Normandy across the English Channel what was left of the German navy did not even attempt to break through an obviously overwhelming naval screen.

Naval protection of amphibiously landed forces is absolutely essential. History's greatest example of what happens when the fleet that was supporting a land force is defeated is the aftermath of the battle of Salamis, when King Xerxes's superior Persian forces were instantly transformed from potential conquerors of Greece to wretches trying to save themselves by walking around the northeast rim of the Mediterranean. By the same token, although World War II's desert campaigns in North Africa are not normally considered amphibious operations, in effect they were, because both sides' supplies came by sea. Allied victory in the sands of North Africa followed victory in the Mediterranean and Atlantic.

Unchallenged naval supremacy makes possible what appear to be strokes of genius. In 1950, General Douglas MacArthur, commander of the U.S.–UN forces in Korea, landed an amphibious force behind the front, at a place called Inchon. The beach was undefended because the North Koreans did not imagine that anyone would land there. Surprise was complete, and in a few weeks the now outflanked North Korean forces lost more than they had gained in the entire war. This event, now forty years old, was the last major victory for American arms.

Amphibious operations, however, are the culmination of a sometimes very laborious process of sea control. In our day, that process must take place in the sky above the sea, in the depths, as well as on the surface. The greatest amphibious campaign in history, MacArthur's island-hopping campaign of World War II, teaches hard lessons: Aircraft carriers can sometimes send their planes to fight against planes from enemy airfields (if they can manage to surprise them). But absent surprise, the carriers themselves must stay out of range of enemy land-based aircraft. The big amphibious landings in the Pacific, where major enemy air activity was expected, were covered by aircraft from American airfields hastily built on islands that had been lightly defended and were captured for this purpose. Then the naval screens were set out, and finally the aircraft and battleships hammered the hostile shore, with seldom a shot fired back. Only then would the Marines "hit the beach."

Naval Operations

While the purposes of naval operations have not changed since the dawn of time, their character is wholly determined by changing technology. In our time, the purposes remain, first, securing the sea for friendly ships and denying it to the enemy's, and second, attacking enemy shores. These goals may be more important now than ever before. In simpler times, land powers did not have to worry about the sea. China after 1433 is the classic example of a one-dimensional land power. But today no nation—even the Soviet Union, the quintessential land power—can expect to fight a major war successfully if its enemies are able to utilize the world's resources to supply themselves and can prevent it from receiving supplies and help from across the sea while landing on its coasts at will. Indeed, the Soviet Union could not have survived World War II if Germany had won the "Battle of the Atlantic" for control of the routes by which American trucks, airplanes, tanks, and food reached Soviet territory.

Coastal or island nations—Britain, Japan, and even the United States—are much more dependent on naval success. Quite simply, for such nations loss of sea control is defeat. Because occupying forces can come only by sea, so long as it is in friendly hands, worse cannot come to worst, and there should be time to repair losses. While the sea is in friendly hands the lifeblood of commerce will provide an unoccupied people the material means to repair losses and prepare for victory. But if an island or coastal nation loses control of the sea, it will run short of materials and necessities and time will become its enemy. Thus, in World War I, the British were right in saying that their First Sea Lord, Earl Jellicoe, whose Grand Fleet did indeed "rule the waves," was the only man on either side who could "lose the war in an afternoon." He could not win it. Only lose it. Germany was largely the mistress of the Continent. Its inferiority at sea was a serious, though not a decisive, liability for its campaign on the Western front. Germany could lose a major sea battle and not be much worse off than before. But if Britain had lost naval superiority, the position of its troops on the Western front would instantly have become untenable. Today this sort of logic is more powerful than ever. NATO troops in Europe are obviously outnumbered and outgunned by the Soviet Union and the Warsaw Pact nations. Yet this inferiority is not necessarily decisive so long as the Soviet Union does not isolate NATO Europe from the support it draws from the United States and the rest of the world.

But controlling the seas today is a vastly different enterprise than it has ever been before. Historically, naval warfare consisted of guessing where the enemy fleet would be, stumbling into it, and getting close enough to enemy ships to strike them with one's weapons—first arrows and then guns. Gradually the range of guns lengthened until, by World War I, guns could shoot to the horizon and beyond. Since that time, war on the surface of the sea has relied on machines (airplanes, radar, and satellites) that can look beyond the horizon and on weapons (guns, but mostly airplanes and missiles) that can reach there. Also, whereas once all naval warfare took place on the surface of the sea, today's technology allows naval operations to take place under and over the sea as well. Let us look more closely at naval technology.

First, consider sensors. Until the twentieth century, ships could perceive one another only by human eyes and ears and could never detect each other if they were farther than the horizon. Today instruments make it possible (though never certain) to perceive ships, aircraft, and even submarines hundreds and even thousands of miles away. The bottom of the North Atlantic, for example, is sown with hydrophones. Similar strings of underwater ears are arrayed across the bottom of key straits in the Pacific as well. These devices transmit to stations on shore the noise made by passing ships and submarines. The ever-changing character of seawater does not allow these electronic underwater ears to tell precisely where submarines are, but they help antisubmarine forces know where to begin searching. Submarines and surface ships now carry large, sophisticated listening devices. Depending on ocean conditions, these can give a reasonably good "fix" on a submarine over a hundred miles away. Airplanes and helicopters, too, can drop into the water buoys carrying electronic ears. This is quite useful for following up imprecise leads provided by underwater arrays. Airplanes also fly low over the ocean carrying Magnetic Anomaly Detection devices, essentially metal detectors, to pick up traces of nearby submarines.

Once a submarine is detected, weapons can be launched at it from far away. The most remarkable example of such a weapon is something the United States calls SUBROC. It is a rocket that a submerged submarine can launch at another submerged submarine. The rocket, carrying a homing torpedo, pushes itself out of the water and travels a ballistic trajectory toward a point above the enemy submarine. Then it dives back into the water and releases the torpedo, which listens for the nearby submarine and then homes in on it. Surface ships and airplanes can also fire rockets carrying homing torpedoes. Improved sensors for long-range detection, as well as the development of sensors that make weapons "smart," have put an end to the era when the only way to destroy a submarine was to drop depth bombs on it.

This is a good place to note that naval warfare was the nursery for "smart," or guided, weapons. That is because the sea, like the sky, is such a featureless background that streams of energy coming from ships, submarines, or aircraft stand out clearly against it, whether they be sound waves, radar waves, or radiated heat. To make any naval weapon "smart" it was only necessary to give it a sensor that could tell the difference between the sound, or heat, or radar coming from the target and those from the featureless background, and then to devise mechanisms for steering the weapon so that it keeps head-ing for the source of the signal. When sensor technology became able to sort targeted objects out of the clutter of signals coming from the ground, "smart" weapons came to be applied to land warfare as well. But because of the peculiar characteristics of the sea, naval weapons are still the "smartest" of all.

High-flying airplanes carrying powerful radars can scan huge swaths of the ocean for surface ships. The Soviet Union even has a Radar Ocean Reconnaissance Satellite. Satellites for detecting heat and the presence of metal on the surface of the ocean are feasible. In addition, satellites, airplanes, ships, and land stations bristle with antennas that can detect and locate the radio signals that ships at sea normally send out. Of course, ships that want to hide (for instance, the Japanese carriers that struck Pearl Harbor) maintain strict radio silence. Nevertheless, as time goes by and various kinds of sensors proliferate, and better computers collate what they report, major naval powers increasingly gain an accurate and timely picture of where ships are located in the world's oceans. The problem of detection in naval warfare is smaller than it has ever been, and it is steadily diminishing.

Almost the same can be said of detecting aircraft in naval roles. Aircraft are normally visible to modern shipborne radar as soon as they come above the horizon. Just exactly when this happens depends on their altitude. That is why any aircraft that wishes to sneak up on a ship must fly low and pop over the horizon only a few seconds' flying time from the ship. Antiship cruise missiles (pilotless aircraft, otherwise known as flying torpedoes) are easy to stop if they fly high enough to give the ships time to aim their antiaircraft guns and launch their antiaircraft missiles. Absolute speed matters much less than speed relative to the horizon. Such speed is highest when altitude is lowest. In naval warfare, as in other kinds of warfare, designers of aircraft and cruise missiles also try to make it possible to avoid detection by shaping their products in ways that give low radar returns (stealth). Modern aircraft can also jam detection radars and carry out other electronic countermeasures.

In sum, modern naval warfare is characterized by generally easy detection and by weapons with increasingly high probability of hitting their targets. This is not to say that every antiship cruise missile launched from a ship or airplane will hit a ship, that every surface-to-air missile will bring down a plane, or that every homing torpedo will sink something. But it does mean that there is a big and growing premium in naval warfare in getting off the first shot. Since the

success of a weapon is more and more taken for granted, the essence
of modern naval tactics consists of taking whatever measures are
necessary to get into position to shoot before the other side can get
ready to shoot back or to protect itself. Submarines win by being
quieter. Aircraft win by flying lower or with better electronic countermeasures. Surface ships try to be quiet in every way, to extend
their eyes and ears as far as possible, and to be ready to repel attacks.
Every naval unit tries for speed, uses electronic communications to
find out from others where the enemy is, and attempts to stay out of
range of his sensors, all the while trying to move its own sensors
quickly into range so that it can strike.

Given these conditions, then, how do modern navies carry out
traditional naval operations? Consider the blockade, and its counterpart, the protection of sea lines of communications. The airplane
is the most common tool of modern large naval blockades because its
speed and field of view allows it to cover wide areas. Satellites
promise to be even more effective. During World War II, German
planes based in western France could not locate and fight American
convoys in the Atlantic because their speed, range, and staying
power were not enough to maintain continuous coverage. Today, if
the Soviet Union were trying to prevent American convoys from
reaching Europe, its Radar Ocean Reconnaissance Satellite would
track the convoys all the way. "Bear" reconnaissance aircraft would
keep them in view, and when the convoys got within perhaps five
hundred miles of the continent, swarms of "backfire" naval
bombers loaded with cruise missiles would head directly for the
ships. The cruise missiles would be launched on accurate headings
well before the ships could see them and would pop over the horizon
seconds before impact. In addition, accurate, high-altitude reconnaissance would have given Soviet submarines time to position
themselves to meet the convoy. It is noteworthy that whereas during
World War II surface ships were usually much faster than submarines and thus were vulnerable only when they ran directly into
them, modern nuclear submarines are actually faster than any but
the very swiftest surface ships.

All of this is to say that the task of securing sea lines of communications today no longer means escorting ships directly, confident
that it would be unlikely to meet an entire blockading force. Since
evasion is unlikely, a convoy can be assured of getting through a
blockade only if its "escorts" seek out and defeat the blockading
forces themselves. Moreover, the speed and reconnaissance capacity

of modern naval forces ensure that the battle to hold or break blockades would be on an oceanic scale.

Thus, given modern naval technology, an advantage for either side would depend on the overall rather than on the local balance of forces. Nevertheless, location remains important, because it seems that the character of modern naval weapons favors the side that is on the defensive, whose job is to stop the movement of ships, especially when it is trying to prevent enemy naval forces from getting near land that it controls. This is true for several reasons. First, submarines that are predeployed in defensive positions need not move much, if at all. Because the submarines that are moving in to dislodge them will be noisier ipso facto, the defense will have an important advantage. Second, even if the attacker is superior in aircraft carriers, it is difficult to imagine any realistic number of carriers that could put enough airplanes in the air at any given time to block a concentrated attack by a major air force operating from nearby land bases.

Conversely, if the defense were to send out a superior number of aircraft carriers, and these carriers were deployed under the cover of friendly land-based airpower, the carriers could project aircraft outward so as to be able to keep the offense from even reaching mid-ocean. Of course, control of the air above the sea also helps a country's own submarines fight underwater without having to worry about threats from enemy aircraft. Naval forces, subsurface, surface, and air, have always been mutually supportive.

Thus we conclude that naval bastions have always made sense, but that the recent extension in the range of sensors and weapons has increased their potential size and effectiveness. At any rate, the lethality of modern naval forces is such that no ship carrying troops or cargo would venture into the battle area, or possibly even out of port, before the battle for control of the sea was decided.

Modern technology has also radically expanded the geographic scope of another classic naval mission: attacking the enemy's shore. Before the invention of gunpowder, navies could batter enemy shores only by landing raiding parties or, occasionally, by shooting flaming arrows into coastal installations. The Byzantine Empire even used to squirt flaming oil at enemy ships and shore defenses: "Greek fire." Since the sixteenth century, naval guns have allowed ships to pound the enemy shore from ever farther away, with ever greater accuracy and effect. American battleships of the *Iowa* class, the Japanese *Yamato*, and the German *Bismarck*, could hurl 2,700-

pound shells 20 miles with the accuracy of a dive bomber. Thus, they could support friendly troops ashore or pulverize an enemy port. In World War II, the carrier-borne airplane extended the range of naval destructiveness beyond the horizon. In the years since, cruise missiles and ballistic missiles carried by ships and submarines have become capable of inflicting major damage from thousands of miles away. The only thing that such long-range weapons cannot do is change their targets rapidly enough to keep up with an evolving military situation. But rapid advances in communications may soon enable a commander looking at a hostile shore through the eyes of small pilotless aircraft or satellites to "call in" and direct fire from faraway ballistic missiles just as his predecessors in World War II used to "call in" fire from battleships, with words like, "Up 200 yards, right 50, fire for effect!"

Battering the shore from very far away has its advantages. One does not have to brave the hazards of a long voyage, which may include facing enemy submarines and aircraft, nor local defenses, which may include the threat of mines. But today one might ask, if the intention is to pound the enemy with very long-range weapons from a safe distance, why go to sea at all? Why not fire missiles from home soil instead? The answer is that probably the safest place for valuable weapons is under a patch of sea close to home, well protected by tons of water, secrecy, as well as both land-based aircraft and submarines. In our time, the Soviet Union has focused much of its navy on one mission: to create a bastion on the edge of the Arctic icecap from which its ballistic-missile submarines may threaten the United States. This way of using its naval resources minimizes the significance of the Soviet navy's technical weaknesses. For example, Soviet submarines are noisier than their U.S. counterparts. But even a noisy submarine is very quiet if it is barely moving. Soviet submarine-launched missiles tend to be even more inaccurate than their U.S. counterparts because of the imperfect way in which they determine the precise location of the points from which they are launched. But the submarines can be more accurate if they do not wander over the ocean and instead fire from pre-surveyed points on a familiar sea floor.

The creation of such a bastion also maximizes some of the Soviet navy's strengths with respect to the United States. For example, although the Soviet Union is almost completely bereft of large aircraft carriers, it has an outstanding fleet of naval bombers. Why then should the Soviet navy try to take on the United States Navy in mid-ocean when it can bombard the U.S. shore from its own home waters and when its own fighting capacity in those waters is incomparably greater than in mid-ocean?

Striking the enemy shore is even more important to the United States Navy. Indeed, beginning with the quarrel over the B–36 bomber in 1947, which it lost, the Navy has fought huge bureaucratic battles to secure for itself as large a share as possible of the assignment to deliver nuclear weapons on the Soviet Union.[6] But the Navy's approach is entirely different from the Soviet Union's. American ballistic-missile submarines seek safety by quietly dispersing throughout the open ocean, while the announced intent of America's "maritime strategy" is to force carrier battle groups, including submarines, into the Norwegian Sea to disrupt the Soviet naval bastion by *force majeure*. The safety of American ballistic-missile submarines depends on the assumption of its continued superiority in quietness (which was undermined in the mid-1980s by significant Soviet acquisitions of propeller-manufacturing technology) and on the assumption that technology will not produce significant non-acoustic tools for broad-area submarine detection. The success of American carrier battle groups versus the Soviet navy in the Norwegian Sea is highly problematic. The only sure fact is that after that battle at least one of the two navies would be seriously crippled for *any* future mission.

Thus, we see that modern technology, by expanding the geographic scope of naval operations, has blurred the identity of the traditional distinctions between them: The fate of blockades and shore bombardments may be decided in naval engagements thousands of miles away from the places concerned.

Technology has also heightened the importance of that least glamorous but perenially important naval operation: mining. The purpose of mining is not so much to sink ships as it is to close narrow waterways. That is why mining, although it is usually done secretly and often by submarine, is almost always announced. Often the announcement exaggerates the extent of the mining. For example, during the Civil War Admiral David Farragut entered Mobile Bay despite the presence of well-advertised mines, yelling "damn the torpedoes [mines], full speed ahead" because he suspected the minefield was thin enough to warrant the risk of going through it. Nowadays, minefields are more deadly. The oldest mines would explode only on contact. World War II's mines would detonate when they sensed the sound, pressure, or magnetic influence of a ship.

Newer mines release homing torpedoes, hence they are deadly as far out as their sensors can hear and their torpedoes can travel—a range far greater than that of any explosive.

Clearing mines, usually by exploding them, is always dangerous, time-consuming, and potentially incomplete. Nowadays, of course, there is always the further danger that the mines may be nuclear. These, whether real or bluff, can cause unprecedented problems. After all, if an enemy claims to have mined the entrance to a port with multimegaton bombs, one obviously cannot clear them by exploding them. What if the enemy claims that the mines are also programmed to go off if moved unless deactivated by a coded transmission? Even if divers found the mines, they could do nothing. Nuclear mines, then, raise the prospect of bottling up enemy nuclear submarines, and indeed whole navies, in port.

Geographically, the Soviet Union is by far the most vulnerable country to mine warfare. But the Soviet navy is also the world's best equipped and most proficient in mine warfare. The United States, by contrast, is only modestly vulnerable to mine warfare. But the United States Navy has shown little interest in the field.

Aerospace Operations

Should air forces be considered in the same terms as armies and navies or should they be considered mere servants of ground and naval operations? This question is not about whether air power can make a decisive difference in battle. Of course it can. Everyone also recognizes that some important battles, for example, the Battle of Britain in 1940, have taken place almost entirely in the air. No one doubts the usefulness of interceptor fighters, fighter-bombers, air transports, and long-range bombers. Rather, the question is whether or not, as air-power theorists of the 1920s (Giulio Douhet) and the 1950s (Curtis LeMay) believed, bombing the enemy's homeland can be the decisive tool of warfare.

Because the "air power theory" came into vogue in the United States during World War II, the United States has an air force that controls most of the nation's fixed-wing military aircraft that do not fly off ships or are especially designed to attack submarines. Indeed, a bureaucratic fight between the Navy and the Air Force in 1947 resulted in the United States having no shore-based naval bombers. The centerpiece of the U.S. Air Force is the Strategic Air Command, which controls both bombers and intercontinental missiles, and which is supposed to be America's principal sword—very much as the air-power theorists thought.

Though the Soviet Union has more military airplanes than the United States, it does not have a separate air force. It has a frontal aviation force, with fighter bombers and air-superiority fighters that serve the army. It has the *Protivovozdushnaya Obrona* (PVO), which contains air defense interceptors and associated radar complexes as well as surface-to-air missiles, anti-ballistic missiles, and space weapons for defending the homeland. Then, it has the Long-Range Aviation and the Strategic Rocket Forces that act as a kind of centrally directed, long-range artillery. Soviet military thought gives much importance to this latter function. But—and this is the point—Soviet military thought does not see strikes by long-range weapons as a principle around which to organize all air operations, much less all military operations. The Soviets are primarily concerned that every kind of military operation that could benefit from the services that airplanes can provide shall have those airplanes under their control. So, because the people who like to think about long-range bombing may not care much about naval matters and be hostile to air defense, the Soviets do not give them control of all or even most air power. Instead, they organize their air forces according to function. As a result, for example, the Soviet Union has naval bombers.

We think it is more reasonable to analyze air operations according to Soviet categories. Let us then begin by considering air defenses, which include various kinds of radars for detecting and tracking aircraft and cruise missiles, as well as the interceptor aircraft and various kinds of interceptor missiles used to shoot them down. Radar waves travel in straight lines. So, when airplanes fly high (say above 25,000 feet), as they must in order to conserve fuel on long flights, they come into view of air-search radars 200 or more miles away. Since such radars are usually set on the periphery of countries, on outlying islands, or, in battle, as far forward as possible, the planes will be evident to the defense many minutes (perhaps hours) before they reach the target. To kill the planes, the defense must keep track of them well enough to direct an interceptor to them. So long as the airplanes are flying high, regardless of how fast they are flying, their speed with regard to the horizon is low, and tracking them is easy.

During World War II, even primitive radars were able to give defenders excellent information about the high-flying airplanes of the day. But tracking bombers was useful only insofar as one's own interceptor aircraft were able to defeat the fighters that accompanied the bombers, since high-altitude bombers were invulnerable to fire from antiaircraft guns on the ground. After World War II, as surface-to-air missiles replaced antiaircraft guns, aircraft designers sought to diminish the vulnerability of bombers and reconnaissance planes by making them fly ever higher. But by 1960, the art of surface-to-air missile interceptors had advanced to the point of making impossible high-altitude penetration of defended areas. Besides, bombing from high altitude is wastefully inaccurate. During the 1960s and 1970s, attack aircraft of all kinds were designed to fly low in order to achieve very high speeds *relative to the horizon* and thus minimizing both the time that radars would have to gather information and the distance at which they could do it. Airplanes also began to be equipped with short-range attack missiles (SRAMS), designed to fly ahead and destroy radars in the airplanes' path. Later, airplanes began to carry low-flying cruise missiles, small and specially shaped to be harder for radars to detect. In the 1980s, long-range attack and bomber aircraft have switched more and more from carrying bombs that are to be dropped to carrying cruise missiles that can be launched. Aircraft and cruise missiles were also equipped with electronic countermeasures to spoof defensive radars.

The response of air defenses to this trend has been to equip radar with the ability to detect spoofing by hopping from frequency to frequency, to increase the number of radars, and above all to interconnect them so that central computers can use many small glimpses to build a comprehensive picture of what is happening. In addition, radars have been developed to be carried on patrol aircraft (AWACS) and to be set on high places that are able to look *down* and pick airplanes and cruise missiles out of the clutter of radar waves bouncing back from the ground. Interceptor aircraft have also been equipped with these "Look down, shoot down" radars. As a result, modern air defenses can cover the air from treetop level to the edges of the atmosphere. This is not to say that air operations are obsolete. But any and every airplane in combat has to be equipped to try to fool radars and also be ready to fight for survival when detected. Whether the airplane or the defenses prevail depends on the quantity and quality of their equipment and on how expertly it is used.

The job of frontal aviation is to keep the enemy under a man-made firestorm while one's own troops can look up at the sky unafraid. Frontal aviation must also operate the elaborate airborne reconnaissance and signal collection system that allows its artillery and aircraft to find their targets. The job of a fighter-bomber, also known as an attack aircraft, is to carry bombs or short-range cruise missiles over the battlefield "low and slow" enough so that the pilot can see where to fire them, yet fast enough so that it can come in and get out quickly enough to evade enemy antiaircraft defenses.

How effective is frontal aviation? One limit case is Vietnam. The United States enjoyed a monopoly of air power over South Vietnam. Enemy soldiers could not concentrate for more than a few minutes without having an American airplane shooting at them. True, the United States lost some aircraft when it bombed. But the United States could choose to bomb any place in the country at any time. This was a potentially decisive advantage. Surely, had it been available in April 1975, North Vietnam would not have been able to drive three main columns totaling some quarter of a million men into the heart of South Vietnam. Nevertheless, the United States never even tried to use this superiority as part of a plan to defeat North Vietnam. There was no such plan. Consequently, this monopoly of air power over the front served only to hold off disaster.

Indeed, between 1962 and 1973 the United States lost 3,706 fixed-wing airplanes and 4,866 helicopters over Indochina.[7] The fundamental reason why so little was purchased at such great cost is that this air power was *not* part of a success-oriented military plan involving other kinds of forces. Take the air war against North Vietnam. Again and again, the fighter-bombers would clear away a set of surface-to-air missiles and bunkers, and lose a few planes doing so. But no American ground force would move through the breach. So, in a few weeks the enemy would rebuild the defenses, and the Americans would lose a few more planes knocking them out. Air strikes also avoided North Vietnam's leadership. They spared the country's vital infrastructure, including the dams on the Red River, without which much of Hanoi would have washed away. There also was no air and sea blockade of North Vietnam. This kind of air war did not shake the resolve of North Vietnam's leaders. It reassured them.

The lesson here is that control of the air, unlike control of the ground, guarantees nothing and means next to nothing unless it is part of a plan to achieve something on the ground.

Another illustration of the function of frontal aviation is the current U.S. plan for aerial follow-on-forces-attack (FOFA) on the Central Front in Europe. The United States has advertised that if superior Soviet ground forces attack across the inter-German border, its arguably superior fighter-bombers will fly deep into East Germany and Poland and, using "smart" munitions, will attack the Soviet tanks and supplies moving up to the front. But would enough American fighter-bombers get through Soviet interceptors and surface-to-air missiles to make a difference? Moreover, if the Soviet Union feared that a U.S. FOFA could put a serious crimp on its projected attack across the inter-German border, why would the Soviet Union not precede any invasion with a ballistic missile attack on the undefended U.S. fighter-bombers in Europe? All of this is to say that marginal air superiority over a front does not make up for the deficiency of the rest of one's forces on that front, neither does it counterbalance the advantages that the enemy gains by seizing the initiative, nor does it make up for deficiencies in an overall strategy.

Now consider modern long-range or "heavy" bombers. The nature of their task differs from that of frontal aviation in that they must traverse considerable hostile territory to reach their targets. Heavy bombers, then, could have serious problems with air defenses—providing such defenses happen to be there.

For example, in the 1950s and early 1960s, the United States built a formidable air defense system against a possible Soviet attack. Eighty-one large radars made up the Distant Early Warning Line (DEW) across the Arctic. Another 280 radars comprised the Pinetree Line across northern Canada and backed up the DEW line. Seaward approaches were covered by radars set on oil-drilling platforms and by 137 radar-picket ships. Behind these radars stood 2,612 interceptor fighters, 274 Nike surface-to-air missile batteries, and 439 long-range nuclear-tipped Bomarc interceptor cruise missiles. If the Soviet Union had launched its two-hundred-odd Bear and Bison bombers against this network, it is entirely possible that none would have gotten through. It is not surprising, then, that by 1959 the Soviet Union stopped building new heavy bombers. But in 1964 the United States began to dismantle its air defense system. By 1974, it was gone. Not surprisingly, in 1976 the Soviet Union went back into the heavy-bomber business with its Backfire and later its Blackjack models.

If a long-range bomber does not have to face serious air defenses it can be an effective, flexible weapon, roaming enemy territory, destroying mobile military forces, nipping military preparations in the bud, and inflicting punishment at will. Thus, for example, heavy bombers would be the weapon of choice for a Soviet Union that had already largely disarmed the United States by a ballistic missile strike. In addition, the long-range bomber can be very useful against enemy bases that may be in the process of being built in faraway places and that are not yet fully defended.

Against well-prepared defenses, however, a force of heavy bombers really has only one reasonable choice: to try to shoot its way to the target by progressively attacking the radars, surface-to-air missiles, and interceptor airfields in its path. Of course, this option entails losses for the bomber force. In a country with many targets covered by a network of air defenses it is not clear whether the bombers or the defenses would run out first. *But more important for our understanding, using heavy bombers in this way in fact reduces their role to that of frontal aviation.*

The U.S. Air Force believes that another choice exists as well: Build heavy bombers capable of evading Soviet radars. Thus, at some half *billion* dollars per copy, the Air Force proposes to purchase the B-2 bomber, a cumbersome, slow airplane whose safety over well-defended territory derives mainly from its peculiar, radar-evading shape. But since no object, least of all an airplane, can be designed to deflect radar from all angles simultaneously, the B-2 bomber is very vulnerable to mobile radars. While it is zigging to present a stealthy aspect to a radar whose location it knows, an unknown radar can betray its location. Our point is that while modern air defenses can be spoofed here and there for brief moments, they have ended the age when bombers could roam the enemy's country at will.

Finally, consider airlift operations. Nowadays it is possible to drive tanks and trucks directly into and out of wide-body aircraft. Since such aircraft are expensive, no nation has enough of them to land a division of 15,000 men, 300 tanks, and 1,000 trucks onto a given airfield in an hour. Nevertheless, modern airlift operations can be strategically significant. The Soviet Union, for example, began its invasion of Afghanistan in 1979 by sending a regiment of special troops via four heavy lift cargo planes into Bagram airfield outside of Kabul on 3 December 1979. After the troops had secured the airfield, the big aircraft shuttled in a division. Nearly all of the nearly eight million Americans who went in and out of the Vietnam theater of operations between 1965 and 1973 did so by air. In 1973, Israel was able to recover from the losses suffered from the Arabs' attack during Yom Kippur because the United States was willing and able to load tanks, trucks, antitank missiles, ammunition and spare parts onto virtually every available heavy-lift aircraft and fly them to Israel.

This shuttle, like the Soviet shuttle of material to Egypt and Syria, did not have to take into account possible military opposition. But, of course, in full-scale war one of the objectives of any military force would be to thwart its opponent's attempts to outflank it by airlift. Hence, during full-scale war, airlifts would likely take place only under fighter escort and they would only go into areas that had been reasonably well secured. This would involve capturing airfields along the route for use by one's own fighters and denying them to enemy fighters. All of this is to say that, air-power theorists notwithstanding, air operations are the operations of war that should be most integrated with other kinds of operations.

CHAPTER
7

MILITARY OPERATIONS IN THE NUCLEAR AGE

The [American] planners seem to care less about what happens after the buttons are pressed than they do about looking presentable before the event.
—HERMAN KAHN
On Thermonuclear War

Nuclear weapons have a decisive significance on the change in the methods of attack and on the employment of other means of destruction: They caused a reduction in their density, especially of artillery.
—A. A. SIDORENKO
The Offensive

WHEN the first atom bomb lit up the sky over Trinity, New Mexico, 16 July 1945, it raised a question that Americans have yet to answer: What should we do with it? It could not be disinvented. Besides, the United States faced the prospect of suffering a million more casualties to finish the war against Japan by conventional warfare. How could the bomb help? Should it be dropped on a Japanese city or on a military installation? The United States planned to use the bomb to shock and overawe the Japanese out of their resolve to resist invasion. But if the United States tried to drop the bomb on ships in Tokyo Bay, the limitations on the bomb's power and the inaccuracy of the parachute drop from the B-29 might well have left every ship afloat. Army bases, for their part, had air-raid shelters, which would surely cut down casualties. On the other hand, if dropped anywhere on a warm-weather city made up of paper-walled houses, the bomb could not help but have an impressive effect. Alas, the policy of destroying cities was well established by September 1945. Certainly there was no moral difference between using the atom bomb or incendiary bombs to destroy cities. So Hiroshima and Nagasaki were hit.

It is impossible to know if these bombs caused the surrender that quickly ensued. Other air raids had been more destructive. Surely the novelty was impressive. But Japan had just as surely been asking to surrender since April 1945, if the U.S. would only spare the Emperor. In July and August the U.S. hinted that it would. Then came the bombs.

Immediately, the debate over nuclear weapons erupted full grown into terms that have not changed much since. Then, as now, the debate was framed in technical terms. But, although technology provides the specific alternatives in using nuclear weapons, the choice between these alternatives can only be made in strategic, political, and moral terms.

The first document in this debate was a little book edited by Bernard Brodie, *The Absolute Weapon*, written within weeks of the bombing of Hiroshima.[1] It held that nuclear bombs could be used in the same way other kinds of bombs had been used. Although they would be more effective, and also more expensive, the logic of nuclear war would be the same as that of other wars: To strike the enemy's bombers and other armed forces on the ground, to shoot down as many as possible in flight, while protecting one's own airfields and other targets with concrete, sandbags, etc. The book made it clear that the power of nuclear weapons did not override the fact that their effect would depend on how they would be used and on the countermeasures the enemy would take.

But the book had another, intoxicating side whose message has had a profound effect. This side of the book assumed that the power of the bomb was infinite, indeed "absolute," and that cities would be the main targets. One bomb could destroy a city. Hence, it would make no difference whether one side had 2,000 bombs or 6,000. Well before the Soviet Union tested its atom bomb, the book postulated that the United States and the Soviet Union would have the power to destroy one another while lacking the ability to protect themselves, and that this situation would never, ever change. Thus, nuclear weapons would be used by not being used. In this role they could establish a perpetual peace that would overshadow ideology and indeed all other sources of human enmity. Why? Because fear of nuclear attack would never be low.

Nevertheless, in the immediate postwar period nuclear weapons seemed to solve a pressing practical problem: how the United States, eager to get back to the pleasures of peace, could fulfill its responsibilities in defending much of the world against a Soviet military superior in numbers and surely far more willing to suffer casualties.[2] Presidents Truman and Eisenhower quickly concluded that if the United States were to attempt to play a global role using only conventional weapons, it would have to keep perhaps seven million men under arms, militarize its society, and perhaps bankrupt itself. But nuclear weapons would allow a much smaller U.S. force to do the job because they provided "a bigger bang for the buck." So, although U.S. presidents from the beginning spoke loudly about putting the nuclear genie back into the bottle, they put the genie to work as fast as they could. But it wasn't easy.

In 1947, President Truman asked the Joint Chiefs of Staff how the United States could use atom bombs to stop a Soviet invasion of Europe. Answering that question had a sobering effect. To stop a three- or four-million-man army, spread out over hundreds of thousands of square miles would require hundreds, if not thousands, of Hiroshima-size bombs (each yielding the equivalent of 20,000 tons of TNT, or 20KT). Each would kill troops and destroy trucks and perhaps tanks in a four-square-mile area, but each would have to be delivered to just the right place at the right time in a rapidly changing military situation. The United States had only some twenty atom bombs at the time, each of which strained the capacity of a B-29.[3] Even if the United States multiplied that number, what would be the chances of getting a B-29 through undiminished Soviet fighter screens to the right places? So the conclusion was that if the United States were to rely on nuclear weapons to make up for its unwillingness to put millions of young American lives on the line around the world, it would have to make its nuclear weapons small enough to be delivered by fighter-bombers and even by artillery. It would have to increase the accuracy and reliability of delivery systems. It would also have to build these new warheads and delivery systems by the thousands.

But wasn't there a shortcut? Couldn't the United States just "nuke" Moscow in retaliation for a Soviet invasion of Europe? Doing that would not stop the invasion, but threatening it might deter the Soviet Union from the undertaking.[4] And besides, how better to fight the Russian hordes than through nuclear-strategic bombing? But even this alternative required hundreds if not thousands of bombs. After all, one bomb would not affect the 100 square miles of brick and concrete that was Moscow at the time the way it had affected 10 square miles of papier-mâché Hiroshima. Also, penetrating thousands of miles of undefeated Soviet territory would be a different proposition than sending a lone B-29 to intrude a few miles from the sea over prostrate Japan. So the United States had to build a whole infrastructure for long-distance nuclear-strategic bombing as well as for battlefield use of nuclear weapons.

Before looking at the preparations that the United States, the Soviet Union, and lesser powers have made for nuclear operations, it is necessary to make two points. First, the success of nuclear operations depends far more on the technology of delivery systems and on the defenses against the delivery systems than it does on the technology of nuclear weapons themselves. There is no factual basis for the widespread view that weapons research has aimed at producing weapons with ever bigger bangs. Almost the reverse is true, because for good or ill, the purpose of any and all military operations is not to destroy but to conquer. Hence, it can be argued that the development of the microprocessor, which is at the heart of delivery system technology, and not the nuclear bomb, is the great development of our time. The development of more reliable and more accurate means of delivering nuclear weapons has resulted in increasing the practical choices available to commanders who are equipped with them.

Second, these technical developments have paralleled the growing hostility of political rhetoric about nuclear weapons. According to that rhetoric, mankind's only choice is whether to "push the button" and perish, or to live happily ever after. At the same time, the military doctrines of states possessing nuclear weapons have increasingly regarded nuclear weapons, their delivery systems, and the defenses against them as practical problems rather than as objects of millennialist fear or hope. The consequence of these conflicting tendencies is that states that are influenced by political rhetoric—chiefly the United States—have pursued policies in preparation for nuclear operations that are both schizophrenic and fitful.

Ground Operations

Nuclear weapons are now thoroughly integrated into the ground operations of the United States, the Soviet Union, Britain, and France. The basic weapon is the nuclear artillery round. The United States Army has some 4,000 of these munitions in Europe alone, mostly for 105- and 155-mm guns and as munitions for fighter-bomber aircraft. The range of the guns is between 10 and 20 miles, and the yield of the warhead is about one kiloton—enough to disable, though not necessarily destroy, unprotected ground forces within perhaps 1,000 feet of where the warhead hits.[5] Then there are short-range, unguided rockets, like the Army's Lance or the Soviet Free Rocket Over Ground (FROG). They can hit targets 30 to 70 miles away with warheads from 20 to 100 kilotons. There are also longer-range battlefield missiles like the Soviet SS-21 and 23, the French Pluton, and the American Pershing IA, which can carry warheads in the hundreds of kilotons up to 500 miles away.[6] In addition, of course, modern fighter bombers can carry nuclear bombs all over the battlefield.

The art of using such devices consists of finding worthwhile targets, hitting them quickly before they move, disperse, or hit back, and then exploiting the holes left in the enemy's order of battle. The scarcity and cost of nuclear munitions demand that they not be wasted. So, even after a commander has received authorization to use them, he must make sure that there are enough enemy troops, tanks, trucks, supplies, and so forth, close enough together to make expending a nuke worthwhile. The enemy, however, is not likely to bunch up and provide an inviting target unless he has the intention of using his own nukes to strike any place from where he thinks the same might be fired at him. By the same token, one is likely to regard an enemy unit thought to be armed with nukes as ipso facto a good target, no matter how small the unit. Hence, much depends on the intelligence, judgment, and speed of both sides.

On the other hand, any target at all is a good target for nukes if one's own plan calls for ensuring a breakthrough at a particular place. A barrage of nuclear explosives will clear a path, providing that one's own troops are ready with the anticontamination suits and equipment necessary for traversing temporarily radioactive areas. All of this is to say that the nuclear battlefield is likely to be as chaotic as other kinds of battlefields. But the character of nuclear weapons ensures that the range at which engagements take place will be greater than in the past and that there will be a greater premium than ever on shooting first and on imposing one's own agenda onto the battle.

Nuclear weapons have increased the importance of mines and of being dug in. Land mines, as always, are useful to channel enemy movement, and most useful when mountains already do the channeling. Hence, the most secure part of the NATO front is the Soviet-Turkish border—mountain country full of passes and canyons where big nuclear mines have been buried. Switzerland's passes are also mined, but not with nuclear weapons. Perhaps their narrowness makes up for the mines' lack of yield.

Radiation, the peculiar characteristic of nuclear weapons, gives a definite advantage to those who are protected by yards of earth or concrete over those who are protected by inches of armor. Hence, in purely ground combat, the nuke tends to restore the kind of advantage to the defense that existed before the tank made it possible to cross fields of fire. In the 1970s, this fact led NATO to procure nukes optimized to emit more penetrating neutrons and fewer blast-producing X-rays. Since neutrons are stopped only by the atomic nuclei of the material they encounter, they travel far through the atmosphere and are stopped only by sheer mass. If that mass is human tissue, they kill. Hence, the occupants of a tank that had survived the blast of an enhanced-neutron weapon would be killed by its radiation. But that same radiation would not affect people nearby who happened to be in cellars or bunkers. Moreover, the reduced-blast feature of this "neutron bomb" tends to spare not just cellars and bunkers, but also buildings. So, even more than other nuclear weapons, the enhanced-neutron bomb tends to favor those in ground combat who have taken refuge underground, meaning those who are not attacking. It is an effective defensive weapon. Conversely, the nuclear weapon of choice for ground attackers would emphasize blast and deemphasize radiation.

The lethality of any and all nuclear weapons places any but the most heavily bunkered of fixed military facilities at an enormous disadvantage. Airfields, command centers, big supply dumps, nuclear weapons storage sites, and above all, fixed-missile launchers, are sitting ducks for any attacker armed with long-range, nuclear-tipped ballistic missiles—unless these installations are defended by antimissile devices, or made mobile, or both. The ability of nuclear-tipped ballistic missiles to destroy much of the defender's infrastructure and thus prejudice the outcome of a war in its opening minutes is an enormous incentive to shoot first.

Naval Operations

Nuclear weapons make a big difference in naval operations. Ships are inherently tough structures. The water they ride on is an excellent shock absorber. They really are hard to sink. During World War II, dozens of direct hits were necessary to sink aircraft carriers or battleships. Even with nuclear weapons, a blast must be fairly close to a ship in order to sink it. Thus, from the beginning of the nuclear age there has been incentive to put nuclear explosives on torpedoes and in depth bombs, as well as on aerial bombs and cruise missiles aimed at ships. The development of technology in recent years has increased this incentive. For example, despite the fact that sea-skimming cruise missiles give ships only a few seconds' warning, nowadays radar-controlled Gatling guns can put up a wall of bullets that will stop the cruise missile a few hundred yards from the ship. This can put conventionally armed, antiship cruise missiles out of business. Only if the cruise missile is carrying a nuclear explosive will it stand a chance of having any effect at all.[7] Moreover, techniques for detecting naval targets at longer distances (say, 800 miles) are most useful only if there are means of striking those targets quickly. Ballistic missiles can indeed be programmed to hit close enough to moving fleets to damage them—providing they are armed with high-yield nuclear weapons. Similarly, a wave of naval bombers poses two different kinds of threats to a fleet, depending on whether their air-launched cruise missiles are armed with conventional or nuclear weapons. In addition, of course, navies can carry out their traditional mission of striking enemy shores much more effectively if their aircraft, guns, and missiles are armed with nuclear weapons.

The United States Navy, however, while it has embraced nuclear weapons wholeheartedly for shore-strike missions, has prepared to

carry out sea-control missions almost as if nuclear weapons had
never been invented. This may be because the existence of nuclear
weapons has made it more difficult for any navy to give equal weight
to both missions and thus has sharpened the conflict between the
two.

During World War II, the Navy's carrier aircraft and heavy guns
inflicted arguably as much military damage on the enemy in the
Pacific theater as did Army Air Corps planes. As mentioned before,
after World War II, the Navy and the Air Force vied for the prestige
and the budget shares that go along with the job of delivering nuclear weapons on the Soviet Union. Of course, in the 1950s and
1960s, it would have been difficult to argue that the United States
needed modern attack aircraft carriers to protect the shores of the
United States when the Soviet navy posed no threat to U.S. control
of the world's oceans, much less to American shores. Nevertheless,
geography alone should have been enough to convince the United
States to maintain the finest possible capacity in this field. The Navy
thus came to sell—and so to regard—the aircraft carrier primarily as
something for the glamorous offensive job of striking the enemy
shore. But even in the 1960s, carriers could expect to get close to a
well-guarded Soviet shore only if Soviet shore defenses, both submarines and aircraft, were not armed with nuclear weapons.

Had the United States Navy sincerely asked itself, as apparently
the Soviet navy had done, how nuclear weapons could be used in
sea-control operations, it probably would have concluded (as did the
Soviet navy) that it is far easier to use nuclear weapons at sea when
defending the ocean approaches to a continent than when trying to
force one's way into enemy waters.

This is not to deny that nuclear weapons can be used offensively
at sea. The U.S. Navy has nuclear weapons for some of its antiship,
antiaircraft, and antisubmarine missiles. Also, the Navy is well
aware that the Soviet Union is vulnerable to having its navy shut in
by nuclear mining, and the United States has the quiet submarines
necessary for doing the job. Still, none of this is as glamorous as five
carrier battle groups shooting their way into the Norwegian Sea.
This shore strike mission is where the Navy's heart—and budget—
are. Yet the United States Navy has never seriously considered how
such a carrier armada would deal with literally hundreds of cruise
missiles and ballistic missiles attacking it at roughly the same time.
The armada could weather the storm only if none of these mis-

siles was carrying a nuclear warhead. Alas, all of them probably would be.

In short, to think seriously about the role of nuclear weapons in sea control (against an otherwise undefeated enemy) is to think in terms of naval bastions and of expanding those bastions methodically by surface, air, and submarine units working together. It also means operating outside the bastions only with relatively cheap platforms designed to deliver nuclear weapons to enemy ships. But, for a variety of reasons internal to the United States Navy and having to do with U.S. alliance politics, it is not U.S. policy to think this way about sea control.

Air Operations

If Germany or Japan had had nuclear-armed cruise missiles during World War II, the United States could never have mounted thousand-bomber raids. By the 1950s the 16,000 U.S. nuclear "Genie" missiles answered a problem that no longer existed. The bombers of the fifties, carrying nuclear weapons, were fewer in number than a decade earlier, and would not travel in big formations. By the fifties, then, nuclear warheads on air-defense cruise missiles and rockets had an entirely different purpose, to hedge against inaccuracy. In some cases (such as the Nike), the hedge was not needed; while in other cases (such as the notoriously unreliable Terrier naval air-defense missile), it surely was. But by the 1970s, advances in guidance technology had shifted the debate from whether or not the interceptor should carry a nuclear or a conventional explosive to whether or not the interceptor should carry any explosive at all, given that it may be accurate enough to smash directly into the target. The swift advance of radar and data-processing technology has made destroying large numbers of attacking aircraft a function of instruments that can track many of them simultaneously and direct interceptors to them.

The only surface-to-air mission in which nuclear explosives are still useful (though probably not for long) is the medium-to-low altitude interception of reentering ballistic missile warheads. We will consider this in greater detail later in the chapter.

The final thing to be said about the effect of nuclear weapons on air operations is that all modern military aircraft have been "hardened" to some extent to operate in a nuclear environment. That means chiefly that all-important electronic navigation, communications, and target-finding instruments have been shielded against the electromagnetic pulse and other effects of nuclear explosions. For some aircraft, such as bombers whose airfields are likely targets of ballistic missiles, this is essential. How effective the hardening turns out to be depends on a variety of factors, not least of which is how fast the airplane can escape the zone likely to be hit by a nuclear explosion.

"Strategic" Bombing

The most talked about aspect of nuclear operations is long-range bombing. Since about 1960, however, discussion of this subject has taken place almost exclusively in terms of the ballistic missiles that have largely replaced the former role of airplanes. We will look at the discussion from this perspective as well as from the vantage point of the struggle over U.S. strategic policy, with occasional glances at the Soviet side of things.

By the mid-1950s, the United States had transformed its nuclear poverty of 1947 into nuclear plenty. The United States had some five thousand hydrogen bombs for its fleet of B-47 and B-52 jet bombers. The United States had more bombs than it had intelligence about places where it would drop them. If "the balloon went up," so the saying went, the United States planned to disgorge its arsenal on everything of value in the Soviet Union, on what the jargon of the day called an "optimum mix" of both civilian and military targets. But beginning in 1957, photographs from U-2 intelligence aircraft showed the United States for the first time how big and spread out the Soviet strategic forces were, and served to identify thousands of important military targets. By this time also, the Soviet Union was building ballistic missiles that could hit the United States despite

American air defenses. Literally no one questioned the need to hit Soviet missile launching pads. The simultaneous increase in knowledge and in the threat caused a shift toward targeting more military and fewer civilian installations. "Optimum mix" targeting had been a compromise between the urge to eradicate communism physically while punishing the Soviet Union for aggression and the need to destroy the Soviet Union's means of doing harm to the United States and its allies. The compromise had been easy to make because there had been lots of American bombs and little detailed information about the places in the Soviet Union where it might be good to drop them. But as the years brought more information, demand increased for "covering" this and that military target, and targeting became more thoughtfully oriented toward the Soviet military arsenal.

By 1959, Secretary of Defense Thomas Gates did away with the ambiguity. The United States would bomb primarily with the intention of defeating the Soviet military—so-called counterforce targeting. By the time President Kennedy and Secretary of Defense Robert McNamara came into office in 1961, the third generation of U.S. ballistic missiles, the land-based Minuteman and the submarine-launched Polaris, were in production.[8] They had not been designed specifically for either counterforce or city bombings, but rather had been made as powerful and as accurate as the technology of the day allowed. Thus, at the time of the Cuban missile crisis of October 1962, the United States, using only a portion of its missile force, could have devastated the Soviet Union's few, highly vulnerable missile-launching pads, as well as much of its long-range aviation.

In 1963, however, the United States came up against a choice that it has yet fully to resolve. The Soviet Union began to put its late second-generation SS-8 ICBMs into underground silos. In order to strike them, the United States would have to increase its own missiles' combination of nuclear yield and accuracy. Unless the United States did that, it was clear in 1963–64 that if the United States were to maintain the strategy of 1962, and its standard for judging forces, it would soon have to regard itself as underarmed. The Kennedy administration chose not to build counterforce missiles but rather to switch both the strategy and the standard. Henceforth, the United States would target the Soviet population and shape its weapons with the objective of killing people. The Kennedy administration did this for a variety of reasons. Among them was the millennialist hope that major war could be exorcised forever by the threat of mutual suicide. But there was also an immediate, concrete disinclination to keep pace with changing conditions by continually innovating weaponry. By adopting a new strategy and a new standard, the Kennedy administration could guarantee the adequacy of its forces without much effort. The Soviets could change both their missiles and their basing modes ad infinitum, so went the reasoning. But they could not remove their cities from under America's nuclear Damocles' sword. Thus, by focusing U.S. strategy on threatening the destruction of Soviet civil society, U.S. nuclear forces would remain adequate forever *regardless of what the Soviets did.* According to this new standard, the United States was seriously overarmed. Of course this fiddling with definitions was the very definition of solipsism.

What does it mean to destroy Soviet society? Robert McNamara defined it as destroying 25 percent of the Soviet Union's population and 50 percent of its industry.[9] He arrived at those figures by examining the demographics of the Soviet Union. According to McNamara, after expending 400 "megaton equivalents" on perhaps as many targets, the United States would be running into the "flat of the curve." That is, any additional nuclear weapons and missiles expended would cost more to manufacture, keep, and launch than the people it would kill and the factories it would wreck were worth. Of course, this entire thought process rested on—indeed consisted exclusively of—arbitrary assumptions about the value of human life and on the assumption that the Soviet leadership shared them.

This targeting strategy raised difficult questions from the standpoint of operations as well. Just what would this "destroyed" Soviet Union be able to do? One thing it could surely do would be to launch its untouched missiles at the United States, whose denser demographic distribution would guarantee a higher percentage of fatalities. McNamara and the national security adviser, McGeorge Bundy, and a whole generation of the U.S. foreign defense–policy establishment did not mind that. Indeed, they saw the United States' obvious vulnerability under their strategy as the guarantee that the Soviet Union would recognize that the United States has no intention of ever carrying out any kind of strike. Hence, with mutual assurance of Mutual Assured Destruction (MAD), both would live happily ever after.

The happy ending, however, required that both sides channel advances in missile technology away from the combination of yield and accuracy necessary to destroy hardened silos and that both sides wholly refrain from developing the means to destroy missiles or warheads in flight. In 1972, many influential Americans believed that the SALT I and ABM treaties guaranteed that both sides would do just that. In 1977–80, when the Soviet Union deployed a fourth generation of ICBMs (the SS-18, 19, and 17) that indubitably possessed those very characteristics, any basis for those expectations collapsed. By the mid-1970s, it was difficult to deny that the Soviet Union, using perhaps one-third of its new missiles, could destroy nearly all of U.S. land-based missiles, half of the U.S. missile firing submarines in port at any given time, and most U.S. bombers on the ground. Thus, the Soviet Union could go a long way toward protecting itself and winning the war.[10]

Even before the collapse, however, the intellectual edifice of MAD had failed the test of internal consistency. As U.S. nuclear targeters tried to follow McNamara's guidelines, they could not help but note that which quarter of the Soviet population lived or died and which half of Soviet industry stood or fell made a big difference in what the Soviet Union could do afterward. After all, although MAD sought to banish the thought that *anything* would *ever* happen after a nuclear exchange, it was obvious that 175 million surviving Soviets might think of *something*. So targeters sought to identify the industries that are particularly crucial to recovery and the workers who would be most difficult to replace. As they did so, they noticed that the Soviet Union had prepared deep, hardened shelters for precisely such workers, and that it had an ambitious program for protecting key industrial machinery (though not buildings). Hence, the U.S. targeters were led to conclude that the missile technologies required to do a thorough antirecovery job were not so different from those required to do the counterforce job.

The targeters also followed another thread of logic. If the purpose of MAD is to deter war by threatening valuable things, MAD works best if we discover *which* things and people the Soviets value most and then seek to threaten them. But satellite photographs showed unmistakably that the things the Soviet leadership most valued and most sought to protect from nuclear attack were military. Hence, even if one had not thought of fighting a war, but merely wanted to deter the Soviets, one would have to have the ability to threaten the military things that the Soviets valued most, especially the Soviet strategic rocket forces and long-range aviation. In other words, one would need counterforce.[11]

The Soviets themselves have never been of two minds about targeting. Back in 1961, when primitive SS-7s still relied on inclined launch rails for their azimuth, U.S. satellites photographed the rails, and photo analysts drew lines from the rails over the globe to get an idea of what the Soviets were shooting at. To their surprise, the lines never crossed American cities—always air force bases. This was at a time when technology did not permit the kind of accuracy that would have assured the success of a missile attack on an air force base. No matter. The Soviets did not want to waste precious nuclear missiles on killing useless people. Nowadays, when technology permits pinpoint targeting of military assets, the public hints of Soviet leaders that nuclear war would be the end of the planet are less convincing than the absence from the Soviet arsenal of weapons (like the U.S. Poseidon) that are optimized for people killing. Soviet weapons are obviously optimized for counterforce.

Thus, in the late 1970s all these threads of logic led the Carter administration formally to renounce MAD and to announce a new strategy. If the Soviet Union ever attacked, the United States would reply by putting at least one high-quality warhead on every Soviet silo. This would deprive the Soviet Union of the accurate reserve force that it would need for a coercive follow-up to its first strike. The prospect of being unable to follow up would presumably deter the Soviets.

This approach had at least three shortcomings. First, the United States did not yet possess any missiles and warheads of the type that would be required to do this—and that could survive a Soviet first strike. This has not changed since 1979, and indeed there are no funds in the latest American five-year defense plan to acquire them in sufficient number. Second, by the mid-1980s the Soviet Union had put the SS-24 and SS-25 mobile missiles into full production, and thus was well on its way to putting all of the missile forces that would not be used up in a first strike out of the reach of American retaliation. Third, even if the United States had intelligence satellites (quite feasible but very different from any existing or planned) that could allow our missiles to be constantly retargeted on missiles moving throughout the Soviet Union, we would have to contend with the growing number of Soviet antimissile defenses.

The growth of Soviet antimissile preparations is the final negation of the McNamara framework. These preparations do not guarantee that the United States could not land an indeterminable number of warheads on the Soviet Union. But they do guarantee that the United States could not carry out a meaningful attack or a meaningful retaliation.

Briefly, Soviet preparations consist of nine huge (200 yards by 300 yards) Pechora-class phased array radars, mostly on the country's periphery. Each of these would "see" incoming warheads from afar, create electronic files for each, sort the files according to the destination of each warhead, and electronically transfer the bundles of files to hundreds of lesser radars around the country, telling each where to look. These in turn would guide interceptor missiles to their marks. These lesser radars and interceptor missiles (named respectively Flat Twin and SH-4 to SH-8) are in mass production. The United States does not know how many copies are being produced, where they are being stored, or what it would take to make them functional. Indeed, there is only a semantic distinction between "storage" and "deployment."

In addition, the Soviet Union is producing the SA-12 surface-to-air missile system. Mounted on trucks, each unit of the SA-12 can intercept a small number of warheads coming into its area. Note that very few targets in the world have more than two warheads assigned to them. On top of it all, the Soviet Union launched a high-energy laser into space on 7 July 1988 as part of a probe to Mars. No Westerner knows its capacity, or how it relates to antimissile equipment. Of course, there is also the modernized ABM system that covers the Moscow area with one hundred rapidly reloadable underground interceptor launchers. What does this all mean?

It is clear that after an initial Soviet attack the United States could not spread the perhaps 2,500 (mostly submarine-launched) remaining warheads among hundreds of targets with confidence that chosen targets would be hit. Indeed, to date the United States has not confronted the problem of targeting a much-diminished arsenal against a Soviet Union that is increasingly protected. No doubt the United States could concentrate its remaining bolts on a few cities, with reasonable hope that at least some would get through. But at what parts of the cities should it aim? And why? The Soviet Union has not ensured its safety from such an irrational American response. But it has reduced any such response to irrationality.

Because no one in the United States has good answers to such questions, anyone who asks what military measures the United States might take to deal with the Soviet Union's capacity to much reduce U.S. strategic forces and then to significantly defend itself, can only answer: Build a serious antimissile defense.

The U.S. government's response has been a research program called the Strategic Defense Initiative (SDI). But while popular opinion has it that since 1983 SDI has gradually risen like a shield to protect America, the reality is different. SDI's official purpose is to investigate whether an anti-missile defense might make sense after the year 2000. SDI has been a decision *not* to build antimissile defenses. But this begs the key questions. Since for some reason the United States has decided not to try to resolve its predicament through ballistic missile defense until the year 2000, why is it not doing something else to try to solve that predicament? The United States has no attractive alternatives for the 1990s. But if the United States has no alternative to ballistic missile defense, why not simply go ahead and do the best job one can of it? One answer is that no one can guarantee that such defenses would be perfect. But surely, although many conceivable antimissile devices cannot be built in the 1980s, many others can be. The same was true in the 1970s and will be true in the year 2000. The only realistic question is what antimissile defenses are available today, and what they can do.

In sum, the United States could produce a mobile surface-to-air interceptor system superior to the Soviet SA-12. Since for this kind of atmospheric interception there is relatively little time for the interceptor's guidance system to achieve high accuracy, the system might have to use a low-yield nuclear warhead. Also, the United States has tested and could produce a very-high-altitude interceptor that is so accurate as not to require any warhead at all. Given the high altitude of interception, each site of this system could protect broad swaths of the North American continent. In addition, since 1983, the United States has had the option of producing an optical system mounted on a high-flying Boeing 767 that is capable of telling the difference between the thermal characteristics of warheads and decoys in space and of transmitting the data to antimissile systems. Of course, the United States can build large phased array radars and the rest of a conventional ABM system much like the Soviet Union's—but superior because of the significantly better data-processing equipment available in the United States. Also, in June 1980, the Defense Advanced Research Projects Agency informed the U.S. Senate that by November 1986 it could produce a prototype of a space-based laser that could kill missiles in space from as far away as 3,000 kilometers. The United States did not choose to take up this option, but it could build such lasers by the dozen.

What good would such devices do? A half dozen space lasers, and a few hundred mobile ground-based interceptor units would so complicate any attack on U.S. strategic forces as to render it unattractive. Perhaps two dozen lasers and, say, a thousand ground-based units would make such a strike unfeasible and protect the population from stray rounds as well as from the collateral effects of the attack, if it were ever carried out. More would do more, fewer would do less.

But would such primitive devices be made obsolete by changes in offensive weaponry or by new defense suppression measures? The answer is almost surely yes—sometime in the future. There is not, and never was, and never will be, any such thing as an ultimate weapon—whether defensive or offensive. Wars, like all other human contests, are won at particular instants in time with the tools available at the time. Robert McNamara and his followers recoiled at the thought of an open-ended contest for improving strategic weapons, and thought that they could freeze for all time an instant in that development. He was wrong, just as those who argue for and against the abstract proposition of a guaranteed SDI are wrong. Strategic superiority is won with concrete, albeit imperfect measures. Those who refuse to do what they can at any given time to secure superiority simply leave it to others.

In 1972, the most impressive of McNamara's defenders, Henry Kissinger, asked "What does one do with strategic superiority?"[12] The short answer is, "Whatever one wants to do with it." Preponderance of power in nuclear weapons, perhaps even more than any other kind of military imbalance, is something that casts a shadow even if it is unused. Nuclear superiority "covers" all of one's military-political moves, and smothers the enemy's. In the jargon of the 1960s, "escalation dominance" produces "extended deterrence." The Soviet Union's ability to drastically reduce U.S. strategic forces and to substantially protect itself against the rest might not keep the United States from shooting at Soviet troop transports if they tried to pull up to the docks in Newark Bay. But it surely could inhibit the United States from doing anything about a defeat of NATO forces in Europe. It could also prevent the United States from overthrowing a hypothetical Soviet satellite regime that had installed itself in Mexico and was effectively ending U.S. ability to concern itself with the rest of the world. On the other hand, the shadow of a serious American missile force backed by U.S. ability to protect itself, its forces, and its allies against Soviet ballistic missiles would not allow the United States Army to march to Moscow undisturbed. But it would cover U.S. military operations all over the world, and perhaps even convince the subjects of the Soviet empire that they could detach themselves from it with impunity.

CHAPTER

8

POLITICAL WARFARE

Phyrrus used to say that Cineas had taken more
towns with his words than with his arms.

—PLUTARCH

For to win one hundred victories in one hundred
battles is not the acme of skill. To subdue the
enemy without fighting is the acme of skill.

—SUN TZU

ARMS are the tools of war—but not necessarily the most powerful
tools. Words, ideas, and reputations, may be even more powerful.
We have said that the foot soldier's bayonet against the enemy's
belly is the ultimate weapon. But bayonets are held by men who can
be persuaded to thrust them home, drop them, or turn them against
others. Men are moved through their minds. One moves one's own
troops mainly by speaking words into their heads. One moves the
enemy to give up his cause by affecting his mind through a combination of words and deeds. The art of heartening friends and dis-
heartening enemies, of gaining help for one's cause and causing the
abandonment of the enemies' is called political warfare.

The term "political warfare" requires some explanation because it
refers both to the *whole* of warfare directed at producing political
results and to that *part* of warfare that employs political means to
attain the political goals of war even without the actual engagement
of fighting troops. Affecting ideas is the very essence of war. But
ideas are also weapons of war among many other weapons of war.
The term "political warfare," often used synonymously with "psy-

chological operations," is often misunderstood as the preposterous proposition that words can substitute for deeds on the battlefield or that the allegiances of peoples in conflict can be manipulated by "dirty tricks" and "big lies."[1] This is seldom the case. Words are most powerful when they refer to powerful realities. Bluff is generally bad policy. Making people attend to one's words is a hard-earned conquest, and it is easily lost. A second bit of nonsense is that the means usually associated with political warfare—propaganda, agents of influence, sabotage, coups de main, and support for insurgents—are not acts of war in the same sense that armies crashing across borders or airplanes dropping bombs are acts of war. They are in fact war whether done in pursuit of victory during war or during unbloody conflicts as serious as war. If these political tools are not used seriously, they are not acts of war. But then again, politically unserious bombings and invasions are not acts of war either. "C'est magnifique, mais ce n'est pas la guerre," someone observed of the suicidal charge of the Light Brigade.

It is incorrect to think that political warfare includes only propaganda, subversion, and related efforts. Every battle undertaken must be calculated to have the effect of strengthening one's own supporters while weakening the enemy's. Planning battles, economic sanctions, and so on without this goal is a sign of either incompetence or a death wish. So, whether it is an atomic bomb, a cavalry incursion into the enemy's rear, a lone saboteur or agent whispering in the right ear, or a frightening set of battle cries, these are useful in warfare only insofar as they form or break ideas in the enemy's mind.

The essence of war consists primarily of neither words nor deeds, but of *intentions*. The supreme decision in war—the one that makes a conflict a war—is designating an objective as important enough to kill and die for. Without such a decision, a country may, as the United States did in Vietnam, mobilize millions of men, shoot off billions of dollars worth of ordnance, and yet not wage war, that is make no progress in bending an enemy's will. When the decision is made to kill and die for an objective, however, it may not be necessary to do very much because the skillful communication of that intention may be enough to marshal support for one's side and to so weaken the opponent that he will either not give battle or will fight it badly.

For example, Mongols developed such a reputation for torturing to death anyone who put up the slightest resistance to them that the appearance of a single Mongol horseman in a Russian village would provoke the inhabitants to line up, docilely offering their necks to be decapitated. Imagine then the psychological effect of Genghis Kahn's Golden Horde, riding out of clouds of yellow smoke generated by hundreds of pots burning sulphur, while the great war drums sounded out doom! The enemy might well have been focusing his mind on escape routes rather than on the impending battle. War is a contest for human hearts and minds.

The objective of this contest is to influence every individual who might become involved in the war. Each is a creature beset by private urges, hopes, and fears and endowed with the capacity to judge better and worse, good and evil. Each wants his own vision of the good life for himself and his loved ones and is therefore eager to relate what is happening in the world to his hopes and fears. He wants to know what the combatants intend to do that will affect him for better or for worse, what it's likely to cost him, and what the chances are that either side will win. Essentially, he wants to know which way the wind is blowing and what this means for him.

Hence, the basic message that each combatant side must get across is as follows: "We are here to win. We have totally dedicated ourselves to winning. We have what it takes and we know what we are doing. You can count on our winning. You and everybody else will depend on us for your lives and for your futures. We have a well-deserved reputation for being kind to those who join us and for making those who stand in our way wish that they had never been born. Moreover, if you think about it, our side deserves your adherence because we are more in tune with the standards by which you live than are our opponents. These people will soon be either cadavers or prisoners. You have a rare and fleeting chance to show you belong on our side and not theirs. Don't miss it!" Regardless of the means employed to communicate it, if this message is well adapted to circumstances it can only help. But we stress that the effect comes from the content. The medium is definitely not the message.

The first element of the message is commitment. The audience must know that they are facing people who have made a basic choice, and hence will not waiver. The Aztecs who faced Cortés would have only been intimidated by someone who burned his ships behind him. What could make this man risk his life so completely? Perhaps he had powers they could not fathom. Such thinking may well have contributed to the Aztecs' defeat. Similarly, the American colonists who read the Declaration of Independence could only have been impressed by the boldness of the signers—prominent men who publicly bet their "lives, fortunes, and sacred honor." If *they* were willing to commit an act for which they surely would be hanged in case of defeat, then perhaps there was a good chance of victory; and the average man could take the lesser risk of joining Washington's Continentals.

Conversely, in 1988 anyone who asked himself whether to ally with Panama's military dictator, General Manuel Noriega, after he was indicted by a U.S. court for dealing drugs, or with his opponents, would have had to ask himself whether or not the United States was actually committed to putting Noriega in a federal penitentiary. Few Panamanians were prepared to die for Noriega. They had not joined his side to be heroes. If the prospect had arisen of Americans coming to get Noriega with guns, how many Panamanians would have risked their lives in an obviously foredoomed cause? Thus, in 1988, Panamanians listened to the U.S. denunciations of Noriega. They were impressed by the sight of additional U.S. military policemen sent to Panama. But they also heard American explanations that this was only a "show of force." Hence, they reasonably concluded that the United States was not going to send any armed men after Noriega, that the only armed men in Panama willing to shoot belonged to him, and that their only choice was to live under Noriega or die. By showing force that was obviously not meant to be used, the U.S. advertised both weakness and stupidity. Under the circumstances, it was natural that the number of Panamanians who cast their lot with Noriega grew, and that Panamanians came to see U.S. economic sanctions against the Noriega regime as gratuitous and personal harm to themselves.

Commitment of resources does not necessarily convey commitment of will. The single Mongol horseman was a sufficient show of force because of the Mongols' reputation. Similarly, in Lebanon in 1984, the Soviet Union was able to convey effectively its commitment to victory by a very small action that sufficed only because of the Soviet Union's reputation. The various factions in the long-festering Lebanese civil war had become habituated to taking citizens of foreign powers as hostages in order to compel those powers to bring pressure against their client states in the area, especially against Israel and Syria, and in turn to bring pressure on *their* clients in Lebanon. Americans, Frenchmen, Egyptians, and Saudis all suffered this fate, and their governments had tried to make arrangements with the kidnappers. In 1984, Soviet citizens were kidnapped for the first time. Soviet agents instantly kidnapped four members of a prominent Beirut family thought to be associated with the party suspected of holding the Soviet hostages, killed one of them, and sent several of his body parts to his family. At the same time, the Soviet Union's local ally, Syria, told prominent Lebanese thought to be involved in holding the Soviet hostages that unless the hostages were released, the Syrian armed forces would destroy their neighborhoods and all of their inhabitants as they had previously done to Hama, Syria's third largest city. The Soviet hostages were released immediately.

Had the United States made a similar move on behalf of its hostages, it would not have had the same effect. It would have been a mere "dirty trick." That is because in the 1970s and early 1980s the United States did not have the reputation of being fearsome to its enemies. For the Soviets, however, one set of severed body parts was no "dirty trick." It was a sufficient measure because it accurately conveyed Soviet commitment and it was able to convey it because the message was entirely consonant with the Soviet Union's reputation. Had the United States developed the same level of commitment in the region, a truckload of gore would not have been enough to convey it.

The reductio ad absurdum of the principle that commitment of resources can have a beneficial effect as a "show of force" was President Jimmy Carter's dispatch of a squadron of F–15 fighters to Saudi Arabia in 1979. This "show of force" was intended to reassure the Saudis against the threat posed by militant Shi'ite Iran. The United States had wanted to show force in a nonthreatening way without exposing itself to accusations of bellicosity. So it compromised by announcing that the F–15s would be unarmed. But the sight of airplanes deliberately stripped of their armaments conjured up the exact opposite of the intended image of a powerful ally ready, willing, and massively able to come to the rescue. Similarly, in 1988, the United States again responded with a "show of force" when the Nicaraguan army crossed the southern border of Honduras. Nicaragua was trying to destroy the base camps of Nicaraguan anticommunist guerrillas located in Honduras, and to frighten Honduras into withdrawing support from the guerrillas. The U.S. sent troops to Honduras while declaring that they were on a training exercise and would not come anywhere near the fighting. Did this show U.S. force? No. The governments of Nicaragua and Honduras can read, and they know how many troops the United States could bring to the area if it wanted to make a difference in the war. Neither knew and both were wondering if and how the United States would exercise its potential power. The U.S. "show of force" told everyone concerned that the United States would not intervene to save either the Nicaraguan guerrillas or southern Honduras. It was a show of weakness rather than force.

Even the commitment of resources to actual operations is politically ineffective unless it is accompanied by the impression that it is part of a consistent, success-oriented plan. From 1981 to 1988 President Ronald Reagan spoke eloquently about the evils of Nicaragua's communist regime and of the dangers it posed to the United States. He also asked for money to support the armed resistance to that regime. Despite occasional successes, he ultimately failed to dry up that regime's support in the United States and to get the American political system to support the resistance. Reagan asked for money to support the resistance's troops in the field. But to do what? Reagan never said specifically. Did Reagan ever desire, much less have a plan for, the military defeat of the Communist government? Since he said repeatedly that he did not, his opponents were able to argue that the money would not accomplish any useful purpose. Reagan claimed that financing the war would bring pressure on the Communists to negotiate and to change their ways. But since Reagan also claimed that the United States planned to get along with Communist leaders in the long run, what sense did it make to bloody them? Because people cannot usually be made to forget past injuries by subsequent aid, it is common sense either to put one's enemies out of action or to get along with them. It is no wonder that Reagan's loud but uncertain trumpet rallied few to his side and strengthened his enemies, both foreign and domestic.

The bottom line in war and hence in political warfare is who gets buried and who gets to walk in the sun. This was illustrated as well as it ever has been by the events that followed the assassination of Egyptian President Anwar Sadat in 1981. From his predecessor, Gamal Abdul Nasser, Sadat had inherited a country deeply enmeshed politically and financially with the Soviet Union. Egypt's principal daily preoccupation was war with Israel. Sadat wanted to turn his country to a worthier agenda. He fought a well-planned campaign against Israel in 1973 to gain leverage for a peace with Israel that would restore to Egypt land that it had lost in Nasser's war. Sadat also expelled the Soviets from Egypt, so that instead of paying for Soviet arms, Egypt became the recipient of some $2 billion of American aid annually. For this he earned the status of public enemy number one of the Soviet Union and of those around the world who see the Soviet Union as the engine of progress and view the United States as the devil. In 1979, the shah of Iran, a longtime ally of the United States, was overthrown by Islamic fundamentalists allied with one of the Soviet Union's allies in the region, the Palestine Liberation Organization. Anti-Sadat propaganda subsequently referred to the president of Egypt as "Shah-dat" and warned him and the world that his end was near. As soon as Sadat died in a hail of bullets in October 1981, anyone in the world who turned the dial of a shortwave radio could not help but hear in a variety of languages and in a variety of formulations the following message: "Anwar Sadat is dead because he was on the wrong side. Who wants to be next? Let him do as Sadat did. Let him oppose the forces of progress in the world, and he will end up as just another corpse alongside the corpses of all others who have thought it possible to go over to the American side in the great worldwide struggle. On the side of progress there is success and life. Against us there is only dishonorable death. Who's next? Will it be Nimeiry of the Sudan? Or Marcos of the Philippines? Who's next?"[2]

In August 1988, the chief ally of the United States in south Asia, Mohammed Zia ul Haq, president of Pakistan, died in a fiery plane crash along with the U.S. ambassador and Pakistani officials in charge of supplying the anti-Soviet resistance in Afghanistan. Legal responsibility for his death will likely prove impossible to establish. But two facts are self-evident: anti-Soviet forces in south Asia lost their principal supporter, and once again America's allies die while their enemies live.

This is war. This is politics.

Let us consider first the tools of political warfare and then the political element in several kinds of wars.

The Tools of Political Warfare

We have already noted that overt policy forcefully explained is the most powerful tool of political warfare, and that for any other tool to be useful it must be used consistently with a clear, well-pronounced policy. This is not to deny the usefulness of minor currents of policy that run secretly against the mainstream. Such undercurrents can prepare for eventual changes in course, or can even fool "some of the people all of the time or all of the people some of the time." But any covert undercurrent always carries the danger of disrupting the main current of policy.

GRAY PROPAGANDA

Gray propaganda is the semiofficial amplification of a government's voice. Foreigners pay attention not only to what a nation's government says, but also to what nonofficial but authoritative voices in the country say. A government can strengthen its hand in political warfare by enlisting the support of these voices. This is what the United States did in the late 1940s when it was trying to convince West Europeans to resist communism. Europeans who were wondering how deep America's official commitment to fighting communism saw that commitment confirmed through a multiplicity of sources: U.S. newspapers, labor unions, chambers of commerce, and letter-writing campaigns by private citizens. These sources had been partly inspired and sometimes paid for by the U.S. government.

Gray propaganda can also serve to help foreigners deceive themselves. Thus the Nazi regime sent "Putzi" Haenfstaengl, Hitler's pianist, and others close to the führer, to mingle in high Western social circles to pass along the "good news" that the regime's ranting and raving, as well as its military preparations, should not be taken seriously. Hitler's antics were just show for the masses. Western socialites, eager to believe the best and amazed that Nazis could eat with knife and fork, preferred to believe what they were hearing to what they were seeing. In our time, the Soviet Union's Georgi Arbatov, Vladimir Posner, and a corps of semiofficial Soviets who could pass for yuppies have served the same "gray" counterreality function with the Western upper-middle classes.[3]

Finally, gray propaganda can provide a government with the dangerous pleasure of saying things that it doesn't really mean, or has not really thought through. For example, in the 1950s the U.S. semiofficial Radio Free Europe and Radio Liberty gave East Europeans the impression that it would be best for them to revolt and that if they did the United States would come to their aid. The United States was not determined to do this. Nor was the United

States determined not to aid an uprising. The U.S. government simply had not faced the question internally and had let its semi-official
voice run ahead of its official mind. When the Hungarian Revolution
of 1956 forced the U.S. government actually to choose between the
danger of aiding East European rebellions and the danger of permanent Communist rule in East Europe, it had neither studied the
consequences of either option nor made contingency plans. The
lesson to be drawn from this is that ideas have consequences,
whether they are white, black, or gray.

BLACK PROPAGANDA

Black propaganda is information (true or false) that appears to
come from a source other than the one from which it actually origi-
nated. Information or suggestions that are black propaganda enjoy
the appeal of appearing to come from a disinterested source when in
fact they do not. For this reason black propaganda can be powerful.
In 1979, in Islamabad, Pakistan, undercover Soviet agents spread the
word that the United States had just committed a mass murder of
Muslims. This ignited a crowd that burned down the U.S. embassy.
In more complex and more important instances the effect of black
propaganda is difficult to gauge. For example, it does not follow that
because the KGB was clearly involved in the 1980s campaign to turn
public opinion in Europe against American nuclear weapons; because certain nominally non-Communist media outlets (for instance, the Greek daily newspaper *Ethnos*) followed the Soviet line;
and because European public opinion *was* turned, that black propaganda played an important role. In fact, there was a massive Soviet
effort on all levels of political conflict, and no one can distinguish the
proverbial straw that broke the camel's back from the other straws
in the bale.

Black propaganda must be consonant with other policy efforts in
order to be effective at all. There is a constant temptation to run
black propaganda, like other secret activities, not as an adjunct to
policy but as a policy in itself. This often happens when an incom-
petent government refuses to choose between two appealing courses
of policy and in effect tries to pursue them both: one policy more or
less openly and the other in the "black." Thus in the early 1960s the
U.S. government used clandestine sources to spread true facts about
the copious sexual misdeeds of Indonesia's dictator, Sukarno. But
at the same time the United States was openly refusing to its own

ally, the Netherlands, the right to land aircraft in transit on U.S. territory when it was fighting Sukarno's attempt to grab the Dutch colony of West New Guinea. Similarly, some U.S. officials have suggested that the United States used sources not known to be working for the U.S. to tell the world (and, perhaps not incidentally, the U.S. news media) the truth that the Soviet Union's chief campaigner against American missile defenses, Yevgeny P. Velikhov, is actually one of the chief architects of the Soviet Union's antimissile defense system. This truth might well be an effective antidote to anti-SDI Soviet propaganda. But given that the main line of overt U.S. policy is treating the Soviet Union as a sincere partner in the quest for mutually advantageous arms control, any U.S. propaganda of whatever color that suggested the contrary would discredit both itself *and* the main line of policy. Just like the black propaganda that disparaged Sukarno's goatishness, it would be a mere "dirty trick." In both these cases the U.S. government's main problem was its inability to choose a consistent line of policy. Sukarno, Velikhov, and many others have prospered by finding the seam between the mutually incompatible lines of policy. No amount of black propaganda, no matter how skillfully employed, could fix this. It could only deepen the delusion.

Agents of influence are people whom the enemy mistakenly believes are on his side. Good ones cannot be bought. Their work is far more valuable, subtle, and dangerous than that of a mere spy. That is because by the very act of exercising influence an agent brings suspicion on himself. For example, the Soviet Union's agent in Norway, Arne Treholt, helped bring about his own downfall in 1985 by negotiating a too obviously one-sided treaty between Norway and the Soviet Union. Such agents can help protect themselves by making their view of the "proper" relationship with the other country into a partisan political position, thus gaining the protection of an entire domestic party. The "other" country can sometimes help its agents by making them the privileged conduits of special favors. Thus in the 1970s and 1980s anyone who wanted access to the Kremlin for special favors knew that the American industrialist Armand Hammer had a record of delivering such things. This certainly helped counterbalance Hammer's record of both helping to transfer U.S. resources and technology to the Soviet Union and lobbying influential Americans on behalf of U.S.–Soviet friendship.[4]

Sometimes when agents are particularly exposed there is no substitute for a great power's extending overt and even physical means to protect them. Thus, in the 1930s, the German government openly encouraged ethnic Germans and their friends in Austria, Czechoslovakia, and Poland to agitate for unification with the Reich. The Reich government then threatened the governments of those countries with invasion if they acted against Nazi agents. Similarly, since World War II, no Finnish government has dared to act against some of its own citizens who obviously look after Soviet interests in the country. Indeed, in the Finnish parliament discussions of the shadow cast by Soviet power are considered in bad taste—like speaking of rope in the house of the hanged. In the 1970s and 1980s agents of influence in Lebanon were so open about their allegiances to Syria, Iran, Israel, Saudi Arabia, and the United States as to be considered outright proxies. Thus, they prospered or died according to the ability of their patrons to convince enemies that killing them would invite deadly retaliation.

Supporting factions in the enemy camp or in neutral countries is the most ancient of arts. Its essence is to recruit allies with the prospect of victory. No one willingly signs on to a losing cause or merely enlists as a paid pawn. True, foreign factions are often used in these ways, and using them like this requires much deception. But doing this is as unwise as it is immoral, because it leads to the discrediting, isolation, and defeat of whomever does it. Furthermore, just recruiting allies requires at least pretending to be committed to victory. For example, in the 1960s the United States gave the H'mong tribes of Laos every reason to believe that the United States had come to Indochina to defeat the government of North Vietnam, which was also the enemy of the H'mong. These tribesmen then made up an army of 30,000 men and, with American arms, held the northwest corner of Indochina until the United States abandoned them.

Sometimes factions will accept—indeed seek out—foreign support even when they are highly uncertain about its purpose and reliability. They do this because they believe they have no alternative to accepting aid, and these factions have a variety of ways to guard against the prospect of abandonment. One way is that pursued by the Nicaraguan resistance in 1981–88, which staked its entire future on shaky support from the United States and prepared for betrayal by arranging places of more or less comfortable exile. Another way is that of Jonas Savimbi, leader of Angola's UNITA party. Savimbi has consistently assumed that all sources of aid are subject to cutoff; he has diversified his resources to the best of his ability and has an endless number of plans for augmenting or cutting back his operations to match his supplies. Because serious groups like UNITA pursue agendas that are undeniably their own, they are sometimes bristly partners. But by the same token, they are more valuable than allies that follow their patron's agenda, as did the Nicaraguans.

In sum, a great power's ability to recruit foreign groups as allies for political and military operations depends on how desperate these groups are for allies, on how they gauge the reliability of the assisting great power, and what are the latter's plans for them. The usefulness of such allies to the great power depends less on their characteristics than on the ways in which it encourages, supplies, and above all supports them while preventing the enemy from concentrating its forces against them.

Political Warfare in Big Wars

The flash of big guns should not blind students to the importance of political warfare even in the biggest of wars.

Few remember Hitler's conquests in Europe *before* he finally unleashed military action in 1939. His conquests between 1933 and 1939 were almost bloodless. They were triumphs of will over victims wanting in conviction, resolve, and courage. Scarcely six years after he had seized power inside Germany from irresolute opponents, Hitler had torn apart the Versailles Treaty of 1919, massively rearmed Germany in violation of it, remilitarized the Rhineland, occupied Austria, and seized Czechoslovakia.

In those six years Hitler did not rule out armed combat. His threats, invariably combined with protestations of peace, broke the will of those who might have combined to resist him. He knew the psychological dimensions of political warfare. As he told a Nazi comrade in the late thirties:

> The place of artillery preparation for frontal attack by the infantry . . .
> will in the future be taken by revolutionary propaganda, to break down
> the enemy psychologically before the armies begin to function at all.
> The enemy must be demoralized and ready to capitulate, driven into
> moral passivity, before military action can even be thought of.[5]

Hitler did not invent the idea of ideological precursor strikes. Classical historians such as Livy have commented on the "anti-imperialist" alliance of the Gauls with Carthage and the Carthaginian "anti-ruling class" propaganda directed at the Romans during the Second Punic War. A strategy of terror can be practiced in both war and peace. Bolshevik military leaders such as Leon Trotsky deliberately exploited latter-day comparisons of their assault on the West with that of the Mongols. A passage in Nikita Krushchev's famous 20th Party Congress denunciation of Stalin in 1956 underscores the importance of terror in Soviet strategy. "The questioning of Stalin's terror," Khruschev said, ". . . may lead to the questioning of terror in general. But Bolshevism believes in the use of terror. Lenin held that no one was worthy of the name Communist who did not believe in terror."[6]

Terror, however, is only one of the factors that shape the minds of men at war. So long as men have been men, ideas have inspired and intimidated. The Roman emperor Constantine, embracing Christianity for himself and his subjects, led his armies to victory after victory, paradoxically by filling them with a peace-loving set of beliefs. Much later, under Bonaparte, French *soldats* plunged across Europe, carrying copies of the "Declaration of the Rights of Man" stowed in their knapsacks. Nazi SS units were outfitted with copies of *Mein Kampf*—presumably to strengthen the soldiers in their beliefs rather than to convince the *Untermenschen* that it would be best if they merged peacefully into the mud.

We should, of course, distinguish the thoughts that animate peoples and armies to fight from propaganda designed to affect the minds and wills of the enemy—civilians and soldiers alike. The first aims to generate and sustain morale. That which is aimed at the adversary in political warfare hopes to persuade or deceive and seeks to detach popular opinion from the wartime government ("we have no quarrel with you people, only with your leaders"). We should take particular note of the *different* forms and manifestations of ideology in warfare; particularistic ideologies—National Socialism, for one—differ greatly in their targets from universalistic ones—Jacobinism and Marxism-Leninism, for instance. And then there are the hybrids of our time—Khomeini's fundamentalism, for instance, its Shi'ite messianism having been artfully merged with Iranian nationalism.

Ideologies, however, do not always move men to wage war, even in self-defense. Even though the power of Bolshevik doctrines inspired the Red Army to triumph over its foes in Russia's civil war of 1918–21, a generation later those very doctrines hindered the Red Army's response to Hitler's invasion. Stalin had to store Marxist-Leninism in a Kremlin closet for the duration of "the great patriotic war." Only after victory in 1945 did the party again proclaim the doctrines of communism and force the patriotic Russian people to repeat its slogans.

One negative aspect of wars that are unusually inspired by ideas is that inspiration may conflict with military strategy. The "flip side of the coin" of Bonaparte's "Rights of Man" carried in triumph throughout Europe was its capacity to arouse homegrown, nationalist, anti-French sentiment in subjugated kingdoms and principalities. The decisive Battle of Leipzig, in 1813, in which Napoleon lost military superiority in Central Europe, was called "The Battle of Nations" because the forces that fought Napoleon there truly felt themselves to be the upholders of their nations' identities against the French "nation in arms." Conversely, Hitler's ideology of German racial superiority feared and despised by most non-Germans, made nonsense of his political claim to be the defender of the European nations against the Bolshevik hordes.

Precisely because ideological warfare (or ideologically inspired war) involves human psychology with all its imponderables, it is not susceptible to fine-tuning. Political warfare, particularly when it expediently opts for a risky "radical" line to achieve battlefield victory, can backfire, have unforeseen effects, or spin out of control.

During World War I, "clever" Imperial German political-warfare strategists transported V. I. Lenin back from Switzerland to wartime St. Petersburg in a sealed train to aggravate an already grave revolutionary crisis and get Russia out of the war in 1917. The stratagem worked in the short term. The Bolsheviks, seizing power, sued for peace and granted Germany an advantageous settlement in Eastern Europe at Brest Litovsk in 1918. But months later, German revolutionaries, Lenin's Comintern comrades, heartened by the Bolshevik revolution, helped to bring the fall of Imperial Germany, and came close to seizing power in Central Europe. The "clever" strategists didn't realize that Lenin's political shock troops also had pamphlets in their pockets!

In this regard, it is useful to recall that terms like "agitator" did not originate with the Bolsheviks. "Agitator" first appeared in the seventeenth-century English civil war; "agitators" were political officers of Cromwell's Parliamentary army, sent ahead of regular troops to mobilize civilian support. The term reappeared in the American Revolution. In a similar capacity Thomas Paine functioned notably as an agitator. His "crisis" papers were commissioned by the Continental Congress to strengthen morale at Valley Forge. Individuals known as *commissaires politiques* first appeared in the French revolutionary regime with the job of looking after the politics of the army, although the political commissar in the French army was more an agent for pre-maintenance of morale than a political monitor.

"Political commissars" as we know them today—"agitators" given authority over professional officers in combat units—are inextricably associated with the Red Army created during the Russian Civil War of 1918–21, and with the armed forces of today's Communist countries. Today, political control of the Red Army officers is exercised by the KGB, acting as the agent of the Communist Party, and not by anyone loyal to "Mother Russia."

Political warfare works best at firming up one's own ranks and breaking down the enemy's when wartime leadership has clear strategic aims that are confirmed by events. It works worst when objectives waver, are confused, or are contradictory. Woodrow Wilson's powerful though brief appeal to war-weary Europeans for peace without victory in 1917–18—the famous Fourteen Points—coincided with the growing popular consciousness that the war had become a tragedy for all sides. By the same token, the appeal of Lenin's Bolshevik propaganda, particularly his seemingly apolitical call for "peace and bread," thundered far beyond revolutionary Russia into all of the belligerent powers of Europe for the very same reason that Wilson's did. In November 1918, when the Armistice took place, Wilson the liberal democrat and Lenin the Bolshevik revolutionary briefly towered together above all other wartime leaders, though they represented wholly antithetical principles in the new political struggle that erupted on the very eve of "victory." But these principles, beguiling as they were for engagé intellectuals, were not the source of their mass popularity. On the contrary, theirs was an antipolitical popularity. When they got to specifics, they lost it.

In contrast, the flood of words from the Johnson and Nixon administrations about the Vietnam War did the very opposite of what propaganda should do. They sounded an uncertain trumpet. They held out no concrete promise of either political victory or justice, and they emitted confusing signals to friend and foe alike. Thus the words of American leaders contributed to public demoralization, and ultimately, to defeat. This was no product of political propagandists. Rather, it mirrored all too accurately the wavering confusions and contradictions of high policy. Because of this, the grim will and relentless political purpose of America's tenacious enemy, inferior in every other way, finally triumphed.[7]

Even outright propaganda can be directly counterproductive. Allied propaganda in its proclaimed insistence on unconditional surrender and punishment of the German nation in World War II was independent confirmation of everything the Nazi regime was itself generating about the Allies' plans for Germany's surrender. In 1944 Goebbels gleefully exploited Roosevelt's proposed, punitive "Morgenthau Plan," with its threat of permanent "pastoralization" of a subjugated Germany. The increasingly punitive language of Western statesmen weakened the case of anti-Hitler opposition in the German public. This teaches that the propaganda of a clearly superior belligerent in wartime must not corner the enemy, giving him no choice but that of total and abject capitulation or resistance to a fatal end.

Political Warfare in Guerrillas, Insurgencies, and Civil Wars

When one looks at small wars (or *guerrillas*, from the Spanish word meaning "little war"), or even at the unbloody side of great conflicts, it becomes unmistakable that regardless of the violence of the means, the proximate cause for ending wars requires persuading people that they really want to be on your side—or at least that they do not want to resist you. Consider the fundamental fact of recruitment. A glance at any civil war or *guerrilla* is enough to remind us that recruitment is not always an automatic process as it was in World War I when national leaders "pushed the button" and effortlessly turned out millions of soldiers. These leaders drew upon and depleted an unusually rich bank of allegiances built up over a thousand years. Moreover, the soldiers did not think they had much choice. Most of the time, however, the allegiances of potential draftees are more scarce, and their choices are more plentiful.

In civil wars or guerrillas, let alone insurgencies, the potential recruit is pulled in at least three directions: to join one side, to join the other side, or to stay aloof. Typically, such wars lead neighbors and even brothers to choose different sides. Also, because the opportunities for desertion are abundant in such conflicts, keeping the loyalty of one's own troops and weakening the other side's is a never-ending concern. Intimidation alone will not suffice.

This is not to say that individuals are not drafted into insurgencies or civil wars. Quite the contrary is true. Indeed, one of the more characteristic and despicable aspects of these wars is that some combatants, especially Communist combatants, force young men to publicly commit murders and expropriations in order to bind their fortunes to that faction's, precluding their return to normal life. Nevertheless, it is clear that since the opportunities to escape from an irregular force are greater than the opportunities to escape from a regular one, irregular forces know that to stand a chance of winning they must gain more and more adherents, and that they cannot do this through intimidation alone. Hence, irregular warfare is quintessentially political warfare aimed at winning over the hearts and minds of potential combatants. The aim of any irregular force is to avoid destruction long enough to persuade enough people by all available means to forsake the enemy and to join its ranks.

Guerrilla, or "little war," is the term Spaniards gave to their ultimately successful struggle against the Napoleonic troops that occupied their country. Spain could not muster an army capable of challenging France's main force in battle. But it could and did muster dozens of small units that achieved local and temporary superiority over small fractions of the French army. By doing so, the Spanish, with the help of an English detachment under the Duke of Wellington, forced the French to move only in large groups, preventing them from becoming a widespread presence in Spain. Although the "little war" could not force French troops out of Spain, it prevented them from drawing a net profit out of their stay. Napoleon soon found he had more pressing needs for his troops elsewhere, The Duke of Wellington's British forces provided the nucleus for victory in a few medium-sized battles, and Spain returned to its native tyranny.

The "little war" has always been the natural recourse of those who know they cannot win a big one. As the Romans advanced deeper into North Africa, they came upon bands of archers mounted on fast horses and camels. The archers could not possibly stand up to the legions' high-tech warfare, but their nomadic camps were always several days' march ahead, and the Romans soon pulled back, figuring that they did not want to be walking pin cushions in the desert.

Still, nothing is more erroneous than the modern view that a determined people fighting from their homes can defeat an occupying army. The Romans, master conquerors, developed the standard for successful anti-guerrilla operations: secure the most valuable parts of the conquered country through a massive troop presence, and offer the inhabitants the choice between reasonably normal lives under Roman rule or certain death. They would then make impossible normal life outside the areas of their control. Over generations the pacified zones expanded gradually. The Soviet Union successfully practiced this pattern against the Muslim Basmachi rebels of Central Asia in the 1920s. In the 1930s, it did so preemptively in its drive to collectivize the Ukraine, causing mass starvation among those who resisted or might have resisted. The Soviet Union repeated the pattern in the 1940s in the Baltic States and in the 1980s in Afghanistan. In the 1980s, Ethiopia's Communist government and Sudan's revolutionary government have applied the same combination of lopping off selected heads in areas they can usually control and making life impossible in those areas they cannot usually reach. To survive in the face of such a strategy, the guerrillas need sufficient arms and food to maintain a semblance of normal life in areas the conqueror does not always control.

The United States lost the military part of the war in Vietnam first because it chose to treat a foreign invasion—a big war that had a base of operations susceptible to attack—as if it were a "little war" that lacked such an enemy nerve center. Having chosen to fight a big war as if it had been a *guerrilla*, the United States also never considered the Roman-Soviet approach. The U.S. found it easy to entice millions of Vietnamese into "secure" areas. But it tried not to upset normal life in areas it did not control, thus forfeiting such control to the North Vietnamese. In fact, the United States in Vietnam allowed its enemy to consolidate in rear areas subject to harassment, but not subject to any strategic threat. This emphatically was *not* a classic *guerrilla*.

Nor can we call the current war in Angola a *guerrilla*. This war, which began in 1975, originally pitted the MPLA, a native political faction supported by the Soviet Union, Cuba, and East Germany, against Jonas Savimbi's UNITA, supported by France and South Africa. The MPLA holds Luanda, the capital city and the most developed third of the country. This does not mean that UNITA merely wanders about the bush. Rather, UNITA has its own remote capital from which it also controls a third of the country. This, even more clearly than Vietnam, is a civil war in which guerrilla tactics are sometimes employed, but by two regular armies both amply supported by outside forces. Interestingly, however, as in the case of Afghanistan, the native army on the Communist side virtually ceased to exist. The Angolan war for the most part has been the Cubans and Soviets versus UNITA, with some South African and token U.S. support.

Rarely are civil wars fought autonomously, as was the American Civil War. Civil wars always represent a diminution of the power that a nation can exercise abroad, and they almost always produce at least one contender that is eager to accept help from abroad. Hence, almost invariably, civil wars lead to foreign interference and tend to make both winners and losers less happy than they would have been without the war. The Romans entered and conquered Greece as a result of being called into a civil war in the third century B.C. The French entered Italy in the fifteenth century when the Venetians as well as the Pope summoned them in. In the 1930s the Spanish civil war squared Italy and Germany on one side against the Soviet Union on the other. But the Spanish were lucky that both sides' "helpers" soon found fighting each other more appealing, and that the civil war's winner, General Francisco Franco, did not pay off any of the debts he had incurred. The Vietnamese were not so lucky. The leaders of North Vietnam could not have fought their war against South Vietnam and the United States without the Soviet Union, and they have apparently been eager to pay their debts, in part by sending over a hundred thousand of their own people to do forced labor as lumbermen in Siberia. Since roughly 1975 the people of Lebanon have been living in perpetual civil war. Israel, Iran, the PLO, the United States, and above all Syria have supported various contenders to some degree. But all Lebanese, except a few factional leaders, live lives that are far poorer, more brutish, and actually shorter than before the civil war began. Interestingly enough, all of the "helpers" except Syria have lost more than they have gained. Syria has been the only winner in the Lebanese civil war.

The least destructive civil wars are the few, like the American

Civil War, in which both sides are organized in regular armies and treat each other as international belligerents rather than as common criminals. Far more pernicious are those like the "dirty war" in Argentina in the 1970s between leftist elements in the population and rightist elements in the army and the police. Both sides hid among larger publics who shared their political views and social preferences to some extent. Each side was bent on annihilating the other because they loathed each other's ways. Hence, neither side particularly cared whether the people it killed were precisely the ones it meant to kill, so long as the intended people were among the victims. But the most murderous civil wars of all are the ones in which at least one side is organized into a regular army and fights to annihilate those who embody the enemy's ways. Thus the Red Armies of Russia and China, as well as the Cambodian Khmer Rouge, sought victory so that they might begin, not end, the serious killing. The small wars are sometimes the biggest killers of all.

Insurgencies are the smallest wars of all. But they are most obviously political because insurgents necessarily begin by representing no one but themselves. Their acts in violation of the law begin as private challenges, and therefore as crimes. To the extent that the insurgents are legitimate, the government is not, and vice versa. The insurgent's hope is to wage a "small war" that will perhaps become a civil war. The insurgent's military task is no different from that of anyone fighting a "small war": to survive long enough and attract enough supporters to win a war.

Special Operations

Special Operations are often misunderstood as consisting of physically demanding acts by specially trained troops. In fact, their special quality comes much less from the character of the troops than it does from the character of the operations themselves. They are special because they are specially crafted to have a bearing on the outcome of the war—especially on its political issues—out of proportion to the small forces they employ. Such operations can hold or gain allies, influence neutrals to stay neutral or stray from neutrality, help resistance movements in enemy-occupied territory, and introduce sabotage and dissension into the enemy country.

In September 1943 King Vittorio Emmanuele III of Italy constitutionally cashiered his prime minister, Benito Mussolini, and appointed a new one who promptly put his predecessor under arrest and imprisoned him in a mountain fortress. Overnight, Germany lost a major ally and faced the prospect that its enemies would soon have safe passage to the Reich's undefended southern borders. But Major Otto Skorzeny, with a group of German commandos, landed by glider under Mussolini's prison. Within hours, Il Duce was having a drink with the führer and organizing an Italian collaborationist counter-government that helped Germany's General Kesselring conduct a brilliant elastic defense in Italy until the end of the war.

Special operations can also be used for strikes deep into enemy territory. During the 1982 Falklands war, Britain sent commandos to sabotage enemy air bases. They had more than military effect. These tactics demoralized the defenders and created dissension among them. That is why such operations are particularly well suited to the opening phases of a war. It is easy to imagine that, were the Soviet Union to attack the United States, it might smuggle into the country some special troops with precision-guided munitions, give them money to rent trucks on the commercial market, and put them in position to take out vital, soft, command-and-control targets at the outset of hostilities. For example, the primary control facility for U.S. military satellites is located on one of the busiest freeways in California. The Soviet Union has up to a million troops who are trained for special operations, who are outside the pattern of life of regular troops, and who are considered especially loyal politically.

Special operations can be used to establish relationships with foreign forces, to coordinate actions with them, and to gather information from them. Of course, during such operations troops can take and interrogate prisoners and, if they can slip in and out unnoticed, emplace and maintain networks of remote sensors.

Those who make clandestine entry must be capable of combat and able to operate a wide variety of military equipment, teach others how to operate it, and organize foreigners into military units. Each of the United States Army Special Forces' twelve-man "A teams" is supposed to incorporate all of the military skills necessary to organize and run at least a battalion of indigenous forces. They are also supposed to be trained in languages and in the political aspects of their work. These "green berets," schooled at the John F. Kennedy Special Warfare School at Fort Bragg, are supposed to bear the brunt of President Kennedy's promise to help any friend or fight any foe for liberty's sake. The Special Forces and their navy and air force counterparts (who make even fewer claims of knowing language or politics or of being able to conduct intelligence operations) were never intended to blend into a foreign environment as third country nationals. Full-fledged capability for special operations would require a cadre of military specialists capable of doing that.

Whether they are helping resistance forces, sowing dissension among the enemy, or influencing third countries, special troops must be able to make genuine political commitments. War, the most constraining of circumstances, makes for the strangest of bedfellows. Only genuinely sympathetic individuals can expect to organize people successfully who are far different culturally during times of high emotion. These people will have their own priorities and idiosyncrasies; and since not everyone can sympathize with, say, both Kurds and dissident Communists, a well-stocked special operations department must have staff officers of widely different backgrounds and widely different personal, religious, and political preferences. One of the strengths of the American OSS in World War II was its political catholicity—it sent leftists to leftists and rightists to rightists. As a result, disparate elements all over the world were enlisted to fight on the American side.

Unbloody Conflict in Peacetime

While in the West political warfare has been a pragmatic adjunct to crisis foreign policy and military operations, in the Communist world, since the Bolshevik Revolution, political warfare has been the essence of politics, identical to politics, and the omnipresent engine of politics. Mass political action, the myriad militant actions of fronts, actions of disinformation agencies, and even the use of special troops against domestic enemies have been part of the normal workings of the Soviet state. At all times, the norm has been struggle and compulsion. Lenin put it this way:

> The dictatorship of the proletariat was successful because it knew how to combine compulsion with persuasion. . . . We must . . . see to it that

the apparatus of compulsion, activized and reinforced, shall be adapted and developed for a new sweep of persuasion.[8]

In our times, the Soviet Union has devoted perhaps as many resources to the *operational management* of ideas in war and peace as it has to its military forces, both to legitimize its rule domestically and to advance its causes abroad. As Vladimir Bukovsky, the Soviet dissident, also has observed:

> The Soviet Union is not a state in the traditional meaning of the word, but a huge and well-organized army of ideological warriors, a fortress with hundreds of front organizations, thousands of publications around the world, and with a gigantic budget, perhaps even a bigger one than their military budget.[9]

The operational form of Soviet political warfare is like a giant wedding cake—a deliberate orchestration of activities on three levels: state-to-state; party-to-party; and people-to-people (front group operation). The triple-tiered division of functions confers a flexibility of operations. Action and emphasis can be shifted from one to another level, and one line of action may be pursued on one level, a contrary line on another. Sometimes these are combined to pursue one unified aim. This can only be done by a bureaucracy rendered flexible by unitary control at the top.

Soviet policy toward the German Weimar Republic during the 1920s vividly illustrates this flexibility. On the level of state-to-state relations, the Soviets wooed Germany into fruitful collaboration. Both states were then pariahs in Europe, albeit for different reasons. Their armies collaborated in secret. Germany thus was able to evade Allied-imposed arms restrictions by developing its war machinery in secluded regions of the USSR, while *Reichswehr* officers trained Red Army forces in advanced weaponry. Commercial ties were also cemented. This mutually profitable arrangement lasted until Hitler came to power.[10]

Yet on the party-to-party level, the Soviets, through control of the German Communist Party (KPD), secretly worked to overthrow the Weimar regime. Nazis and Communists in Parliament and on German streets collaborated to destroy German democratic institutions. This pattern was paralleled by Europe-wide front organizations pursuing the never-ending Soviet goal of "peace." These logically contradictory campaigns were nevertheless unitary, and have been replicated again and again, in peace and war, in many parts of the world since that time—sometimes successfully, sometimes not.[11]

One of the most impressive successes of political warfare in our time is the reversal of the U.S.–Soviet military balance regarding long-range ballistic missiles and bombers through the arms control process that began about 1969. This process has involved not only state-to-state negotiations but the full panoply of political warfare: manipulation of the other side's data through managing exposure to its intelligence collection; white, black, and gray propaganda; bureaucracy-to-bureaucracy influence; the intervention of Armand Hammer to reopen a blocked channel of communication;[12] as well as campaigns aimed at selected groups of American elites (lawyers, physicians, and scientists), even at whole towns or sister cities.

We do not mean to imply that the changes that have taken place in this military balance have been due exclusively or even primarily to Soviet activities. On the contrary, perhaps the primary mover of the arms-control process has been the desire of one faction of Americans to impose their view of military policy upon another faction while gaining the reputation of peacemakers at their domestic competitors' expense.[13] This is the reason that, as former president Jimmy Carter's defense secretary Harold Brown has said, "when we build they build, when we stop they build." It is also the reason that, rhetoric aside, the United States has pursued a steady path of arms control regardless of what weapons the Soviet Union builds. Nevertheless, it is undeniable that the Soviet Union has contributed to the success of the American arms-controllers' agenda within the United States by taking part in the arms-control process as it has.

The reversal of this military balance is of momentous importance both in and of itself and because of the ensuing change of official American attitudes regarding missiles and bombers that has accompanied it. The numbers speak for themselves: In 1969 the United States had 1,054 ICBMs and the Soviet Union had 1,140, each with one warhead apiece with roughly the same military capacity. The United States "built down" to 1,000 in 1987, but the Soviet Union "built up" to 1,398 fixed launcher models, in addition to an unknown number on mobile launchers. Furthermore, in 1987, while the United States had 1,720 multiple ICBM warheads, only 100 of them were of the highest type of military utility; the Soviet Union had 5,840, all but 620 of which were of the highest type of military utility. Regarding submarine-launched ballistic missiles, in 1969 the United States had 656 to the Soviets' 185, while in 1987 the figures were 640 and 1,003, respectively. The United States still held a narrowing lead of 5,632 warheads to 3,623 for the Soviet Union, but SLBM warheads are of the city-busting type and of low military utility.[14]

Note well that these changes occurred not in spite of the United States' best efforts to prevent them, but with the full, conscious agreement of the United States government. The series of operations that brought this about were *political*. Those very operations also helped bring about a remarkable change in the way the U.S. government views nuclear weapons. Readers of the Defense Department's two flagship annual publications for 1989, the *Annual Report to Congress* and *Soviet Military Power*, cannot help but note that they describe U.S. weapons strictly in terms of their relationships to arms-control treaties and do not contain any reference to how, if worse came to worst, they could be used to the advantage of the American people.

No bomb caused this turnaround. No bomb could have. The ultimate ends of war are political, but so are its ultimate weapons.

Conclusion

Political warfare may serve as a surrogate for actual war, but it does not work without actual force backing it up. Sun Tzu proposed that the "supreme art of war is to subdue the enemy without fighting." This canny advice seems to clash with Clausewitz's description of war as "an act of violence pushed to its utmost bounds." But the two conceptions need not be taken as polarities. Fighting is a tool of war. It is not war itself. Clausewitz's more famous dictum, that "war is a continuation of politics by other means," which refers to war itself, is quite compatible with Sun Tzu's political vision. The practical meaning of all this was perhaps best summed up by a Soviet theoretician: "A state official is offered a choice—to attain this or that political aim, whether to act along lines of peace or with the help of armed violence. . . . [W]hat is important is to select the means which is the most suitable under the given conditions." This is what it's all about: when war comes, a lot of tools are always lying around or can at least be fashioned. Some are more violent than others. The political art of war consists of judging when and how each can best be used.

CHAPTER
9

INTELLIGENCE

How can any man say what he should do himself if
he is ignorant of what his adversary is about?
　　　　　　　—ANTOINE HENRI JOMINI

KNOWLEDGE of the enemy's purposes and plans does not guarantee victory in war. But nothing so enhances one's forces or detracts
from the enemy's as piercing his secrets while protecting one's own.
History is full of spies who have helped their masters' cause.
Throughout the American Revolution, Benjamin Franklin's personal secretary in Paris was a British agent, as was one of George
Washington's staff officers, Benedict Arnold. Before and during
much of World War II, the Soviet Union had excellent access to
German plans through a spy in the German entourage in Tokyo. But
history is also full of spies who may gain good access and yet so
misunderstand the information they gather that they harm their
side's cause. According to the Book of Deuteronomy, Moses' spies
returned from the Promised Land with overestimates of enemy
strength so gross that they disheartened the Children of Israel. By
the same token, ill-trained Union spies furnished General George
McClellan with exaggerations of Confederate strength that accen-
tuated the general's already excessive caution. To act on knowledge
from spies is almost as big a gamble as acting on no knowledge at all.
Such uncertainties are in the very nature of conflict, and decisions
must always be made on the basis of less-than-complete knowledge.
　　This chapter outlines the principles of intelligence in war. First
among them is the need for humility in the face of the unknown and

willingness to humbly make the best of what is at hand. Thus King George VI ended upon such a note in his 1941 New Year's message to the British Empire: "I said to a man who stood at the Gate of the Year, 'Give me a light, that I may tread safely into the unknown.' And he replied, 'Go out into the darkness and put your hand into the Hand of God. That shall be to you better than light, and safer than a known way.' "[1]

The conduct of war, that is, the pursuit of political objectives and the preparation and management of battle, depends substantially on knowledge of the enemy. The purpose of war is to convince the enemy to abandon the aims for which he fights and to place himself at the winner's mercy. But what would bring about such a development in the enemy's mind is not self-evident. The enemy's counsels on such matters are sure to be his most guarded secrets. Hence, anyone who fights must pierce his enemy's secrets in order to learn what it takes for him to win and how best to fight. Fighting without good intelligence consists, at best, of mindless campaigns of destruction conducted in the hope that indiscriminate damage to the other side's arms and body will somehow affect vital but unknown pressure points.

For example, perhaps the biggest policy mistake committed by the Allies in World War II was the policy of "strategic bombing," premised on the false beliefs that (a) enemy soldiers at the front would slacken their efforts if they knew that their homes were being attacked; (b) war production could be crippled; and (c) the Axis governments would decide to stop the war before their societies suffered excessive harm. As we have noted, strategic bombing strengthened morale in the enemy soldiers and did not seriously affect enemy war production. As for inflicting pain upon civilian populations, Italy switched sides in the war without being seriously battered. Japan's decision to surrender flowed from feelings of helplessness rather than suffering. But Germany's Nazi leaders, though incapacitated, spent their last weeks trying to make sure that their own country's suffering would be a total Götterdämmerung. A better understanding of the Axis governments' relationship with their societies, as well as a better assessment of their military capabilities, clearly would have allowed the allies to employ resources more efficiently.

A more contemporary example is the current controversy over the meaning of the Soviet Union's extensive preparations for sheltering its industry and key personnel in the event of nuclear war.

The official position of the U.S. Department of Defense is that the United States should not consider such preparations as evincing Soviet willingness to fight a nuclear war. According to this view, the Soviets "must realize" that nothing they do could keep Soviet society from suffering unacceptable damage in nuclear war. But do we know what the Soviet leadership considers acceptable prices to pay or acceptable risks to run in order to achieve a goal? To suggest that someone else "must realize" something that you do not *know* he realizes is the definition of mirror-imaging—or of whistling in the dark.

Fighting with good intelligence means knowing where your enemy's jugular vein is. One extreme case of an operation that made sense only because knowledge of the enemy was thorough and secure was Ho Chi Minh and Vo Nguyen Giap's decision early in the winter of 1968 to commit all of their forces in South Vietnam for a frontal assault against U.S. forces. Because of the Americans' overwhelming firepower, the attack (since known as the Tet Offensive) was doomed to fail, and Communist forces in South Vietnam never recovered from the losses sustained in that attack. Had North Vietnam's leaders been mistaken in their assessment that the shock of the Tet offensive would have a decisive effect on America's "effete elite," the casualties they suffered would have meant losing the war. But their assessment of the U.S. government's domestic vulnerability proved correct.

Good intelligence also means knowing your enemy well enough to surprise him—or at least well enough to keep him from surprising you. Thus, competent commanders planning an attack always seek to know what the enemy does *not* expect. Clearly the main focus of this attempt is to determine where an attack will stand the best chance of success regardless of the physical difficulties. This is why German knowledge that the French had not seriously defended the area southwest of the Ardennes forest made it reasonable for the Germans to push columns of tanks through the area in 1940. Given the terrain, the French could easily have turned this masterstroke into disaster—if only they had known about it beforehand.

Hence, one of the major preoccupations of any military force must be to guard its secrets. This can be done by concealment or by deception. One of many examples is the Germans' preparation for their May 1918 breakthrough on the Chemin-des-Dames. As forces assembled for the attack, large groups moved only by night. When they moved by day, soldiers would instantly turn and march away

from the front whenever an airplane appeared. All rolling stock had
joints wrapped and muffled against noise. Even horses' hooves were
wrapped. Movement by the river was timed to coincide with the
croaking of frogs.[2]

Combatants' needs for intelligence vary somewhat depending on
whether they are engaged in offensive or defensive operations. In
the first two years of World War II Hitler had much less need for
intelligence than he did afterward when his fortunes waned. An
attacker must simply scout out his plan. True, the defense can complicate this task by deception or by sowing confusion, thus raising
questions as to what its own plans are. But the attacker can deceive
and confuse as well. Even if the attacker does none of this the
defender, waiting for the blow to fall, must scout out all the different
possible ways by which the attack might come. The attacker is also
in a better position to pre-position his spies and observers to keep
him supplied with information as the attack develops. The defender,
on the other hand, is lucky if his intelligence assets survive the
outbreak of war and must shift whatever survivors there are under
enemy fire and according to the enemy's timetable.

For the rest, attacker and defender are in the same boat. During
wartime, when governments want to know more about their opponents than before, they tend to classify more information as secret.
"Loose lips sink ships" was a popular World War II saying in America, the world's least security-conscious society. Even liberal governments declare areas "off limits" to casual traffic, ask people to
curtail casual conversations, and encourage suspicion about those
who may be curious. Hence, all information is much harder to obtain. Travelers, magazines, and diplomats become less useful as
sources of information. On the other hand, war spawns new sources
—troop communications, refugees, prisoners of war, and traitors.
Wartime intelligence is driven by the tempo of events. Most information is useful only in relation to the next battle or to the next
political ploy. There is not enough time to collect and analyze facts
to one's full satisfaction. Leaders must make do with the information
at hand. This puts a premium on their ability to shrewdly interpret
sketchy data. It also produces success for simple deceptive schemes
that would not stand up to calm examination. Finally, each side is
sure to compromise some of its secret agents because of the urgent
need to use them for subversion of the enemy.

Let us now consider the role that intelligence plays in the conduct
of war by examining how each of the four elements of intelligence

—collection, analysis, counterintelligence, and subversion—function during wartime.

Collection

Although the technology of intelligence collection has changed over the years, its purpose has not. Today's agents do not usually have to travel for weeks, as did George Washington's spies, to report handwritten or memorized secrets. They may use encoded satellite communications beamed from packages that can fit into briefcases. But today, as always, agents have the nasty but indispensable job of posing as friends of the enemy, at least long enough to learn the enemy's intentions and his own views of his situation. Today, a military commander who wants to reconnoiter an enemy army does not have to rely on a fast horseman with a good memory. Airplanes or satellites equipped with cameras and electronic sensors are instead at his disposal. A military commander in the midst of a battle today still wants to know what Napoleon and Alexander the Great wanted to know, namely, what effect they were having on the enemy, where and in what state were the enemy's reserves, and how he was planning to use them. Just as we count tanks rather than chariots today, and missiles rather than siege engines, intelligence collection on modern battlefields does not rely on human ears listening on the ground for the beat of hooves. Rather, it relies on picking up the signals emitted by modern weapons. Hence we will consider each aspect of collection, broadly divided into collection by machines and collection by human beings.

COLLECTION BY MACHINES

Battlefield Intelligence. The primary requirement for modern military intelligence is the timely identification and location of enemy targets. Nowadays, once a target is identified and located, chances are it can be hit.[3] Most modern weapons (ballistic missiles in silos being a notable exception) either emit or reflect some electromagnetic energy themselves or depend for their direction on other equipment that emits it. Hence, a great deal of tactical intelligence on the modern battlefield consists of intercepting emissions from enemy equipment. These emissions could be an air-defense radar or the radio of an artillery battery or command post. Battlefield intelligence then processes the intercepts to identify and localize the emitters, and forms a picture of the tactical situation. The modern battlefield also abounds with broadcast oral communication—much of it necessarily not encoded. This must be intercepted, quickly translated, and fit into the tactical picture. On the basis of such intelligence, weapons can be assigned almost automatically to attack those emitters, priority being given to the ones that pose the most immediate threat.

Electronic emissions can be collected by a variety of aircraft behind the front lines, as well as by troops on the lines. These collectors can vary in number and differ in level of protection. Processing, however, is the heart of any system, and here there can be no substitute for speed. Ideally, any time a piece of equipment begins to radiate or a military unit reveals its location by going on the air they should be targeted. To accomplish this, tactical processing centers must first have linguists able to instantly translate the words they hear into information about what and where it is happening and also include reception terminals that can interpret and diagnose various technical sensors. Skilled commanders must then supervise a tactical fire-control network that automatically, or almost automatically, assigns weapons to every enemy unit that is located. Even the best equipped modern forces can do this sort of thing only approximately. Otherwise the modern battlefield would be the equivalent of a video game.

The effectiveness of modern battlefield intelligence depends somewhat on the number, security, and effectiveness of individual collection sensors. But its effectiveness hinges more upon the reliability of communications between the collectors and the processor than upon the processor's efficiency. Some suggest that the weakest link in modern battlefield intelligence is the physical vulnerability of processing centers. Since the entire system ceases to exist if these centers are destroyed, reason suggests that they should be designed for mobility and hardness—even at the expense of capability—and, of course, that they be defended. The Soviet Union's battlefield processors in Eastern Europe, for example, are mobile. Israel's are not, but they are heavily bunkered. NATO's are neither mobile nor bunkered—a sure sign of unseriousness and a portent of battlefield blindness.

Reconnaissance of the Rear. The mere existence of airborne and spaceborne sensors makes good reconnaissance of the rear theoretically possible—but only theoretically. You need enough sensors to cover the enemy's rear to actually see what you want. Even when a war is geographically very limited, as in the Arab-Israeli wars, the Iran-Iraq War that began in 1981, or the Falklands/Malvinas war of 1982, the combatants may not have enough aircraft for constant surveillance. The one or two satellites that could be available, directly or indirectly, to any of the belligerents would make eighteen revolutions per day and, given the earth's rotation, would scan the war zone about once a day, assuming good weather. Electronic satellites can give more continuous coverage. Still, this is not much. But the problem of quantity is even more pressing in larger wars, or in any war where ocean going navies are involved. Consider a hypothetical case of a war between NATO and the Warsaw Pact, whose front would stretch from Norway's North Cape to Turkey's Lake Van, and whose rears would literally be the world.

The success of reconnaissance in such a war would depend largely on the quantity of airplanes and satellites available to either side, *and* on each side's ability to protect or replace its reconnaissance assets. Even if each side did not attempt to interfere with the other's assets, the problems of rear reconnaissance would be enormous. In wartime, ships—even armies—do not broadcast radio signals while moving in the rear. They either do not go "on the air," and simply *listen* to encoded orders broadcast from national headquarters, or they beam their communications to relay satellites. Land forces would use land telephone lines. This means that various kinds of electronic ears pointed to rear areas may hear nothing, or hear broadcasts emanating from place x that are normally associated with a particular military unit, while that unit has moved on to place y. Electronic deception is not a possibility on the battlefield. It is a certainty. Hence, both sides must try to visually scan each other's rear area.

We must digress a bit at this point. Not all imaging satellites are created equal. Satellites like the French SPOT operate in relatively high orbits, cover much ground, are relatively cheap, but can barely make out a big truck. Others, like the American KH-11, fly relatively low, can pick out a duck in a pond, but are terribly expensive and cover relatively little ground. Of course neither can see anything at night or through clouds. In the future, night vision from satellites using infrared cameras may become possible and even be quite good over relatively small areas. But any satellite that sees through clouds will require radar and hence will be grossly expensive and very limited in coverage. Good radar coverage of the oceans, however, is now feasible, since satellites there need only to produce blips from large ships. They can therefore fly high, with relatively cheap, low-resolution radars. All of this is to say that with considerable expense it is possible to give frequent coverage to huge areas with low-resolution imagery, but prohibitively expensive to try to do so with high-resolution, KH-11-type satellites.

So, how would NATO and the Warsaw Pact forces see where each other's reinforcements were, which fixed long-range missiles had and had not been fired, and where their mobile missile launchers were at any given time? Unless either side had inflicted massive damage on the other's air defense system, reconnaissance aircraft sent to the enemy's rear—except as part of a massive reconnaissance-in-force operation—would not likely return. Even if some did, it is impractical to try to maintain surveillance of large areas with aircraft. Because they have narrow fields of view, many would be needed, especially if they had to shoot their way in. Perhaps a score of high-flying satellites, however, could do a reasonable job. But to keep that many in the sky in the face of a determined antisatellite campaign would require successfully shooting down antisatellite devices *and* reserving satellites to replace the ones that would inevitably be lost. A serious reconnaissance effort, then, would be at least in part a contest between the number of replacement satellites and the number of antisatellite weapons each side had stockpiled. In the end, neither side would have full information about the other's rear, and each would have to make the best of what each of its satellites yielded before getting shot down. This is not so different from the way it was in the days when armies relied on expendable second lieutenants as forward observers.

There is nothing preordained about the vulnerability of space-based reconnaissance assets. True, because it is technically easy to achieve orbital intercepts, it is technically easy to build killer satellites. But by the same token, it is also relatively easy to deploy space-based defenses for satellites.

The simplest way to escort key satellites is with packages made up of optical instruments to sense the approach of interceptors and of defensive rockets that would be sent out to intercept the interceptors. Such packages are well below the state of the art.

Approaching the state of the art are even more effective means of defending satellites: space-based lasers with sufficient range to protect any object within thousands of orbital miles from any physical interceptor. Of course, neither defensive rockets nor defensive lasers could safeguard an intelligence satellite that flew within range of a powerful ground-based laser. But heavy shielding might well do. In sum, considering the effort required in protecting reconnaissance aircraft or reconnaissance satellites from enemy action, it becomes apparent that satellites are inherently more protectable.

Communications Intelligence. Communications intelligence (COMINT) is essential in war because it is a primary means of gaining insight into the enemy's intentions. Means of collecting COMINT have increased in importance and sophistication, apace with the growth in communications technology. The growing science of cryptology serves the purposes of those who want access to electronic communications but even more for those who want to guard such communications.

Modern war involves a huge volume of electronic communications. Because volume alone naturally works against security efforts, war—in addition to increasing the likelihood of mistakes—normally produces a lot of valuable COMINT. Moreover, since so much modern communications security depends on complex equipment, especially computers, strikes against enemy forces deep into the enemy's homeland would likely reduce the operational readiness of that equipment and result in reductions in the amount and proficiency of encryption. Thus a lot of urgent messages that would be worth protecting would go on the air "in the clear." Although some COMINT is collected by stations on the ground and by aircraft, much of it nowadays is collected by satellites. These are naturally prime targets. However, it may be feasible and worthwhile to build and escort COMINT satellites over enemy forces and territory during wartime. Each side could expect to suffer and inflict losses on such satellites in a bid to protect its own communications and put the other's at risk. Hence, much of the battle for COMINT in the next major war may well be fought in outer space.

Communications intelligence, however collected, is often meaningless without massive amounts of electronic processing. Processing is essential not only for cryptologic purposes, but also for picking out valuable conversations out of high volumes of low-grade traffic.

Translation is a vital part of processing. Even if all peacetime means of collecting COMINT were to survive the outbreak of war, the destruction of the computers necessary for processing it would leave the collector without most of its COMINT. From this follows the wisdom of the Soviet Union's military planners who located their COMINT computers in deep caves and the imprudence of American planners who located them in thin-walled buildings outside of Washington. The Soviets experience inconvenience in peacetime. The United States would suffer a loss of intelligence in wartime.

Scientific and Technical Intelligence.   Although the fruits of peacetime intelligence gathering to figure out the technical characteristics of enemy weapons would be useful in wartime, it makes little sense to continue much of this work during a conflict. Knowledge of telemetry from new weapons, precise measurements of missile silos, and calculations of the thrust-to-weight ratio of aircraft engines can be of little consequence. When war does not allow time for engineering entirely new countermeasures, however, a good supply of scientific and technical intelligence gathered in peacetime is still essential for probing the meaning of the surprises that are sure to be encountered in war.

The controversy of the early 1980s concerning the Soviet Union's use of chemical warfare in Laos, northeast Cambodia, and Afghanistan provides a good example. According to Sterling Seagrave,[4] thousands of reports by Asians who had been attacked by "yellow rain" falling from Soviet-built aircraft were discredited in the United States because American intelligence was not aware of any chemicals previously used in war that would cause the reported symptoms. And, in fact, no such chemicals had ever been used in war. Of course, American intelligence should have asked immediately what chemicals *might* have caused the reported symptoms. When Mr. Seagrave asked that question, the correct answer, mycotoxins, was waiting in the library. Collection of evidence then corroborated library research.

However, any nation must expect that its forces will be confronted by chemicals, weapons, procedures, frequencies, and so forth not described in any libraries. To avoid this, peacetime data bases must be built imaginatively, with an eye to what the other side *might* do if it really put its mind to the task.

If a nation's intelligence agencies are on the lookout for the unexpected, and have prepared the data bases necessary for understanding the unexpected, they will be able to ask the right questions to understand quickly what they are up against and to minimize the surprise. This preparation consists of basic research on the outer limits of certain technologies. Nothing so cripples understanding of new phenomena as the judgment that what one has just observed "doesn't fit with anything we know."

HUMAN COLLECTION

In the absence of excellent, consistently available communications intelligence, human agents are the only means of addressing the key questions of political warfare. Under what conditions will the enemy decide to cease hostility or surrender? At what point will he think he has won? What will he do if he thinks he's won? Where does the enemy consider himself vulnerable? What and whom does he fear? Is the enemy trying to foment a coup d'état in a third country? If so, is the coup a prelude to the entry of the enemy's troops into the country? If troops do come in, is the enemy willing to make a major strategic commitment to that sector or theater? What do the enemy's allies expect to get out of the war? Under what conditions will such allies desert the enemy? Who are the people in the enemy camp who would likely disrupt the war effort if they were strengthened? Where does the enemy plan to strike next? How does he plan to do it? How does he expect other nations to act? By what means is he managing to purchase embargoed goods? Only well-placed people can answer such questions well.

Let us consider three categories of such people: (a) agents recruited to "stay behind" in enemy-conquered territory or simply to infiltrate through enemy lines; (b) agents in enemy territory; and (c) agents in third countries.

"Stay behinds" must be trained and placed before the enemy's advance. Foresight, humility, and self-discipline are required to realize that the enemy is likely to attack certain areas successfully, and to decide to commit resources to find, train, and pay people willing to stay there under enemy rule. For the sake of security, sensitive communications equipment need not be issued until the enemy's move is imminent. Successful stay behinds must be people who would least likely be suspected of being an agent, and who would probably not be included on a purge list. They would probably not be the sort of people one might meet at diplomatic receptions. Recruitment of such assets would have to be done largely by people with no known connections to foreign embassies. In other words, a truly covert net can only be built covertly. This often entails "spotting" potential recruits, but not approaching them until necessary. The speed with which a clandestine stay-behind net could be assembled would depend largely on how thorough were prior preparations.

In his book *Honorable Men*, William Colby describes how, during the 1950s, the United States recruited agents in parts of Europe it expected to be overrun by an eventual Soviet attack.[5] They were to supply invaluable information about the identity and detailed intentions of invading troops as well as to pinpoint any obvious vulnerabilities they might have. Of course that attack never occurred, perhaps because the United States was prepared in this and in many other more obvious ways. But recruitment of stay behinds is prudent in places susceptible to enemy attack.

Agents willing to slip through or parachute behind enemy lines can be recruited from among people who have fled ahead of enemy forces, or among individuals such as students and businessmen who found themselves away from their homes when these were occupied and who wish to return. Normally, such agents are fairly easy to recruit on the spot when the time comes. But before the first approach can be made, the intelligence system that employs them must have made preparations for assigning properly trained case officers to them, as well as for giving the agents rudimentary training and not-so-rudimentary equipment. To be useful, such agents seldom need what might be called high access. Rather, their usefulness consists in providing the sort of indispensable basic information about occupied areas that in times of peace and free movement would have been provided by travelers and newspapers.

News of troop movements, together with reports of unguarded remarks, can signal the particulars of an impending attack and especially its scope. Even rumors can help target more sophisticated and valuable intelligence resources. The enemy's morale, his concerns, and the weak points of supply lines all can best be signaled by friendly agents behind the lines. Moreover, although intelligence collection and resistance activities theoretically should not mix, collection agents are often involved in partisan activities and can provide valuable links to them. Communications with such agents is always difficult. But the marvels of space age communications have eased this problem considerably.

When wars disrupt normal population-control systems, cause floods of refugees, destroy records, and so forth, they greatly facilitate penetration of enemy territory by intelligence collectors. This is what happened throughout Central Europe toward the end of World War II. Nuclear war would likely scramble populations at least as radically. With proper prewar preparations, the confusion could be used to infiltrate agents under various kinds of cover. It is not clear whether it is possible at all to infiltrate societies that are thoroughly regimented on the Soviet model, with every person accounted for and every lodging place surveiled. The best chance for success would lie in using third country nationals with "cover" that would give them plausible reasons for being where they are. The diplomat, the businessman from a third country who retains good relations with the enemy but who has been recruited to one's own service can potentially be exceptionally valuable in mingling with and reporting the mood of the enemy's ruling class. Communications with such agents could also be less difficult than with other "inside" agents.

Even when the target is a non-Communist or imperfectly Communist country, training someone to survive in enemy territory and giving him plausible cover requires years of prior preparation. Also, such missions are inherently so dangerous that they have almost nothing in common with the missions of, say, U.S. intelligence officers deployed in peacetime under the cover of the U.S. embassy.

The value of intelligence officers infiltrated into enemy territory is limited. Infiltrated agents who capture a key leader, shake key information out of him, and radio it home are the stuff of movies. It might happen occasionally, but normally such agents try to provide answers to what's happening at a certain location by mingling with locals. They also report on the people's state of mind, levels of nutrition and health—in short, on the valuable things that everybody in the country knows but which an adversary otherwise would not. Of course, the intelligence officers might try to contact native agents who had been recruited before the war but who had somehow lost the ability to communicate. At best, such infiltrators would position audio devices in places where they might pick up important conversations. But one could not expect them to get close enough to important people to gain information from them. Surely, any activity that does not conform strictly with their cover is very dangerous.

It is impossible to know beforehand what opportunities or requirements must be made for such infiltrators in the middle of a nuclear war. A nuclear war might cause a deep schism in the enemy regime or among the population. Individuals on the ground might know more about what was going on than those who monitored radio broadcasts and troop movements. Agents sent into areas controlled by presumed rivals for power would not have to obtain high-level information in order to report back on the basic viability of such rivals. They could report valuably on which way the political wind was blowing.

The technical requirements for handling such penetrations would be the same as those for handling agents in enemy territory who had been recruited before the outbreak of war. Except for rare occasions when the agents could come out of enemy territory, communications with them have to be done electronically.

Human operations in third countries have been and will remain a staple of wartime intelligence. That is because in third (neutral) countries it is possible to approach the enemy's diplomats, to surveil their premises, and to watch them as they carry out their country's foreign policy. Even if enemy diplomats in a third country don't know everything about their country's war aims and plans, their knowledge is sufficient to be worth attention. Moreover, the strains of war might weaken their loyalty. The enemy diplomats' principal friends in third countries are also inviting targets for recruitment or surveillance.

However, preparations for such activities must begin with the assumption that at the outset of war third countries will break diplomatic relations with at least one belligerent party. Of course, they may not. Then, like Portugal and Turkey in World War II, they could become meccas of intrigue. But, if they do break diplomatic relations, they automatically and totally eliminate a country's intelligence presence under diplomatic cover just when it would be most valuable. The only way to avoid being liable to such a drastic reduction in one's intelligence presence abroad is to recruit and train a cadre of human intelligence collectors who pose as something other than diplomats, and hence who could move about in countries when other officials are not welcome. These people could be international businessmen, journalists, philanthropists, or scholars; indeed, anyone who had a legitimate reason to travel. They could also be permanent residents of the country they are assigned to cover. The alternative to building such networks in peacetime is to face the prospect of having to try to build them hurriedly under harsh wartime conditions.

Wartime Intelligence Products. Policymakers, military commanders, and diplomats look to intelligence agencies for information. This information comes in different formats, each designed to be useful in a particular context, such as in a meeting where bombing targets are picked or on the bridge of a warship. These formatted packages of information are known in the trade as "intelligence products." Wartime products may be divided into four categories. First are what we might call static products: descriptions of the military, political, and economic means that are at the enemy's disposal. Foremost among these are the lists of what equipment and manpower the enemy has and how it is organized, called "order of battle" books. Then there are books containing biographies of the people who matter in the enemy's war machine. In addition, there are files on industries and management and labor organizations and records of political alignments, factions, and so forth. Of course these static products require constant updating.

Second, there are dynamic intelligence products. These are reports of troop movements, changes of command, changes in administration and production, as well as discussions of latest events. Third, strategic products study what the enemy is *capable* of doing in any given functional area (for example, how many tanks or nuclear warheads it can produce) or in any geographic area (how many antiship missiles it can put at the entrance of the Persian Gulf). There are also studies of any given situation from the enemy's point of view, and estimates of what the enemy is going to do. Finally, there are tactical products—reports on how the enemy behaves in specific situations and, occasionally, predictions of tactical moves.

In major wars, each part of a government engages in the fighting. Each pays attention to its area of concern and brings unique insights to it. During wartime the operating departments of government, especially the military services, gather more intelligence than usual through direct contact with the enemy and heightened attention to every opportunity to collect it. Consumers of intelligence, such as major military commanders, contribute data to the intelligence product and *insist* on being the final analytic authority on intelligence papers that address matters that concern them. But any "shop" in the government, perhaps only as a hobby, may cultivate outstanding knowledge about an individual, a unit, an industry, or a location. The official source of "all source knowledge" may lie elsewhere. But in the bowels of some ministry, there may be someone who knows nothing but the proficiency of every Ruritanian pilot who ever flew a plane! The trick in wartime is to channel information so that it flows from the various collectors and consumer-collectors up to some central point where it is integrated with all other *relevant* information and then down again to those who need it. In practice, information does not flow so neatly.

For Americans, the most poignant example of this was that during the first days of December 1941 there was more than enough information in the hands of the U.S. government to have led a reasonable person who looked at it to conclude that Japanese aircraft carriers would strike at Pearl Harbor on or about December 7. But the information was not all where one person could consider it as a whole. Hence, the proper conclusion was not drawn. The intelligence service established at the outbreak of World War II, the Office of Strategic Services (OSS), was too busy with other matters to be concerned with analytic integration. But the CIA, established after World War II, was designed largely to prevent a reoccurrence of Pearl Harbor.

The CIA represents surely the biggest effort ever made to rationalize the flow of intelligence. The CIA's Directorate of Intelligence—which is in charge of production—is supposed to contain the country's central files for production and analysis, as well as expert analysts in every field of intelligence. Its analysts have no attachment to any operating department. But, for example, a CIA analyst covering the Ruritanian navy is supposed to know not only about all information in the United States bearing on that subject, but also about the U.S. Navy's needs for information about Ruritania. Thus, in wartime as in peacetime, he is supposed to act as the authoritative guide and supplementer to his counterpart in the Navy, as well as the National Security Council's expert on the Ruritanian navy. Before computers became the primary tools for storing and transferring intelligence data, this system would have been hampered by lack of speed during war even if it employed the very best analysts. However, if the CIA's central computers and the links to them were kept in operation during wartime, the technical possibility exists that the system would work.

However, even given technical perfection, two human conditions might cause the system not to operate as planned. First, the Navy might not trust the naval analysts in the CIA to notice everything that might be of naval significance and to enter it into the computer in the right way. The Navy might even be reticent about sending some of its intelligence to the CIA. Second, even if the CIA analysts were trusted with all the intelligence, they would certainly not be trusted to "do" any intelligence products that would affect naval operations. Naval officers, after all, might complain that the CIA does not know the U.S. Navy's own capabilities and plans intimately and is not responsible for the success of U.S. naval operations. In wartime, the CIA's analysts on the Ruritanian navy might therefore write what they wished, but the U.S. Navy's thoughts on the subject would be shaped chiefly by its own analysts. In this hypothetical case, as in real life, CIA analysts would be no more than an additional source of information to the analysts in the effective operating department of government. The situation might not be so different than before Pearl Harbor, when naval intelligence was so jealous with its facts that it would give only oral briefings (nothing written) to the White House itself.

Chaos seems to be endemic to the intelligence business in wartime. The operating forces tend to rely on their own analyses. The intelligence services that report to the national leadership each have different analyses. Not only does each data base differ from another, but more important, the perspectives and the bureaucratic interests of the several centers of analyses differ. This naturally leads to interdepartmental differences of opinion. High decision makers influenced either by *their* department's analysis or by central analysis argue against other high decision makers who defend their own department's analysis. Such conflicts are mitigated by the fact that during war bureaucrats are sometimes too busy to fight one another. Modern data-processing systems offer the hope that at least in the future all centers of analysis and production will work from the same data base.

Sometimes in war an intelligence question is so important that it requires a decision binding on all departments. Winston Churchill's resolution of the question of the German air force's strength in 1940–41 is an example of good intelligence management. The Air Ministry, reacting to its own shamefully low prewar estimates, gave a figure for German first-line aircraft about twice the actual number. If that figure had been correct, it would have been good reason for Britain to husband all its aircraft at home and virtually forget the rest of the world during 1941. Churchill, spurred by this and by his own knowledge of German war production, disagreed. The central analytical body, the Joint Intelligence Committee (JIC), knowing the prime minister's view, re-analyzed the evidence. But without fresh insights it only knocked the number down a bit. Churchill then established an ad hoc group under his personal adviser, Professor Frederick Lindemann, which forced the Air Ministry and the JIC to overhaul the basic assumptions behind the definition of air force

strength, namely the concept of "first line aircraft": how many operational aircraft were in each squadron and how frequently each
plane would fly a mission. This done, it became possible to reinter-
pret the signal intelligence data (SIGINT) about the number of aircraft actually on mission at any given time. The Lindemann committee's final figure was very close to the actual truth. The point
here is that although there had been more than one source of analysis on the German air force, and no shortage of will to please the
prime minister, there had been a shortage of insight. The prime
minister's personal representative was armed not just with a mandate to come up with a different answer, but evidently with more
ingenuity and honesty than the bureaucracy. Had he not, Churchill's eventual decision would have produced the wrong result.

There is no best or worst way of organizing the flow of wartime
intelligence. War tends to decentralize that flow. The top intelligence manager's job may then be summarized as making sure that
all the various users receive the intelligence relevant to their missions in a timely manner, monitoring the clashes of views to see
whether some kind of national-level arbitration is necessary, and
making sure that no single department works on the basis of unchallenged intelligence assumptions.

PRACTICING AND DETECTING DECEPTION

The certainty of deception shadows all collection and all production of intelligence about war aims, "statics," strategy, or tactics.
Because deception is usually cheap and its success pays enormously,
it is always attempted.

In the fall of 1939, for example, Hitler gained a serious advantage
over France, Britain, and the Low Countries, finished off Poland,
secured his maritime flank in Norway—and secured cooperation
from Italy and Russia—by dissimulating his war aims as mere German racism. The dictators of Italy and Russia, confident that mere
German racism would never drive Hitler to a destructive world war,
reasonably figured they could make a few gains (the Mediterranean
and Africa, Poland and Finland, respectively) by riding a tiger that
was frightening the Western powers. The Western powers continued
to hope that if they did nothing to provoke Hitler, the war would
continue to be limited to areas that were, had been, or conceivably
could be ethnically German. Hence, the war would continue to be a
phony war, at least for them.[6] But Stalin and Mussolini, no less than

Chamberlain and Daladier, were mistaken. Hitler was not an extraordinarily artful deceiver. After all, his plans for the world had been spelled out in *Mein Kampf.* Rather, during the early part of World War II just about everybody deceived themselves about Hitler's war aims because they resisted believing propositions that, if accepted, would have compelled them to undertake dangerous, uncomfortable actions. Hitler did not have to do much to encourage this massive self-deception.

Even self-interest is not a reliable barrier against self-deception. It was clearly in the interest of most Americans between 1965 and 1975 to keep South Vietnam out of the Soviet orbit. That was the professed goal of four U.S. Presidents—two from each party. But this did not keep many Americans from deceiving themselves about the Communists' war aims. The Communists professed to be working for the same end as the U.S. government, namely the self-determination of the South Vietnamese people. By the time the North Vietnamese, with Soviet help, were overrunning South Vietnam, the elite American press and the U.S. government had accepted de facto that the Soviets and the North Vietnamese were sincere about South Vietnam's independence and that the South Vietnamese people supported them. So strong was this acceptance that it overcame obvious evidence to the contrary. For example, the American press erroneously explained the sight of populations fleeing Communist lines for the U.S. side as fear of U.S. bombing. When the flow of people in the same direction continued, even after U.S. warplanes had left Vietnam's skies and the South Vietnamese air force had been grounded, the widely accepted explanation for why the Vietnamese people fled the Communists was that the South Vietnamese were childlike, excitable, and did not know themselves why they were fleeing. After the Communist victory in Southeast Asia, the spectacle of the Communist government's murder of millions of their own citizens, and the flight of more millions into the sea, has convinced some journalists in the West that they had taken part in deceiving their readers about the war aims of the Communists. But the fact that such spectacles have left many other opinion makers unconvinced is further evidence for the proposition that deception consists in simply giving people even a meager excuse to believe what *they* would really like to believe anyway.

The most common deception about war aims, practiced since the dawn of time, seeks to convince sectors of the enemy population that *they* are not the target of military operations, that only their leaders, their policies, their system of government, or their allies are the targets. This line of argument may not be deception at all. In most cases it is wise policy. But in *all* cases it is indispensable. Its absence can only be expected to strengthen the enemy's hold on his people. Thus, the great Russian author, Alexander Solzhenitsyn, chastised the Reagan administration for giving the impression that the United States opposed not so much the Soviet Communist regime but historic Russian ambitions. He went on to criticize the American military for making plans not to defeat the Soviet regime but rather to inflict casualties upon the Russian people. The very fact that people of good will characterize American policy as such is a serious indictment of that policy.

Let us turn now to strategic deception. Its purpose is to induce the enemy to deploy his efforts in a way that leaves the main axis of attack relatively undefended. The most common fruit of strategic deception is surprise attack. The most common means of achieving surprise are military maneuvers, attacks announced on axis *a* that suddenly turn on axis *b*, and attacks launched under the cover of negotiations for the reduction of tensions.

The United States, the victim of the third kind of deception in 1941, has developed elaborate means for detecting surprise attack by ballistic missiles and has created a set routine to provide for a near automatic response. But that routine assumes that the indications of attack will be unambiguous. Since the means of detection are exclusively technical, it is easy to imagine an attack accompanied by basic deception, such as a huge satellite-dispensed cloud of chaff attended by a simultaneous call from the enemy that some solar condition is hampering long-distance radar. These stratagems would be recognized for what they are relatively quickly—but perhaps not before the enemy had gained the first fruit of surprise: time.

In 1940–41 the British JIC misinterpreted Hitler's deployment of troops in the Balkans for the invasion of Russia as a preparation for directing the left half of a pincer movement at the Suez Canal. The British understandably saw themselves as Hitler's main target and tried to interpret every move he made in terms of a strategy to defeat Britain. This was not an unreasonable conclusion, given Hitler's plans for a cross-channel invasion in the summer of 1940. But by 1941 the conclusion was mistaken. Hitler helped this self-deception by continuing to rattle a few swords on the Channel coast. The point here is that the easiest kind of strategic deception in the course of conflict is a shift away from a strategy that the enemy is aware of and in terms of which the enemy evaluates his intelligence. The deception consists of the enemy's own judgmental fixation and inflexibility.

Another possible example of this is the conventional wisdom in the United States since the early 1970s about Soviet strategy regarding Europe. Since about 1956 some Americans have believed that the Soviet Union aims to detach Europe from the United States by gaining control of U.S. oil supplies in the Middle East. Therefore, the United States has invested much political capital in the region and has gone so far as to earmark military forces for action in the inhospitable sands around the Persian Gulf. However, though Soviet activity in the Middle East had hardly ceased in the late 1970s and early 1980s, an entirely different, simpler Soviet strategy toward Europe seemed to be at work. By the 1980s the Soviet Union was presenting Europe with overwhelming Soviet military power not in faraway places but on its borders, to convince Europe that any effort to ever redress the military imbalance would be too dangerous, and to let Europeans slowly draw the inevitable conclusions. And indeed, some Europeans, impressed by Soviet military superiority along the inter-German border, have urged the United States to bring the Soviet Union into negotiations on the future of the Middle East. This shows the good sense of Soviet strategy. It also shows that American officials in effect deceived themselves by their inability to abandon an outdated way of looking at a problem.

As for tactical deception, it is easier to implement under modern conditions than ever before, given the mobility of modern military assets and the fact that the performance of military systems often cannot be discerned by technical means of intelligence gathering. Indeed, modern technical intelligence seems to be particularly vulnerable to deception. For example, cruise missiles directed against ground targets must be programmed before launch. This programming takes into account the location of air-defense sites, whose effectiveness against cruise missiles depends to some extent on the *angle* from which the "cruise" approaches. Of course, some of the "cruises" can be targeted on the air-defense sites. But the direction from which they come would make all the difference. Anyone programming a cruise missile would rely on satellite pictures of the air-defense sites to determine their location and the best angle of approach. But if the owners of the air-defense sites know that they are being observed by satellite, and given that these sites are mobile, they can move them after passage of an imaging satellite. Or they can simply deceive the satellite by temporarily posing for it in false orientation. Thus any cruise missile that is programmed to reach its target according to that satellite's data would be flying into a trap. A similar effect can be achieved in cloudy weather by turning on air defense radars when an enemy electronic intelligence (ELINT) satellite is in range and then moving the radar. Similarly, by purposely radiating a false, "signature" signal, the enemy may be deceived into thinking that units are armed with a different type of air-defense missile, again setting up a mismatch. The same sort of deception can also be employed against the B-2 stealth bomber for the same reasons. The possibilities for such deception are limited only by imagination.

SUBVERSION

As we have already discussed, the exercise of political influence on the enemy is the proximate goal of waging war. Hence, it would be incorrect to think of such political manipulation under the narrow category of intelligence. Nevertheless, intelligence is precisely involved in exercising the kind of political influence that the enemy does not know is being exercised. This kind of influence is popularly known as subversion. Intelligence is involved in subversion in two ways. First, those who are in position—i.e., who have the physical and social access—to gather intelligence are in effect in a position to subvert. Any side that can put people behind enemy lines to gather intelligence can also put people there to subvert. Second, in order to subvert in a competent manner it is necessary to have very good intelligence about a target. In other words, subversion is like intelligence work; it is intelligence-intensive work, and it often uses the same people.

Subversion—etymologically, the act of turning from underneath —consists of actions ranging from the spreading of rumors (either true or false), to building up or tearing down the influence of key people or factions in the enemy camp, and possibly to sabotage and assassination. Its distinguishing feature—the "sub" in subversion— is that the actions do not appear to be the work of an enemy. Thus, whereas some injuries rally the victim by focusing its anger on the enemy, the defeats inflicted through subversion confuse the victim as to who the enemy is, and thus further erode the victim's moral energies.

Action of almost any sort is dangerous to spies. Their safety lies in being unobtrusive. Highly placed spies who openly take the side of an enemy power in internal deliberations cast suspicion on themselves ipso facto. Those who "run" spy rings generally resist suggestions that the spies be used for subversion. Yet, because the spies are often the only agents in the "right" places when the need for subversion arises, they must either recruit and run the subverters or become subverters themselves.

Secret agents in the enemy's camp have always been rare and invaluable. Usually, unless one has made preparations, the only people on whom one can count in a foreign court are one's own diplomats. In his history of the Peloponnesian War, Thucydides writes of Athenian and Spartan ambassadors who lodged with friends in cities throughout Greece and secretly mobilized groups to influence the host city's government. One of the goriest episodes in that war was the partisan strife in Corcyra, on Corfu, fomented by ambassadors who promised each of the island's factions support that encouraged them to fight one another. During the wars of the Reformation, ambassadors did little but stir up court intrigues and partisan warfare. Today, embassies are still the bases of choice for subversion because diplomatic personnel enjoy both wide social access and almost complete personal immunity. For example, in 1963 American diplomats and CIA officers worked out of the U.S. embassy when they met with South Vietnamese army officers who were plotting against President Ngo Dinh Diem and provided them with the green light for the coup d'état; specifically, the assurance of continued U.S. support. By the same token, in 1986 the Soviet embassy in Aden was the headquarters for a coup d'état—indeed, a mini–civil war in which one faction of the ruling Communist party seized power from the other.

Perhaps the most complete example of diplomatic subversion was that of Count Diego Sarmiento Gondomar, Spain's ambassador to London at the beginning of the seventeenth century. Gondomar not only induced many of England's leading personalities to accept handsome, secret "pensions" from the Spanish treasury; he also became so close personally to King James I that he was able to steer England's foreign policy. Although Spain, Protestant England's great rival, was in the process of putting down a Protestant rebellion in the Netherlands, Gondomar succeeded in keeping England neutral. Indeed, the king of England even arrested anti-Spanish Englishmen. Compared to this example, Henry Kissinger's grant of a privileged parking space in the State Department's basement to Soviet Ambassador Anatoli Dobrinyin seems mild. The former example illustrates an important point about subversion. Subversion is not magic, it is not "brainwashing," and it does not involve "making" people act against their will. No one was ever subverted against his will, just as no one was ever deceived, converted, or for that matter, seduced against his will.

Less dramatic but no less real instances of subversion occur daily in embassies around the world. It is not easy to draw a line between subversion and the customary function of embassies: influencing affairs in the host country through wide-ranging contacts. The distinguishing mark of subversion, however, is choosing not to accept the decisions that a foreign government might make but to attempt to influence those decisions secretly. In effect subversion is warfare within a foreign government's decision-making process.

Dispatching agents of subversion who magically transform a foreign country is normally the stuff of fiction. Since the dawn of history subversion has relied upon people within a target government or society susceptible to the suasions of a foreign power. If these people have a grievance or a state of mind that predisposes them to act in accordance with a foreign power's designs, it is then up to the foreign power to send operatives able to turn the potential for subversion into reality. The Athenian democracy would send words of encouragement to democratic parties throughout Greece, while its rival, oligarchic Sparta would intrigue with oligarchs. The Soviet Communist party does not simply send out agents helter-skelter, but rather sends them to those persons in foreign countries whose ideas or whose "class" presumably predispose them to work against the "main enemy," the United States. Nor does any competent government send forth missionaries to convert foreign groups who are not inclined to it. It is difficult enough to convince people to work for the things they want. It is almost impossible to convince people to work for things they do not want. Indeed, competence in subversion consists of talking with the people who are to be used about *their* agenda. The subverter's art consists in advancing his own agenda by harnessing it to the locals' eagerness to realize their own. Thus, American agents working in Kurdistan in the early 1970s did not vaunt the wonders of America or the glories of Iran, but rather their willingness to support a war against the Iraqi Arabs whom the Kurds hated. The American agents who persuaded the H'mong tribe of Laos to fight against North Vietnam would have moved no one with talk of democracy. But they enlisted a nation by showing it the possibility of achieving freedom from its oppressor. It is important that agents, whether they are government employees or people specially engaged for a particular assignment, be able to understand, visibly sympathize with, and give malcontents the necessary tools to act.

To be in a position to subvert an agent must be credible to those he is trying to influence. This can be achieved by appearing as the representative of a purposeful, powerful foreign country. Or it can mean hiding that fact and appearing as another kind of friend. Whatever guise is chosen, it is indispensable that the agent be trusted as someone who knows what he is talking about and as someone whose counsels are friendly. Thus, in 1986 when President Reagan sent former senator Paul Laxalt to Manila to entice Philippine president Ferdinand Marcos into giving up power, Marcos believed both that Laxalt and Reagan had his interest at heart and that they were in a position to deliver an honorable retirement rather than the gilded cage—and the prosecution—he actually got. Similarly, when various Iranian intermediaries approached the U.S. government in 1985 with the hope of purchasing U.S. arms, they did so as representatives of groups that they said were ready, willing, and able to take certain actions contrary to the regime of Ayatollah Khomeini.

The "trick" of subversion, then, consists in knowing what will impell target groups to act and what will impede them. The subverter must also know what kinds of people or styles will inspire trust in them and what will alienate them. Often it's a close call. For example, in 1939–40, when the British government sought to enlist U.S. help against Germany, it had to overcome the coolness and even the hostility of the State Department and of Ambassador Joseph Kennedy especially. The British government knew that President Roosevelt favored aid, was hostile to Germany, and unfriendly to Ambassador Kennedy. British intelligence tapped Kennedy's telephone and recorded remarks that were both grossly pro-German and anti-Roosevelt. The British naturally wanted to share these recordings with the President. But would Roosevelt's tendency to pounce on a chance to squash a disloyal subordinate and push a favorite policy be counterbalanced by unhappiness at having had the U.S. embassy's phones tapped? The British judged that Roosevelt was the kind of man who would put substance over form, and they were correct. They knew their target.

During World War II, the U.S. preceded its landings in French North Africa in 1942 with agents whose purpose was to secure the noninterference of the French authorities. The American agents had a lot going for them. The United States was at war with the same Germany that had crushed the French army two years earlier and now occupied Paris. Every Frenchman in North Africa knew that a U.S. victory would liberate France. But American agents had a lot going against them, too. American policy at the time was to work with the Vichy regime, which was ruling France on Hitler's behalf, because the State Department believed that this regime retained the loyalty of most Frenchmen. Thus, the U.S. agents in North Africa did not work with the allies of General Charles de Gaulle's Free French movement. They instead tried to persuade the Vichy government's leading representatives in North Africa to come over to the Allied side, avoiding attacks on the legitimacy of the Vichy regime. Ambassador Robert Murphy displayed the talents of a world-class diplomat in the service of a self-contradictory policy. Its logical consequence was that on the day of the American landings, the official chargé of the Vichy regime ordered French troops to fire on the Americans and told American agents that he would have to get permission from Hitler's puppet, Pétain, to change sides. American agents failed because they tried to subvert the Vichy government's control of North Africa without really subverting it. Finally, as American troops were landing in force and Frenchmen had to decide whether to risk their lives by fighting them, the fundamentals of the situation asserted themselves. French forces in North Africa aligned themselves under de Gaulle's banner against Germany and the Vichy regime, but not because of American policy, whose brilliant execution was vitiated by ignorant conception.

What will move—or steady—a target group? Who is inclined to be of assistance, and how can they help? These are the intelligence questions that underlie subversion. Without correct answers even technical virtuosity in operations will be counterproductive. Suppose that a country wishes to bolster a foreign regime by weakening its dissident groups. It must know the factions it supports well enough to insure that strengthening them will weaken rather than merely incite their opponents. For example, during the 1960s and 1970s the United States sought to undergird the regime of the shah of Iran by encouraging it to secularize the country—something that displeased most Iranians, who are devout Muslims. But at the same time, American advisers discouraged the Iranians from adopting the dictatorial measures secularization entails, such as banning the wearing of veils and eradicating or subsuming religious endowments, that Mustafa Kemal had undertaken half a century earlier in Turkey. The Americans thus encouraged the arousing instead of the destruction of Islam, the country's most powerful force. This counterproductive result, which ultimately led to the Islamic Revolution of 1978–79, came as a big surprise for the same reason that it happened at all—ignorant intelligence. U.S. intelligence was not in contact with or intellectually capable of comprehending the religious mentality that made Iran into what it is today. The United States unwittingly helped to subvert those Iranians who were on its side.

Who is on whose side? War naturally narrows the "sides" to two. What will the various people who support a country's enemy do when the immediate danger is over? What can that country do to make sure that they stay on its side in subsequent conflicts? The answers require inside knowledge of the parties involved. Armed with that knowledge, a country can firm up allies and weaken enemies. Machiavelli's favorite example, Cesare Borgia, presents a case in point. Borgia had allied himself with the King of France, Louis XII, and the Orsini family against the Colonnesi family of Rome. He realized that in the long run he lacked the power to manipulate France, so he resolved to have as little to do with it as possible. He knew that the Orsini, though unreliable, were venal, so he showered them with the spoils of war. He also knew that the Colonnesi could be enticed to negotiate for a share of his spoils, but that he could not actually deliver that share without alienating the Orsini. So during the negotiations he assassinated the leading men of the Colonnesi. This left his enemies much weaker and his allies more in his power than ever.

Contrast this with the obtuse way in which the United States dealt with its allies in World War II, by relying on the ones it could not influence and weakening and alienating the ones it could. Not only did the United States place its bets for the postwar order on the Soviet Union, which it could not control. The United States also chose which political factions to support materially and politically in wartime Europe strictly on the basis of their ability to fight the current enemy, Germany, without regard to their relationship to the Soviet Union. Thus the United States and Britain are largely responsible for the prominent positions that Yugoslav, Italian, Greek, and French Communists—allied with the Soviet Union—occupied at the end of the war. Theoretically, it is possible to wean another power's allies away by treating them better than they are currently being treated. But whether or not that can be done, and what it will take to do it in any given case, can only be determined by accurate intelligence. Borgia knew that the Orsini could be bought with material goods. He also knew that to keep them bought he had to kill the Colonnesi. And he was willing to do it. Any country serious about subversion has to have the kind of knowledge and the kind of determination Borgia had. Subversion is a part of war. It is not a cheap substitute for war.

This point is easiest to grasp when one looks at examples where either intelligence, determination, or both, are lacking. Unfortunately, the quintessential example is the perennial fascination of the U.S. government with promotion of the "moderate faction" in the Soviet leadership and indeed throughout the world. The unexamined assumption of American policymakers is that "moderates" are intrinsically preferable and that they have a better chance of prevailing. But the term "moderate" begs, indeed hides, all the tough questions. What does the United States want these people to do? What are they disposed to do? What will it take to get them to do it? Is the United States willing to do what is needed to make it work? The term "moderate" is attractive to policymakers precisely because it begs these questions. Thus, unserious policymakers can tinker with foreign situations as fancy strikes them without having to know or commit very much. Presidents from Franklin Roosevelt to Ronald Reagan have imagined that each dictator of the Soviet Union, whether it be Josef Stalin or Mikhail Gorbachev, represented the "moderate faction" and that the United States ought to do what is necessary to strengthen him lest "hard liners" take over. Never mind that the United States has next to no knowledge of who belongs to what faction in the Soviet Communist party or what the factions represent (if anything) for the interests of the United States. Certainly the United States has nothing to offer or to inflict that would make a difference in Soviet factional struggles.

Similarly, in the 1980s, American policymakers have fancied that they could subvert the existing order in Iran and South Africa by supporting, respectively, moderate factions of the Shi'ite fundamentalists and moderate factions of the African National Congress (ANC). Leave aside for the moment whether it makes any sense to call anyone associated with such organizations "moderate," and assume—though this is not the case—that the United States had private, secure knowledge that the people with whom they were dealing were ready to take over their organizations and turn them into servants of U.S. policy. Still, what could the United States do to help these "moderates" achieve that end? The sine qua non of such an accomplishment by the moderates would have been the rather extreme act of killing or helping to kill the "extremists." But surely the "moderate" Shi'ites and the "moderate" members of the ANC were not prepared to commit fratricide. If they had, the United States would not have been willing or able to help them do such immoderate deeds. So what could this American subversion have amounted to? Nothing but self-deception.

This brings us to the bottom line on subversion. Subversion is a human activity that cannot be calibrated in terms of money, promises, propaganda, or, indeed, in any rational way at all. It consists of somehow inducing human beings to induce others to act in one's interest, wittingly or unwittingly, for whatever reason compels them to do so. No one can know for sure beforehand whether everyone assembled for a particular purpose will do the job. Hence, it is not unusual for people to deceive themselves about the reliability of a subversive scheme that they have devised—no matter how competently they have designed it. People being people, no intelligence can foretell who will be one's friends at the time of trial. Machiavelli's rule of thumb, however, has proved valid through the ages: "If one will have good arms, one will always have good friends."

CHAPTER 10

JUST WAR

Love thine enemies.

—Luke 6:35

CAN IT ever be right to set in motion events that can reasonably be foreseen to lead to the death of thousands, many of them innocent? The answer clearly must be "That depends" . . . let us see on what. The paragon of justice in our civilization is the Good Samaritan. Christ tells us that a certain traveler was set upon by robbers, who beat him and left him for dead alongside the road. Priests and scholars saw him as they passed by but moved to the other side of the road. Finally, the Samaritan arrived. He bound his wounds, took the victim to an inn, and paid the innkeeper to nurse him the rest of the way back to health. Our civilization invites us to imitate this active Samaritan, rather than the passive priests and scholars.

But what would this exemplary Samaritan have done if he had come upon the scene while the violent robbery was still in progress? Would charity have been satisfied if he had sat and watched until the robbers had finished with their victim before moving in to help? Wouldn't the Good Samaritan have attacked the robbers? On the other hand, if the robbers had been so many that by joining the fray he would only have committed suicide, he might have stayed hidden in the rocks. Charity and suicide are two different things. However, if he had been traveling with his own friends, he probably would have judged the strength of his band against the robbers' before deciding whether it was prudent to ask his friends to join him in war against the robbers.

As for the priest and the scholar, although they did not put themselves out in any way for a stranger, one might well surmise that if they had come home from their journeys to find the same band of thieves looting their farms and raping their wives, they would have used all prudent force to put a stop to the evil. Nor can one imagine that Christ would have condemned anyone for using all necessary force—though doing so would involve the commission of some evil —to stop a greater evil from occurring. "Turning the other cheek" is no virtue when it means offering up someone else's cheek or life to be smitten.

Hence, the civilization that has risen on the teachings of Christ has always sanctioned war, providing that sufficiently valuable goods are at stake, that they are seriously enough threatened, that the danger is such that violence is necessary if the goods are to be protected, that there is reasonable chance of success, and that any evils committed in the defense of these goods not outweigh them.

Of course, if all Western rulers who ever contemplated war had made these dispassionate judgments about the justice of their cause, the world would have suffered only a small fraction of the wars that it in fact has suffered. But war has happened so often precisely because when men judge their own case they tend to be inspired more by interest, fear, and hatred than by a thirst for justice. Still, without the above criteria not only would the number of wars have been greater, but there would have been no way for third parties and mere citizens to distinguish between Good Samaritans, aggressors, defenders, the prudent, the mad, and the criminal.

Western thought has divided questions of justice regarding warfare into two interrelated sets. One asks whether it is right or wrong to fight for a particular cause in a particular circumstance—*jus ad bellum*. The other concerns whether particular actions taken in the course of a war are right or not—*jus in bello*. Let us examine each set in turn.

Jus ad Bellum

The worth of the goods at stake—human and material—is a necessary element in considering whether it is just to break the peace. But substantially elevating the quality of life for all concerned does not by itself justify breaking the peace. This is because in the Western tradition peace and settled arrangements are themselves of great value. Xenophon tells cf the Socratic teacher asking his pupil, the young Cyrus (the Great), what he would do if he came across a small man with a big coat and a big man with a small coat. When Cyrus replied that he would take the big coat away from the small man and give it to the big one, and vice versa, the teacher beat him to drive home the point that although both parties would benefit from Cyrus's distribution, the big coat actually belonged to the small man and Cyrus had no right to take it away from him, nor the small coat from the big man.

Likewise, Abraham Lincoln, while he had no doubt that Negro slavery was a great evil to be done away with, was determined to do all he could to avoid fighting a war in order to eradicate it. He knew that war would cause death and suffering and might permanently break the U.S. Constitution. He also realized that no one had the right to dispossess the masters of the property in which they had invested and on which they based their livelihood, and that no one could adequately manage the instant transition of millions of slaves to lives of responsibility. So he sought to arrange laws and public opinion so that the extinction of slavery would happen both gradually and peaceably. When the southern states resisted these peaceable measures to the point of making war, Lincoln then prosecuted that war at the cost of carnage (Antietam, Gettysburg) for the sake of two worthy goods: the integrity of the United States and the abolition of slavery. The abolition of slavery became necessary both as a measure of war and in order to eliminate the bone of contention that had led to the war. Lincoln did not issue the Emancipation Proclamation simply because slavery is evil. For their part, the southerners who started the Civil War were not unanimously convinced that slavery was good. Rather, they were defending the only way of life they knew against a threat that, although nonviolent, was just as certain to end that way of life. They broke the peace for this legitimate reason. The fact that the order they were defending was less just than the order they were resisting is important but separate.

The American Founding Fathers, though committed to the proposition that the American form of government was the only one fit for free men, that it was the "new order of the ages" and the future of all mankind, resolved to be at peace with all the despots of the world. A large part of the reason is that they recognized that weak America had no other choice. But as Thomas Jefferson's letter to his friend

Thomas Leiper indicated, they looked forward to the day when they would have "a rod to shake over their heads that will make the stoutest of them tremble."[1] Nevertheless, it did not cross the Founding Fathers' minds that the United States would ever fight a world war to "make the world safe for democracy." Who were the Americans to claim the right to force, say, the Chinese to be free? And how could they assume responsibility for making sure that such vast works of cultural revolution would not yield something worse?

Only in the twentieth century, when American leaders had channeled the fervors of their vanishing religious faith into secular pursuits, did they fight wars for "unconditional surrender," to "end all wars," and to "make the world safe for democracy." Perhaps because American leaders valued the earthly goods at stake too highly and lacked prudence in making political strategy, the two world wars left more people under worse governments than before.

Early America did fight a distant war against North African pirates in order to defend the small but concrete good of unmolested navigation. It also went to war with the Indian tribes and with Mexico to secure for Americans the safe enjoyment of the lands they were settling. Did this good justify breaking the peace? The unofficial war with Mexico over Texas in 1836 and the official one of 1846–48 pose ethically straightforward questions. Mexico laid claim to vast, largely empty lands in North America. It did not try to restrict settlement by English-speaking Americans, nor did it warn the Americans that they would have to learn to live under Mexican rule. The Americans who poured into these lands preferred to live as they had and to resist Mexican despots. The U.S. government's support of American settlers in Mexican territory was no doubt influenced by the desire to spread the good of the American form of government. But the U.S. government did not send the settlers and it did not instigate the quarrels. When the quarrels came, the U.S. government's choice was between the evil of watching Mexican despots crush American settlers and the evil of joining a war that was already raging.

Much less straightforward are the issues surrounding the wars between Europeans and the Indians of America and the aborigines of Australia. The case of the Spanish conquest of America is an exception, because the Spaniards came unambiguously to exploit, enslave, and kill. The conquistadores treated the Indians as they had treated the Muslims they had earlier dispossessed or chased out of

Spain—and worse. In all other instances the Europeans did not enslave but sought to work the colonized land themselves. To say that these lands "belonged" to the natives is to use a concept entirely foreign to those natives. At the time, only Europeans, not Indians, bought, owned, and sold land. The "land deals" between European settlers and natives, including the one for some twenty-four dollars for Manhattan Island, were surely examples of different cultures talking past each other. The natives had no idea that the white man intended to have exclusive use of the land or that he intended to stay. On the other hand, the Europeans wrongly expected the natives to behave as Europeans. Add to this the natural preference for one's own way, and disdain mixed with fear of peoples so different, and it is not surprising that friction and massacres on both sides fueled wars as cruel as they were unequal. But where did justice lie?

In general, both the natives and the Europeans believed that they were endangered and fought for the defense of their ways. Moreover, because the civilization of the Europeans was superior in its capacity to accomplish things, it attracted the natives and thus destroyed their ways perhaps more efficiently than did violence. Violent and nonviolent conflict alike were less the result of decisions that can be judged just or unjust and more the consequence of events that flowed naturally—and tragically—out of the proximity of irreconcilable human differences.

In most wars, however, fighting for particular goods is never as urgent as fighting for the survival of a civilization. Which of the two princes claiming kinship to the deceased king shall rule? Will the Burgundian peasant pay his taxes to the duke or to the agent of the French king? Will Venetian or Genoese ships carry the bulk of silk and spices from the East to Europe? Will the French or German flag fly over Strasbourg? Will the Italian peninsula be ruled by various French- and German-speaking princes or by an Italian-speaking king? Thus stated, these "goods"—for which the majority of wars in our civilization have been fought—do not begin to justify breaking the peace. Yet, things are not so simple.

The various parties in former dynastic struggles were not morally equal (although in most cases they were not as unequal as they thought). Who would deny that it was just to raise an army against the mad and murderous Richard III? Surely anyone who lived at the time when Cesare Borgia appointed Remirro d' Orco to terrorize and "pacify" the city-states of Romagna would have been able to make a case to the duke of Milan (who was not a nice guy) and the Council of Venice—Borgia's opponents at that time—that it was their moral duty to send an army to end this oppression. In our time, few would dispute that the Tanzanian tyrant Julius Nyerere acted justly when he sent his army to help depose Idi Amin, the tyrant of neighboring Uganda, a man whose cruelty was of truly historic proportions.

There is no doubt that the various kings who gradually turned France into a unified state broke the peace and destroyed a relatively benign medieval order to do so. But the moral arguments that supported their actions cannot be easily dismissed. For hundreds of years English armies had been crisscrossing the land, causing much grief. Perhaps the principal reason they had been able to do so was the autonomy the duke of Burgundy and other nobles enjoyed. Moreover these nobles found much of their fun in life by fighting each other over insults, real or imagined. Thus, the kings who made war to subjugate their nobles saw themselves as farsighted defenders of the peace. Human nature being what it is, however, the kings then raised armies for bigger quarrels abroad, quarrels usually without moral significance.

The Genoese's and the Venetians' greedy wars over seaborne trade followed directly from clashes between individual merchants in foreign ports or between rival argosies at sea. These in turn were fueled by envy and the desire to reduce commercial competition. Ships' captains would return home to both cities, demand protection, and assure their fellow citizens that without it the city's economy would wane and everyone would starve. Fight, they would say, or watch the enemy starve your family. Only wisdom, prudence, and fortitude made war between these two cities sporadic rather than constant.

But what happens when people of one race, language, or religion are being ruled by people of a different race, language, or religion? Is it then not just to break the peace in order to change an unjust status quo? In fact, the wars of the nineteenth century were fought on the premise that the answer to this question is yes. But common sense requires distinctions. On the one hand, there was Muslim Turkey's rule of Christian Greece. Each year until the eighteenth century Turkish troops would exact from Christian communities a "tax" of their best boys. These would be taken away from their families forever and brought up as Muslim janissaries in the service of the sultan. Some would be castrated and employed as eunuchs. The only argument against waging war to topple this system was not whether the end was just, but whether there was a reasonable chance of success. The reasonable likelihood of success is a sine qua non of *jus ad bellum*. Human life is not to be hazarded lightly.

On the other hand, Austria's rule of Lombardy in the eighteenth and nineteenth centuries provides a contrary example. It is true that the prince spoke German and the subjects spoke Italian. But Milan was governed about as well as Vienna. The Italians who lusted for war with Austria adhered to the nationalistic (and neo-racist) tradition in which good government is no substitute for government by one's own kind. The wars of the Italian Risorgimento were not especially bloody. But, then again, they affected the moral tone of government on the peninsula little, if at all.

The extreme example of nationalist-racist reasoning applies to the British dominion in India. In 1919, after a British officer had put down a riot in Amritsar at the cost of 317 lives, the British viceroy, Viscount Chelmsford, objected on moral grounds. Previously, the British had no qualms about killing people by the hundreds in order to swiftly suppress mobs, reasoning that if they did otherwise, the Hindus, Muslims, Sikhs, Tamils, Dravidans, Afghans, and other groups of the Indian subcontinent would kill each other by the millions and the British by the thousands. In fact, the governor's decision in 1919, motivated by his sincere view that British rule in India was not morally defensible, opened the floodgates. During the 1920s and 1930s, as British units gradually withdrew from enforcing order in India, the toll from interracial rioting rose into the many thousands. When Britain finally withdrew in 1947, the ensuing intercommunity violence uprooted perhaps one hundred million people and claimed uncounted lives. The carving out of Pakistan in 1947 and the bloody secession of Bangladesh from Pakistan in 1970 did not end the intercommunity violence. The massacre of 1919 looms large in historical consequence, but imperceptible in quantitative comparison with what continues to happen in the area.

Nationalism is the most widespread excuse for war in our time. From Algeria to Indonesia people have convinced others to break the peace to take power in the name of their "kind." The notion of self-determination grew during the eighteenth and especially the nineteenth centuries and became somewhat associated with the idea of democracy. But in practice, few of those who have started wars in the name of nationalism have turned out to be democrats. Nor does democracy guarantee or even imply fair treatment of minorities. For example, had nineteenth-century Americans followed

Stephen Douglas rather than Abraham Lincoln and adopted a utilitarian attitude toward Negroes, the United States would not thereby have ceased to be a democracy. Indeed, the scope of popular choice would have been even wider. Douglas was "pro choice" on slavery, and argued that Lincoln would restrict the scope of private and public choice on the matter. Lincoln did not dispute that. Lincoln rather argued that a good democracy should not have certain choices.

Because race and nationality are morally neutral concepts, no argument can be made that any suffering is justified simply to give power and glory to one race or nationality. Indeed, any such argument would seem to be a good definition of injustice.

Another frequent justification for war is the fulfillment of obligations to others. World War I is often assumed to have started because of a system of alliances, and the formal cause of World War II was Britain's commitment to Poland. But in fact, few break the peace simply to keep their word. Nor can the moral worth of a personal commitment weigh in the balance against the horrors of war. So in fact, when leaders take their followers to war pursuant to a promise, the real reason is whatever led to their making the promise in the first place.

Perhaps the most common excuse for war is self-defense. If an army is marching toward one's home, one will naturally prepare to prevent armed men from roaming the streets as conquerors. Common sense says that conquerors can and often do take and destroy anything they want. Protection of the normal, decent order of a community is among the worthiest good that may be safeguarded by war. And indeed, a high percentage of those who have fought wars throughout the ages have done so because enemy armies were bearing down on them and they feared what would happen if they did not fight. The right of individual and collective self-defense is explicitly recognized in Article 51 of the UN Charter as the only justification for going to war.

But many more people throughout the ages have taken up arms while deceptively citing this fear. Still others have feared honestly, but mistakenly. Surely, leaders of aggressive states often try to convince their peoples that their attacks are really acts of defense. The German military surely succeeded in doing this in World War I. How does one evaluate the moral worth of preemptive attacks? In June 1967, immediately after trouncing Egypt and Syria in hostilities that had begun with a preemptive Israeli strike against their airfields, an interviewer asked Israel's General Moshe Dayan, "Who started this war?" Dayan told the TV cameras that Egypt had started the war by excluding Israeli ships from the Suez Canal, blockading the Gulf of 'Aqaba, and preparing for an invasion. All of that was so, and Egypt's media were full of threats to wipe the Jewish people off the face of the earth. Israel had merely beaten the Arabs to the punch. Dayan was correct, and Israel's attack was defensive, just as the United States Navy would have been acting defensively had it been able to attack the Japanese aircraft carriers that were moving into position to strike Pearl Harbor without waiting for their bombs and torpedoes to hit. The governing fact here is that the peace is broken by whoever makes the decision to break it. If the party that is to be attacked learns of this decision and strikes out first, its action cannot be called an act of aggression.

Perhaps the most common excuse for breaking the peace has been this claim that the other side was about to attack. The fact that most of these claims have been false does not deny that some have been true, while others have been authentic cases of misperception.

Yet not even a clear victim of aggression, like the United States after Pearl Harbor and Hitler's declaration of war, can escape the questions: What are our war aims? What are we fighting to achieve, and are these aims just? As we have seen, one of the characteristics of war is that people redefine their aims, and sometimes their character, in the course of the fighting. A country may at first attempt to simply protect itself. But what then? Perhaps the rarest outcome of any war is the reestablishment of the *statu quo ante bellum*. Hence, the moral quality of a country's goals necessarily changes as one's goals change.

For example, while the causes for which Britain and the United States entered into World War II—essentially self-protection against attack from Hitler and Tojo and, incidentally, reestablishing the rights of lesser nations from Poland to the Philippines—was just and achievable, by the end of the war U.S. aims had changed to making the world safe for the U.N. system. For the sake of this new "good," which required above all accommodating Stalin, the United States and Britain committed a variety of injustices—including abandoning the immediate goal for which several of the Allies had entered the war, namely, protecting Poland. Thus, at the end of World War II the United States and Britain were fighting on an ostensibly much higher, but actually much lower, moral plane than that upon which they had fought at the beginning.

The ends in themselves, however, justify nothing. Violence will not suffice if the fight is hopeless or if there is another way to achieve just goals.

During the Peloponnesian War, for example, the representatives of the neutral city of Melos were besieged by the much stronger Athenians, who sought to occupy their land and enlist them in an alliance. The Melians tried to dissuade the Athenians, until the latter ended the dialogue by declaring: "The strong do what they can, while the weak suffer what they must." At that point, was it right for the Melians to wage a hopeless fight? The Melians' goals were morally unexceptionable: to be left alone in peace in an honorable neutrality. But fighting could not bring peace—only death. The Melians fought anyway. As a consequence, their men were put to the sword and their women and children were sold into slavery. Surely the Melians' just ends did not justify their decision to resist, because the resistance was hopeless and out of proportion to the Athenians' demands.

Just ends and the absence of peaceful alternatives do not justify breaking the peace unless a plan has been reasonably formulated to bring success. For example, some have argued that between 1937 and 1941 the United States, together with the British and Dutch empires, so restricted Japan's access to raw materials, especially oil, that Japan was forced to choose between war and economic strangulation. But even if one accepts this theory, one is still compelled to agree that the Japanese never formulated a war plan to achieve anything. They knew that they could conquer the Philippines, Indochina, perhaps Singapore and Malaya, and perhaps put a big dent in the U.S. Pacific Fleet. But what could they expect after that? How could Japan compel Britain and, above all, the United States to let it retain any portion of its gains? The Japanese navy estimated the U.S. overall potential advantage over Japan at ten to one. Japan could scarcely think of conquering Hawaii, much less California or Washington, D.C. Nor did Japan build submarines and distribute its troops in the Pacific in order to form a strong defensive perimeter that would tire the United States and force it to negotiate. It just simply struck out ferociously to the very limit of its reach. And then it awaited disaster. If for no other reason, Japan's war was grossly unjust because it stood no chance of success.

In our day, the U.S. government under President Reagan repeatedly argued that the cause of the anti-Communist forces fighting in Nicaragua, Angola, and Afghanistan was just. Because these causes were just, said Reagan, it was also just for the United States to publicly associate itself with those causes and to send them some aid. But to achieve what? President Reagan never seriously addressed the question of what results could reasonably be expected from any given kind of association and any given level of aid. The United States never formulated any plan by which it could have caused these forces to win in any sense of the term. Over a period of years the United States consciously refused to supply these forces with the kinds and amounts of supplies that would have allowed them to make a serious try for victory. Nor did the United States ever consider isolating Nicaragua's and Angola's Communist governments from Soviet supply routes by air or sea blockades. Indeed, throughout the struggle, the United States maintained an embassy in two of these three countries under Communist regimes, recognizing them as the legitimate governments of their peoples. President Reagan's domestic opponents had more than a rhetorical point when they berated him for in effect making war against legitimate governments. Arguments for their illegitimacy were ready at hand, and Reagan sometimes voiced them. But his official acts belied them.

Thus, granting that the causes of the anti-Communist sides in these civil wars were just and weighty and that there was no alternative to war, one could still conclude that U.S. involvement on their side was unjust because it was not done as part of a plan reasonably calculated to bring about a new peace. The purpose of war is not to fight and die, or to temporize among contradictory lines of policy, but to win a peace worth winning.

Jus in Bello

Whereas the question of whether it is just to enter into a given war in a given set of circumstances is complex, the matter of just behavior in the course of war is governed by simple, straightforward rules. Alas, those rules are rarely observed, because even when war does not spring from hate, it inevitably engenders hate. As various exceptional leaders throughout history have shown, from Nicias in the

Peloponnesian War to Douglas MacArthur in World War II, it is possible not to succumb to hate's temptation to simply inflict pain on the enemy. But the sad fact is that the longer a war lasts, the more likely will hate drive it to irrational ends and unjust means.

The general rule is that the means used to fight the war may not outweigh the good that victory might bring. In other words, the means must not be allowed to dishonor the ends. The point of the rule is that the enemy in war is not so much a set of persons—much less whole peoples—but rather a set of evil intentions. It is imperative to defeat these intentions without hate. This rule of public life is identical to the private commandment to hate the sin while loving the sinner.

The specifics of the rule are that one must make reasonable efforts to spare noncombatants from harm and, indeed, that the harm inflicted in order to achieve the worthy ends of the war, even upon combatants, must be as minimal as possible. The rules boil down to discrimination, economy, and mercy.

DISCRIMINATION

Discrimination means that armed forces should fight armed forces and not ravage the enemy's countryside, cities, or economy. While it is permitted to "starve out" an army, blockades of whole countries, such as the ones that kept food from Germany in World Wars I and II, have traditionally been considered unjust means of warfare because they do not discriminate between combatants and noncombatants. By the same token, it has been a traditional rule of Western warfare that when an army takes possession of a city with the intention of using it as a fortress by which to fight another army, both armies must allow the civilian population of the city to depart in an orderly manner. This is what General Charles George ("Chinese") Gordon and his enemy, the Mahdi, Mohammed Ahmed, did before fighting the final battle of Khartoum in 1890. In other words, the corollary of the rule that armies may not make war on cities full of civilians is the rule that armies may not hide behind civilians.

Both the French and German armies respected this rule with regard to Paris during World War II. But in the battle of Leningrad the Soviet Union violated that rule, with disastrous results. The German army besieged the city. But on the northeastern side Leningrad has access to the rest of Russia through Lake Ladoga, which remained in Soviet hands. In the winter, good truck roads crossed the frozen lake, and ferries plied it in the summer. The Soviets could have let the civilians depart at any time. Instead, to maintain the fiction that the city was functioning normally, they prevented the population from leaving. Nor did they give adequate supplies to the population that they were forcibly keeping in harm's way. As a result, almost a million civilians, kept on a minimum diet of as little as 100 grams of black bread per day, died of starvation and disease.

Of course, discrimination above all means not intentionally killing civilians. Yet this is precisely what the United States did in World War II. Hiroshima was picked as a target for the atom bomb according to criteria laid down by James B. Conant, later Harvard's president: a factory complex full of workers, surrounded by closely packed workers' housing. Eighty thousand died. Upon Soviet request, the United States also carried out the most destructive raids of World War II against Dresden in 1945, specifically to kill Germans who were fleeing in front of the advancing Soviet armies. In a little over twenty-four hours, 135,000 people perished. The policy of strategic bombing, which meant the outright murder of millions, was ordered by the same President Roosevelt who at the outset of World War II had written to all combatants asking them not to bomb cities.

Why did this happen? In general, the Roosevelt administration was overcome by hate, an irrational and unjust desire to punish rather than to win, by a millennialist streak in President Roosevelt, and by a demagogic desire to show the American people that the relatives of those killing their relatives were being killed. In the specific case of Dresden, Roosevelt simply killed at Stalin's request. This, along with Roosevelt's delivery to Stalin—and certain death —of millions of prisoners of war and displaced persons, was intended to reassure Stalin of America's friendship. U.S. officials called this "Operation Keelhaul." There is no clearer example in history of two sets of murders—Dresden and Operation Keelhaul— executed to achieve the same end. One was undertaken as an act of war and the other as a peace offering. But murder delegitimizes peace just as much as it delegitimizes war.

The essence of both the practical and the ethical problem of warfare is "Whom shall we kill and why?" As the American nuclear targeters who tried to make concrete Robert McNamara's plan for killing 25 percent of the Soviet population discovered, random killing of an enemy population stands about as much chance of winning a war as a monkey at a typewriter has of tapping out a novel. The craft of the military leader is to cause death and destruction in the

manner most likely to prevent the enemy from effectively continuing the fight. Even shooting as many simple soldiers as possible all
along the line—imposing attrition—is such an inefficient, uncertain, and slow means of winning a war as to be immoral. Certainly
the specialized weapons, strategy, and training developed in the
history of war have been designed expressly to concentrate the killing at key points. Going after those whose death is most likely to stop
the killing is not only more ethical but also more effective militarily.

Taking this point to its logical conclusion, it is clear that the higher
the rank of the persons killed, the more likely they are to be carriers
of the purpose that is the legitimate target of hostilities. Hence, the
most discriminate, economical, effective, and moral act in World
War II surely would have been the killing of Adolf Hitler. The conclusion that follows from this runs directly counter to the conventional wisdom that has grown up recently about war, namely that
among its worst features is the assassination of individuals. But what
could be more just *and* economical than that those who are most
actively engaged in promoting a particular end should be the target
of those who oppose that end? What could be more unjust than going out of one's way to spare the leaders while targeting the poor
draftee—or, worse, his hungry family at home? No doubt leaders, or
those who fancy themselves as such, have a stake in defining war as
a kind of chess game in which the opposing kings (and their staffs)
are never taken, while they coolly maneuver their bloody pawns.
But the common sense of mankind, and the Western tradition of just
war in particular, reject this.

The high tide of this foolish reasoning may have come during the
Vietnam War. The CIA ran a project, code-named Phoenix, to secretly identify and to clandestinely kill the leaders of the Vietcong
infrastructure in South Vietnam. The numbers killed under this
program ran into the hundreds. When the program was disclosed,
editorials in the leading liberal dailies of the Western world den-
ounced it as the epitome of immorality. The chief complaint was
that the people killed were identified as enemies without the benefit
of trial. In other words, the killings were insufficiently discriminate.
No doubt, without attorneys and impartial juries (or for that matter,
with them) it is always possible to mistake someone's involvement
in an enterprise. Personal vengeance, mistaken identity, and mis-
leading circumstances often skew judgment. There are always more
perfect ways of assigning individual responsibility. But surely the
people killed under Project Phoenix were far more carefully chosen

than the rank-and-file Vietcong who fell by the tens of thousands on the battlefield. Did the moralists who attacked Project Phoenix mean to assert that the rank-and-file Vietcong, many of whom were draftees, should be killed while their leaders were spared? They certainly did not say this. The moralists were not advancing a particular view of justice, they were blaming the U.S. government for being on the side they opposed. The U.S. government, for its part, did not force a serious debate by asking the moralists, "Whom do you suggest that we kill in order to end this war?"

If there had been a debate rather than a shouting match the moralists' answer would have boiled down to this: we oppose this killing precisely because it begins to strike at the heart of the anti–U.S. forces in Vietnam—forces we want to see succeed. Of course, the critics of Project Phoenix were not eager to talk about whom they wanted to see win the Vietnam War, so they used expressions of moral outrage to batter the United States while partially hiding their anti–U.S. partisanship.

To expose and counter this, the U.S. government's position would have had to boil down to this: We want to kill these people because killing them is the quickest, most effective way to win the war. But if Presidents Johnson or Nixon had argued this, one might well have asked them: "If you are really interested in winning this war quickly, at the lowest cost in lives, while killing only those who most fully embody the purpose you are trying to frustrate, why then don't you bomb or invade to destroy North Vietnam's politburo?" But the U.S. government was not interested in victory, and it did not want to explain why. Thus, it was uncomfortable explaining why it was killing anyone. So both sides, each for their own reasons, avoided a debate that would have been enlightening.

For similar but somewhat reversed reasons the U.S. government and its critics in the mid-1980s avoided debating the morality of assisting the Afghan mujahedeen's efforts to assassinate Soviet officials in that country. The same moralists within the U.S. government who had opposed the Phoenix program were aghast that the Afghans were using U.S. weapons for assassinations and argued internally that U.S. assistance to the Afghans violated an internal government prohibition against direct or indirect assassination. As in the Vietnam War, they were unwilling to suggest that it would be better to shoot enemy draftees while sparing Communist officials. But this time they were also unwilling to entirely oppose U.S. involvement in the war. So they did not argue the matter in public. On the other hand, since the U.S. government was again unwilling to consider the topic of victory, it once again welcomed the chance not to debate the matter.

The U.S. government did not have such an easy time in 1986 avoiding the question of whether it was (or should have been) trying to kill Libya's dictator, Muammar Qaddafi. In 1981–82 official Washington accepted intelligence reports to the effect that Qaddafi had dispatched "hit teams" to kill the U.S. president. During the following years, the United States gathered incontrovertible evidence that Qaddafi had ordered or sponsored a series of murderous acts against U.S. and European citizens culminating in the bombing of a Berlin discotheque frequented by Americans. The United States launched a strike by a squadron of FB-111 bombers against Qaddafi's headquarters. Qaddafi was not killed, but about one hundred of his men were. A baby girl described as his daughter was also reported killed. The president and the secretary of state categorically denied any intention of killing Qaddafi or of overthrowing his government. What, then, one may ask, was the point of bombing his headquarters? Did the United States intend to kill the one hundred Libyan soldiers and the baby girl? If so, why? And if not, then whom had the U.S. government intended to kill and to what end? The U.S. government's official explanation that it had struck at the "infrastructure" of Libyan terrorism did not dispel doubts about the government's moral sense, or about its competence.

The proposition that leaders should be spared the consequences of war, then, is a product less of moral and practical reasoning than of the contemporary lack of willingness (or perhaps capacity) to think through difficult questions.

The most shocking case of lack of discrimination in warfare is terrorism. Indeed, it is precisely the willingness to target noncombatants, rather than enemy officials, that qualifies one for the label of "terrorist." The terrorist may argue that his ends are very worthy, that given his relative weakness he cannot afford to fight with the enemy's armed forces, and that hence he is compelled to kill those who cannot defend themselves. By detonating bombs in marketplaces or machine-gunning airports, bus stops, and schools, he may argue that he can force the enemy either to give in to his demands or take self-destructive measures in an effort to establish security. But the terrorist is wrong. He does not *have to* fight. Indeed, if the only means at his disposal are the intentional harming of innocents, the Western tradition says that he *must not* fight. Nothing in Western tradition sanctions the intentional as opposed to the collateral (un-intentional) harming of innocents. Of course, most terrorists come from outside the Western tradition and openly intend to tear it down. This does not change the character of their acts. Much less does it warrant the judgment that there is no moral difference be-tween striking innocents and sparing them or that innocence is a matter of opinion.

By far the largest acts of nondiscrimination in modern history have been committed by governments. During World War I, the German government enslaved—there is no better word for it—400,000 civilians in occupied Belgium and France and deported them to Germany to work. Conditions were so harsh that one in ten died. By World War II, the practice of enslaving occupied popula-tions had become almost normal and had acquired a deadly twist: the slaves were literally used up and their remains recycled. By deriving maximum work for minimum food and shelter until the slaves died, the enslaving power both increased war production and freed itself of potential trouble in the future. In World War II, Ger-many, the Soviet Union, and Japan together may have enslaved 30 million human beings, perhaps two-thirds of whom had their lives sucked out of them. Needless to say, the Western tradition judges that if this is what it takes to win a war, winning is then absolutely not worth it.

MERCY

Mercy is a duty not only toward noncombatants but to enemy combatants as well. No one can set out precisely beforehand how much violence, how much killing, will be required to cause an enemy to stop resisting, and how much restraint it will be possible to exercise. But the rule of the West has been not to go beyond what the battle against combatants requires and that as soon as resistance stops one should show mercy.

The issue of mercy chiefly concerns prisoners of war. The tradi-tional Western teaching is that as soon as an enemy is wounded, lays down his weapons, or otherwise ceases to pursue the purpose of the war, he ceases to be an enemy to be killed and becomes someone to be treated in a brotherly fashion. This is more easily taught than done. An enemy may have just finished killing a soldier's friends. Because of him the soldier will have suffered fear, privation, expo-sure, fatigue, and pain. Hatred and the desire to kill the enemy have helped to sustain the soldier in battle. What should compel him to reverse violent feelings just because the enemy is wounded or has surrendered, just when the occasion is at hand to satisfy them all? Only the Western tradition of the just war, inspired by Christianity.

In the West, the incidence of this difficult, demanding mercy has been remarkable. In the best of times regarding these matters—the wars between King Louis XIV of France and Queen Anne of England—prisoners of war were often released to return home on "parole," that is, in return for the promise that they would not fight again in that war. As late as World War I, the German army picked up Captain Charles de Gaulle, who was severely wounded on the battlefield, and provided him with conditions under which he not only recovered but wrote a book while giving a course on military history to his fellow prisoners. Even under Nazi influence, the German army of World War II lapsed only occasionally from its proper treatment of *Western* prisoners of war.[2] American troops, for their part, might well win the prize as the group by which one would most enjoy being captured. Any number of German (not to mention Italian) POWs shipped to the United States during World War II fell in love with the country. Lieutenant Hans Sennholtz of Germany, for example, became an honorary citizen of the town in New Mexico where his prison camp was located. Upon repatriation he applied for U.S. citizenship, returned to the United States, and taught economics. He was one of about 5,000 (out of 375,000) Germans held in the United States who later managed to emigrate to the land of their captivity.[3]

But the lot of most prisoners in most wars is one of cruel abuse and death. It is noteworthy that the great abuses have not resulted from overflowing passions on the battlefield, but rather from policy and culture on the homefront. The greatest act of cruelty in Thucydides' Peloponnesian War was the imprisonment of the entire Athenian expeditionary force in the Syracusan quarries. There, without even the capacity to dispose of their comrades' corpses, much less their own excrement, the Athenians suffered all the worst things that can possibly befall men.

The crusaders and the combatants in the religious wars of the sixteenth and seventeenth centuries, for example, did not believe that the rules of war applied to infidels or that they had any obligation to keep their promises to infidels. Under this misunderstanding, tens of thousands of prisoners were put to the sword. Another common error was committed by General Santa Ana at the Alamo. In

order to encourage surrender, he set a deadline after which surrender would no longer be accepted. Then he sounded the *deguelo*,
the order to slit the throats of all who were wounded or captured.
Perhaps just as famous is Shakespeare's rendition of Henry V's
warning to the people of Harfleur:

> The gates of mercy shall be all shut up,
> And the flesh'd soldier, rough and hard of heart,
> In liberty of bloody hand shall range
> ... mowing like grass
> Your fresh-fair virgins and your flow'ring infants.
> . . . .
> If not, why, in a moment look to see
> The blind and bloody soldier with foul hand
> Defile the locks of your shrill-shrieking daughters;
> Your fathers taken by the silver beards,
> And their most reverend heads dash'd to the walls, ...
>
> (*King Henry V* 3.3.10–37)

But encouraging surrender is no excuse for killing harmless human
beings. The point of war is supposed to be the peace of the living, not
of the dead.

Totalitarians, however, do not understand this. If they have any
concept of peace at all, it is indeed the peace of the dead. Because
they fight wars to extinguish enemy classes or races, they embody
the opposite of mercy. While German generals treated prisoners
on the western front well, they boasted that they had reduced their
Russian prisoners of war to "eating each other." The survivors had
the life sucked out of them through slave labor.[4] Of course, those
who survived this ordeal were handed over to Stalin at the end of
the war; he then had them killed because they had committed the
crime of surrendering in the first place! The Soviets, for their part,
also efficiently "used up" their millions of German POWs. The most
typical, though far from the biggest, act of deliberate totalitarian
cruelty was the Soviet Union's murder of 15,000 Polish officer prisoners in the Katyn Forest (and in two camps) in order to deprive
Polish society of its leadership. Even if the totalitarians' ends had
been noble, such means wholly discredit them.

The behavior of Japanese troops in World War II toward all their
captives demonstrates another sad fact. Some people simply get satisfaction by making others suffer. The Japanese were not out to

exterminate any class or race. They simply went out of their way to kill, rape, maim, starve, and humiliate. Southeast Asia will remember them for a thousand years. When this Asian style of warfare blends with the totalitarian style, there occurs the treatment that American POWs received in Korea and Vietnam. Now, the Western tradition, codified in the Geneva Convention, states clearly that not only are prisoners to be left unharmed, they also may not be compelled to act against their country or to be used as hostages in any way. Yet these two Asian Communist regimes literally "used up" a significant proportion of its American POWs by torturing them into making statements injurious to their country's war effort and to turn them into pitiable objects that should be ransomed in a hurry. In the end, North Korea and North Vietnam let out of captivity only those they had not crippled or disfigured. The others may be dead. Or they may be held as amusements to confirm their captors' peculiar kind of self-esteem.

Proportionality and Punishment

As if *jus ad bellum* and *jus in bello* were not concepts difficult enough in themselves, the Western tradition holds that for a war to be deemed just, there must be a reasonable proportion between the ends sought and the means used, even when these means are just and necessary in themselves. Clearly, there can be no strictly defined rules. Rather, the rule is that one must constantly ask: Is this worth it? Would any reasonable man unaffected by the passions of the moment think it worthwhile to go through all of *this* for *that*?

Who is to judge? In practice, the victors often punish the vanquished. But all men can exercise their judgment at all times. The just war tradition aims less at prescribing the punishment imposed by winners than it does to forming the consciences of the combatants. The attempts to enforce the laws of war after World War II show why.

In the Pacific theater General MacArthur prosecuted and the U.S. government hanged General Yamashita for his mistreatment of prisoners and for the rape of Manila. One soldier imposed on another soldier his standards of soldiering, period. But the trials of the German leaders at Nuremberg were problematic—above all, because the Soviets were among the judges. Surely, the Soviets were winners. But they had no other claims to judgeship. If nothing else discredited the Nuremberg trials it was Molotov helping to hang Ribbentrop for the offense of having joined him in signing the Molotov-Ribbentrop pact that started World War II. Moreover, the Allies had weakened their moral basis for judgment through their policy of bombing civilians. If Germany and Japan had won, they would have had a good case for hanging Generals "Hap" Arnold and Ira Eaker of the United States Army Air Corps, as well as Roosevelt, for breaches of *jus in bello*. Of course, Ribbentrop would have hanged Molotov for breaches of *jus ad bellum*. But that would have been no more ludicrous than what actually happened. In sum, the flawed attempt to apply ethical guidelines as if they were criminal laws brought undeserved discredit upon those guidelines.

Justice and War in the Nuclear Age

How can there be proportion between ends and means if the means of war happen to be inherently disproportionate wreckers of the planet? The question carries its own answer. But the premise of the question is wrong. For better or for worse, nuclear weapons are not necessarily disproportionate tools any more than are fire and sword. With nuclear weapons, as with all others, the primordial question remains: Whom should we kill and why?

As we have seen in chapter 7, there is no basis for the speculation that the widespread use of nuclear weapons would alter the world's climate or significantly poison the environment beyond the areas where they were employed for more than a few weeks. Nuclear weapons certainly do inflict collateral damage. But the effects of nuclear weapons, both direct and collateral, are finite and calculable. Moreover, these effects vary widely according to the design of the weapons and how they are used. Thus, to speak about the ethics of using nuclear weapons as if there were no difference between a 1-kiloton-enhanced radiation weapon delivered precisely on tanks attacking a town and a 1-megaton weapon delivered on a square mile of high-rise apartments makes no sense. Nor will it avail to overlook such distinctions by declaring that any use of nuclear weapons by anyone will lead all parties to disgorge their stocks of them onto residential areas while neglecting rational military uses. Clearly, it is no more likely—and it may be less likely—that people will jeopardize their own interests when nuclear weapons are used than when other kinds are involved. The issue, then, is which uses of nuclear weapons that self-interest may inspire are more just and which uses are less just?

This question, like all the others regarding *jus in bello*, is logically dependent on the reasons why the combatants may be fighting, which falls into the domain of *jus ad bellum*. It so happens that nuclear weapons have become prominent during a time when the "issue" dividing the great powers of the day are as important as any that ever set nations against one another. The Marxist-Leninist objective of the Soviet Union, emblazoned on buildings in every city and taught in every school, is the destruction of every non-Communist regime on earth. The official position of the Soviet Union is that this destruction need not necessarily occur through war, indeed, that it would be desirable for other "ruling classes" to give way to the new order peacefully, but that this cannot be expected. If a transition were to be peaceful, this would happen, in the words of the 20th Party Congress, "not because the capitalists have become wiser and more benevolent," but because they have become militarily weaker. The shadow of the Soviet Union's military power is the only hope for peace and the only assurance of victory. This victory does not necessarily involve running new flags up flagpoles. It does involve physically eliminating the people who had helped mold the former society, and then changing the lives of the survivors. It means doing away with religion, emplacing a new history on the lips of adults and in the minds of schoolchildren, and instituting compulsory public obedience to Marxism-Leninism—regardless of the leadership's private unbelief. The declared objective of the U.S. government, and of the North Atlantic Alliance, and of all non-Communist governments, is that none of this shall come to pass.

From the point of view of the Soviet Union, the question of justice with regard to nuclear war is straightforward. One cannot make the world safe for Marxism-Leninism by destroying it. But short of wholesale destruction, the question is framed in Lenin's words: "Justice? For what class?" In other words, with or without nuclear weapons, the most just course of action is the one that best advances the interests of the vanguard of the world's proletariat, the Communist party of the Soviet Union. The end justifies the means by definition.

In operational terms, this means that nuclear weapons are to be used like any other weapons—to defeat the enemy while paying reasonable attention to avoiding collateral damage. But nuclear weapons are not considered efficient, discriminatory tools for physically eliminating the class enemy. That is the job of commissars.

But what does the Western tradition have to say? Surely it recognizes that preventing the physical murder and mental subjugation at the heart of the Soviet objective is worth killing and dying for. But how much? Surely the Western tradition also rejects the notion that the ends justify the means. So the ethical question for the West with regard to nuclear weapons depends in large part on a practical one. Can it or can it not devise ways of using nuclear weapons that are in fact effective in bringing about victory and that cause no more harm than is proportionate to the good that victory brings or to the evil that victory avoids?

The great problem in the West is that utopian hopes and fears regarding nuclear weapons have obscured the moral dimensions of practical choices with regard to what nuclear weapons we should have and how we should prepare to employ them. With nuclear weapons, as with others, the question is, "Whom do we shoot and why?" Few realize that the question, "Do we nuke Moscow?" is meaningless in practice. Where, in a Moscow area that has grown to 50 miles by 50 miles (2,500 square miles), do you want to put down our four- to ten-square-mile circles of destruction? Are we after the population? If so, which sector? Are we after industrial plants? If so, which ones? How about the military? But the Moscow area has perhaps 300 distinct military targets, most well hardened. Which should be hit? The moral significance of such questions is no smaller than their military significance.

The doctrine of Mutual Assured Destruction (MAD), which grew out of Bernard Brodie's academic speculation in 1946 and which Secretary of Defense Robert McNamara imposed on the U.S. military in the mid-1960s, attempted to get away from both the military and moral problems by threatening to make nuclear war so overwhelmingly destructive that no one would contemplate it as a rational alternative. We have previously examined the practical difficulties of the "MAD threat" designed to kill 25 percent of the Soviet population and 50 percent of Soviet industry. But the moral problems with this threat are as great. On what *moral* basis could the United States choose those whom it intends to kill? Surely, the fact that a person happens to live in a place that is both heavily populated and unprotected does not make him a carrier of the evil purpose, the negation of which is the legitimate purpose of war. On the contrary, those whom Communist regimes leave unprotected are precisely the ones *least* connected with their purposes. So, simply trying to fill the MAD quota by killing those who can easily be killed is doubly unjust.

As soon as one begins to ask *which* sectors of the population—other than simply the ones who are most accessible—ought to be the targets for one's nuclear weapons, one has already crossed an intellectual divide. Even if the questions are formulated in MAD terms —for example, "Whose deaths will delay national recovery longest?"—one has already begun to discriminate. And if one admits discrimination, then one cannot help but face the question, "Is it worse to kill someone because he may do some good to his country in the future, or is it worse to kill someone because he may do some harm to our country in the present?" But the moment that one accepts the notion that the only justification for killing in war is to prevent harm, one has clearly left MAD behind. At that point, even though one is still talking about nuclear weapons, the focus of the discussion returns squarely to the central question of *jus in bello*: how to achieve victory while causing, and allowing, the least possible harm.

The practical solution stems from the fact that nuclear weapons and the means of delivering them are relatively rare and expensive. Instead of people, they themselves are the most reasonable targets. Other, non-nuclear, military forces would be secondary targets. Ideally, these things could be destroyed without killing anyone unconnected with their operation. But in practice, nuclear weapons, just like other kinds of weapons, will always cause collateral damage. But how much?

Because nuclear-tipped ballistic missiles and planes loaded with nuclear bombs have always been based in out-of-the-way places such as Siberia and North Dakota, the expected collateral damage from attempts at striking such devices has always been small, even when the accuracy for striking them was low (about half a mile) and the bombs had to deliver a huge payload of about 25 megatons. Nowadays, ICBMs can hit within 200 yards of their targets and hence need to carry carry only between three-tenths (U.S.) and seven-tenths (USSR) of a megaton. The extent of probable collateral damage has therefore shrunk. Certainly the collateral damage expected in a nuclear attack on a missile field in Siberia would be much below the civilian devastation that resulted from the U.S.-British iron-bomb raids on the ball-bearing plant in Schweinfurt during World War II. Expected increases in accuracy and decreases in yield can be expected to shrink collateral damage even further. Of course, the ideal means of completely disarming an opponent of his nuclear arsenal without collateral damage is to intercept that arsenal in flight. Thus antiaircraft and antimissile systems are the most discriminating, most effective, and least harmful means of combat in the nuclear age.

Yet in the West—certainly not in the Soviet Union—there is an influential body of opinion that holds that the more discriminating and less collaterally damaging a weapon is, the more immoral it must necessarily be. This is because its very effectiveness and reasonableness make it more likely to be used. According to that point of view, a weapon that produces indiscriminate, mass destruction is much more just, because ipso facto, it is less likely to be used. Now, this view rests on the distinction between threatening to use and actually using weapons. Nobody contends, or could ever contend, that to actually try to kill innocents is a good thing. But many contend that it is acceptable to *threaten* to kill innocents, *so long as there is no intention to ever carry out the threat.* The moral status of a bluff advertised as a bluff is equal to its effectiveness. The enemy is certain to disregard the threat. Why should he not? The only people who are likely to believe this advertised falsehood are the ones who advertise it.

But why would any country promise that it would slaughter innocents, which would be at once counterproductive and immoral, and at the same time promise not to do it? Clearly this is not a strategy. It is an intellectual game that serves to push out of the forefront of our minds the fact that certain unpleasant choices exist. Yet they do exist. Nuclear weapons exist. They have finite effects. Hence, no country can avoid choosing where they should be shot, what they should destroy, whom they should kill, and whom they should spare. Those who follow this line of logic argue that it would be most moral and effective for the West to prepare—should war come—to destroy Soviet nuclear weapons both on the ground and in flight.

Those who oppose this logic argue that such preparations would provoke the Soviet Union into war. Sometimes they note the Soviet Union's preparations for a disarming strike, but always they recommend that the West should maintain only enough nuclear weapons so that a few would survive such a Soviet disarming strike, to inflict mindless damage upon Soviet society. Such weapons should threaten, but under no circumstances should the United States actually inflict such damage. This line of logic concludes that the Soviet leaders would be deterred by the knowledge that this capability existed.

But why should they be? They know that the Western moralists who follow this line of logic intend not to shoot. More important, they know that circumstances would prevent these moralists from changing their minds. Anyone who faced the alternative of shooting or not shooting nuclear weapons at useless targets would be forced to confront the practical choices they had fled from in the past. In the glare of war, Western leaders would realize that their previous choices now left them with only two alternatives: murder and suicide on the one hand, and surrender on the other. Surrender would make more sense to any rational human being.

In sum, nuclear weapons, like all other weapons, have moral implications not only because they can be used to kill some and spare others, but because they can be the object of miscalculations so great as to render unjust basic choices about war and peace.

PART III

How Wars End

CHAPTER
11

MAKING PEACE

Both parties deprecated war; but one of them would *make* war rather than let the nation survive; and the other would *accept* war rather than let it perish. And the war came....

... with malice toward none; with charity for all; with firmness in the right, as God gives us to see the right, let us strive on to finish the work we are in; to bind up the nation's wounds; to care for him who shall have borne the battle, and for his widow, and his orphan—to do all which may achieve and cherish a just, and a lasting peace, among ourselves and with all nations.

—ABRAHAM LINCOLN

FIGHTING STOPS when at least one of the parties to the war changes its objective enough so that *it appears* that mutual satisfaction can occur without further violence. At the very least the loser gives up his quest and claims. Perhaps he pays a ransom. Often, he gives up his means of future self-defense as well. The loser asks for the armistice in the hope of cutting his losses, to stop the winner from doing any more damage. The winner, for his part, gives certain assurances in exchange for the surrender, rather than forcing every last man on the losing side to fight to the death.

Contrary to the belief of many, finishing off a war is even more painful and problematic than starting one. That is because the cessation of hostilities is fraught with the possibility of betrayal. The winner fears that the loser may just be gaining a respite, while the loser fears that as soon as he lays down his arms the winner will fall on him and destroy him all the more easily. Either or both fears may be well grounded. In peacemaking, precisely as in warmaking, everything depends on intentions, capacity, skill, and luck.

Regardless of the outcome, the ending of a war involves some kind of agreement between the winner and loser. The immediate consequences of the capitulation depend on how the agreement is carried out, which in turn shapes the kind of peace that follows. Let us look in turn at negotiations, at the various consequence of capitulation, and at several kinds of peace.

Negotiations

Since surrendering an army, a cause, or a nation is a complex matter, negotiations are almost always necessary. Yet thinking of negotiations as the harbinger of peace is at least premature and often mistaken. When two sides meet to negotiate an armistice, each side's intentions are still not obvious, even in the clearest of circumstances. Gibbon, for example, tells of the meeting in A.D. 410 between Alaric, king of the Goths, and the ambassadors of a Rome whose armies had ceased to exist. The Romans demanded a fair and honorable surrender. If Alaric refused this, they said, he would have to confront a warlike people who would sell their lives dearly. Alaric knew that the Romans were blowing smoke, and he quickly blew it away. He laughed, expressing "his contempt for the menaces of an unwarlike populace, enervated by luxury before they were emaciated by famine." He made it clear that he wanted to sack Rome. "The ministers of the Senate," says Gibbon, then "presumed to ask in a modest and suppliant tone, 'If such, O King, are your demands, what do you intend to leave us?' 'Your lives,' replied the haughty conqueror."[1] The Romans knew perfectly well that once they opened the city gates, the Goths would be able to take their lives as well, and even more easily. But they correctly decided that under the circumstances the best chance of saving their lives lay in appeasing Alaric.

Sometimes there is even less to negotiations than that. In 1945, especially after Hitler's death on April 30, the German high command was frantic to surrender to the Western Allies. Any man who surrendered to them, they reasoned, was a life saved. By contrast, any man who surrendered to the Soviets was a life likely to be lost in captivity far more painfully than in battle. However, the policy of the United States, enforced on Britain and France, was that only "simultaneous and unconditional" surrender of German forces on all fronts would be accepted. Nevertheless, in the final weeks individual Allied commanders were accepting the surrender of countless individual German military units. Commanders from sergeants to generals were not about to waste the lives of their men killing Germans who wanted to lay down their arms. Thus, in the final week of the war, Allied forces moved into Germany virtually without opposition, "capturing" millions of willing prisoners, while in the east, Germans resisted Soviet forces as best they could or moved westward to surrender to the Americans. Grand Admiral Doenitz, on whom authority had fallen after Hitler's suicide, and the German military representatives at General Eisenhower's headquarters in Reims, France tried to prolong talks to allow this process to continue. Finally, threatened with the prospect that the West would stop accepting military surrenders, the Germans at Reims signed a general cease-fire that included an order for all German troops, including ones facing the Soviets, to stay where they were. The Germans had gotten the most they could from the negotiations under the circumstances.[2]

The most common fear among those who are about to lay down their arms is: Will the winner now slaughter us? As we have mentioned, this sort of thing is all too common, even when the winning commanders try to prevent it. For example, on the evening of Waterloo some Prussian troops bayoneted disarmed French soldiers. Negotiations, however, can do little to ease this fear or to prevent slaughter. At most they can serve to get a clearer picture of the winner's intentions. But there is no insurance. In the end, armistices are acts of faith, good or bad.

Often, however, there is much more to negotiations than protecting lives and easing the transition to peace. That is because the disparity of power is seldom so great as to really convince the loser that he has lost, or the winner that he has won. Often, the very process of negotiation serves not so much to ratify the verdict of arms as to contribute to it. The outstanding examples are from our own time, namely, the protracted "peace" negotiations between the United States and various Communist powers. The first of these concerned Korea.

By 1951, the military situation on the Korean peninsula was clear. The United States had so much firepower that any Chinese offensive across the front on the 38th parallel could only result in mass slaughter of Chinese troops. But the United States had decided that it did not want to advance beyond the 38th parallel. Yet those who expected the negotiations to quickly ratify these fundamental facts and lead to a peaceful division of Korea were surprised by the attitude of the Chinese Communists. The Chinese harshly raised points of protocol, charged the Americans with every imaginable wrong-doing, used the suffering of American prisoners of war as a lever, and demanded everything from territorial concessions to a say in the future of South Korea. Above all, during the negotiations the Chinese kept fighting. They did not attempt a breakthrough. This might have forced the United States to reassess its policy of not conquering North Korea and not supporting a challenge to the newly established Communist regime in Peking. Instead, the Chinese launched local attacks to cause American casualties. In fact, about as many Americans died in Korea during the negotiations than before the start of negotiations.[3]

Surely the Chinese negotiators were not interested in stopping the fighting. Rather, they used the negotiations to reinforce American reluctance to wage a decisive war against them. Meanwhile, they themselves continued to fight in a way that could not be militarily decisive but that would pile up casualties the Americans could only regard as meaningless. The longer this process continued, reasoned the Chinese, the likelier that the Americans would give them "peace" terms under which they could eventually win the war. Thus, the negotiations wore on in an entangling mess of meaningless detail. However, in 1953, after the Eisenhower administration took office on a platform of "rolling back" Communist influence world-wide, and the Chinese government was informed that B-29 bombers armed with atom bombs were warming up on American runways in Japan, the complexities melted away. The Chinese quickly agreed to formalize the status that had existed since 1951.

During 1965–73, the government of North Vietnam wholly learned the lessons of Korea, while the U.S. government mostly forgot them. The United States fought the Vietnam War for two objectives: to achieve a negotiated settlement, and to "let South

Vietnam choose its own form of government." From the very beginning, these objectives (which for the most part were mutually contradictory) competed for primacy within the U.S. government. Since North Vietnam's sole objective (other than the survival of its regime) was to take over the South, the U.S. government could achieve both of its objectives only by defeating North Vietnam and threatening the Communist regime there. But the U.S. government refused to contemplate this. Thus, the U.S. government's eagerness for negotiations amounted to an incipient preference for agreement with North Vietnam over the independence of South Vietnam. This had been clear since 1968, when the United States first stopped its already very limited bombing of targets in North Vietnam in order to "signal" its good faith and to entice North Vietnam to the negotiating table. North Vietnam came to the table with the intention of turning the U.S. government's preference for an agreement into an active abandonment of South Vietnam. The North knew that the U.S. government valued negotiations not so much for what they could bring about in Southeast Asia as for its own internal reasons. Thus, because the United States would be reluctant to carry out any military act that might break them off, the negotiations assured North Vietnam that the war would drag on indecisively. North Vietnam was quite content with that, precisely because the United States could not be. Thus, between 1968 and 1972, the Vietnam negotiations followed the Korean pattern.

In December 1972, the newly reelected Nixon administration brought the negotiations to a climax by seemingly retracing the steps the United States had taken twenty years earlier in Korea. It resumed, and drastically changed the pattern of bombing in North Vietnam in a way that augured the collapse of the regime. Instantly the complexity that had bedeviled the negotiations vanished, and North Vietnam agreed to all American demands. But there was a vital difference between the Vietnam and Korea negotiations: the nature of the American demands. In Korea, the United States had held off the Damocles' sword in exchange for the enemy effectively giving up the fight. The U.S. Eighth Army has remained in Korea to guarantee that result by threatening war against the North Korean regime lest it renege. But in Vietnam the price for withholding doom was simply to allow the United States to withdraw from the entire area with a semblance of honor—that is, the return of some, if not all, U.S. prisoners plus a "decent interval" between America's withdrawal and North Vietnam's final, victorious offensive.

It is impossible to know in retrospect how North Vietnam would have reacted to the Americans' final act of pressure in the negotiations had the United States meant to enforce the terms of the agreement so that North Vietnam would have had to give up the objectives for which it had fought the war. At the time of the Nixon bombing campaign of December 1972, North Vietnam *could not have been entirely certain* that the United States had abandoned its commitment to South Vietnam. *Conceivably* the United States might have insisted, as it did after signing the Korean armistice, that its adversary abide scrupulously by the agreement. But whereas the United States had left the Eighth Army in Korea as a living pledge, in 1972–73 the U.S. government advertised that American combat troops would not return to Vietnam no matter what happened. So why would North Vietnam not have been in a hurry to sign a piece of paper that relieved it of an immediate threat, made it much less likely that the threat would ever return, and portended the achievement of all its war aims? The winner surrendered to the loser. This was one of the rare instances in which what happened at the negotiating table was out of proportion with what was happening on the battlefield. However, the outcome reflected very accurately the results of a decade of political struggle between the Soviet bloc and the United States.

The experiences of Korea and Vietnam show unmistakably how silly it is to regard negotiations as anything but part and parcel of the war effort. The American leaders' blind faith in compromise and their unwillingness to realize that any agreement with an enemy is meaningful only insofar as it is based on both a willingness and an ability to continue fighting can only be characterized as ignorance about the fundamentals.

The whole point of negotiations at the end of a war, just like negotiations prior to or during a war, is for each side to determine what the other side is and is not willing to kill and die for, to relate that to what one's own side is willing to kill and die for, and then to make a deal with the other side to advance one's own interests as best one can. In fact, at the outset of negotiations one does not know whether the end of the war is at hand because one does not know the other side's intentions. As the examples of Korea and Vietnam show, it is possible to influence an opponent's intentions by and during negotiations. But the chief means of doing this is to somehow drive for victory. Absent this, one is really negotiating one's own defeat.

The clearest example of this is the negotiations held in 1988 between the United States and the Soviet Union over the future of Afghanistan. Immediately after the Soviet Union invaded Afghanistan in 1979, the United States began to supply arms to the many Afghan resistance groups that sprang up. Until 1986, when the United States finally began to supply serious antiaircraft missiles to the Afghans, the Soviet Union regarded the U.S. effort as the mere irritant it was. But in 1987, faced with a reasonably well-supplied resistance, the Soviet Union began a diplomatic effort to end U.S. supplies to the Afghans. The Soviets proposed to withdraw their troops in exchange for the cessation of aid to the Afghans. Did the Soviets intend to stand by and watch the destruction of the Afghan government they had created? The principal American negotiators did not ask. They *assumed* that the Soviets had decided to give up their war goals. They *assumed* that the Soviet objective in the negotiations was merely to lessen the resistance's military pressure during their withdrawal so that the Afghan mujahedeen would not chase Soviet troops back to the Soviet border.

Yet these assumptions did not make sense. If the Soviets really wanted to give up their war aims, why did they not say so? If they really wanted to be rid of the war and of Afghanistan, why did they not simply pull out their troops? But although some troops left, other troops stayed. If they really wanted to cover the withdrawal, why did they not simply ask the West to restrain the mujahedeen during the withdrawal? Indeed, they might have asked the mujahedeen directly. After all, few mujahedeen would want to risk getting killed to liberate a country that was obviously being liberated anyway. They would save their sharp knives to settle scores with the collaborators whom the Soviets intended to abandon, just as the U.S. government abandoned thousands of its collaborators in Vietnam. Yet the Soviet negotiators asked for none of these things.

Instead, they insisted on a commitment that the United States cut off aid to the mujahedeen. Everything else in the negotiations was nebulous except that. The American negotiators hardly noticed that the Soviets were making no commitments to stop helping their Afghan puppets. No doubt, the very mention of the possibility of Soviet withdrawal must have depressed the puppets' morale. Nevertheless, the Soviets made it clear that the relationship with their Afghan clients would continue, while the relationship between the Americans and their Afghan clients would be broken. The U.S. negotiators eagerly accepted these terms. The U.S. Congress objected to

cutting off the Afghans while the Soviets maintained their commitment. The U.S. negotiators reluctantly made a unilateral statement
that the United States would maintain "positive symmetry" in the
aid going to both sides in Afghanistan. But this was merely a bow to
Congress. In fact, the flow of antiaircraft missiles to the resistance
stopped immediately. Nor did this unilateral statement lessen the
impact of the formal agreement, which consisted merely of a pledge
by Pakistan and Afghanistan to stop interfering in each other's internal affairs.

Since the agreement was signed, the Soviet Union has warned,
and Afghanistan has bombed Pakistan to force it to stop harboring
mujahedeen. All of the possible consequences of the agreement
favor the Soviet Union. At the time of this writing the Afghan war is
fought by an Afghan government in control of the only productive
parts of the country, amply supplied with Soviet weapons and enjoying support from Soviet air strikes against a group of mujahedeen
increasingly bereft of food, weapons, and sanctuary and whose
principal supporter, Pakistan's President Zia, has been killed, while
the U.S. government has put good relations with the Soviet Union
ahead of the mujahedeen's interests. At the very least, the Soviet
Union succeeded in driving a wedge between the United States, the
mujahedeen, and Pakistan. In October 1988 the Soviet Union formally announced that it was "suspending" its withdrawal from
Afghanistan and restated its commitment to the political objectives
for the sake of which it had invaded Afghanistan. Of course, the
Soviets could hold on to the most useful parts of the country, and
continue to base its action on charges of bad faith and noncom-
pliance on the part of the free world—charges it has made ever since
the day the agreement was signed. But for the United States and
Pakistan to go back on the agreement would be difficult because the
agreement and the murder of Pakistan's President Zia have changed
Pakistan. The agreement also created a vested interest in the U.S.
government in acquiescing to whatever happens. In sum, the resistance, the Pakistanis, and the U.S. gave up much of what had pres-
sured the Soviets into negotiations.

In the face of such tempting diplomatic prospects for striking decisive blows at the Afghan mujahedeen, one would have to marvel
at any Soviet decision to accept defeat in the war. At any rate, the
Soviet Union still rules most of Afghanistan. If the Soviets had ever
been tempted to give up control of Afghanistan, the negotiations

must have convinced them otherwise. In sum, it seems at this writing that the Afghan negotiations were not the end of the war, but a very effective operation of the war.

Indeed, it seems that "peace" negotiations by antagonists who are not in clear and present danger of rout, starvation, or some other catastrophe tend to be themselves acts of war aimed at changing the balance of power. In the Peloponnesian War, for example, the Athenian navy cut off a substantial Spartan army on the island of Sphacteria. Both sides agreed to a truce for peace negotiations, during which time the Athenians would allow food to reach the trapped Spartan forces. The Spartans gave up some ships as collateral on condition that they would be returned at the end of the negotiations. But the Athenian assembly voted against the peace proposal, in part because now that the ships were in their hands they could safely break the truce deal and thus deprive the Spartans on the island of any hope of escaping captivity or death. The Athenians figured correctly that once the Spartans on the island had surrendered, Athens would be in an even better bargaining position.

In our time, by the same token, Arab states have negotiated with the United States and the United States has negotiated with Israel concerning the future of the Middle East. A generation of U.S. diplomats has characterized these talks as a "peace process." But the substance of the negotiations is quite a different matter. Various Arab leaders and their allies in Europe have tried to convince the United States to induce Israel to give them various kinds of advantages, mostly land. Once the Israelis have given that up, say these leaders, the Arabs could discuss peace. But of course they would do so from a stronger position from which to wage war. It is easy to see why Israeli statesmen would want no part of such a "peace process," and it is difficult to see why any American would want to guarantee its results—unless he was not serious about the guarantee. Then one would have to wonder why the American negotiators were so eager to destroy their ally. An elementary principle of negotiations would appear to be not to give up things that, once given, cannot be taken back and that by possessing the other side loses the incentive for good behavior. It is always prudent to ask, "But will you love me tomorrow?"

One of the most notable aspects of peace negotiations involving greater and lesser powers is that the greater power may sacrifice the interests of the lesser power. For example, using Spartan captives as a bargaining chip, Athens induced Sparta to restore the Macedonian city of Amphipolis to the Athenian sphere of influence. That quite simply meant the slaughter of the pro-Spartan party in that city.

Similarly, in 1938 when Stalin perceived that Britain and France were going to sacrifice Czechoslovakia to Hitler, he promptly ordered the end of Soviet involvement in Spain and ordered the world's Communists to sabotage the anti-Hitler side in the Spanish civil war (and, incidentally, to blame the defeat on Trotskyite treachery). This meant the death of thousands of Spanish leftists, but it enabled Stalin both to husband his forces and to seek a rapprochement with Hitler. In the same year, Britain and France doomed thousands of their Czech allies to death when they negotiated peace with Hitler for their own interests at the price of letting Hitler have his way with Czechoslovakia unopposed.

The Munich negotiations, at which Britain and France handed over the Sudeten region of Czechoslovakia, are worth special notice because although the Munich betrayal on the surface seems to resemble Stalin's betrayal of the Spanish republic, in fact it was much less intelligent. Whereas Stalin's cruelty was meant to achieve a reasonable objective, Britain and France's cruelty was the result of mere incompetence and cowardice. The British and French asserted (and perhaps believed) that while they had led the Czechs to give up the security of their own fortresses, they had given the Czechs something even more solid: international guarantees of the little that remained. But what remained of Czechoslovakia after Munich was much harder to defend. When Hitler invaded in 1939, the Czechs found it impossible to defend themselves, and Britain and France found it impractical to help. George F. Kennan, then U.S. ambassador to Prague, reacted with an excess of equanimity and a dearth of common sense when a Czech Jew he had known sought refuge from the Nazis at the U.S. embassy and, finding none, went out, in Kennan's words, to "face the music" alone. This shows the foolishness of inducing an ally to give up military power in exchange for guarantees that the reduction of military power manifestly render less credible.

Any small power drawn into peace negotiations with a big-power sponsor is well advised to keep its hands firmly on its weapons. However small its armaments, they are nevertheless more real than any promise could ever be. Israel has always understood this. In early 1988, the Nicaraguan contras forgot this. In their wholehearted attempt to win support from a divided U.S. body politic, they agreed to forgo U.S. weapons, to observe a cease-fire, and to respect an ambiguous understanding between the American and Nicaraguan governments. They thus ceased to be important in Nicaragua. Because they let American politicians off the hook, they ceased to be important in the United States as well. When in mid-1988 they turned to the White House to request arms once again, their request was not even forwarded to Congress. They forgot the maxim that only he who has good arms is likely to have good friends.

Rarely do negotiations between two undefeated antagonists end rather than advance the struggle. Yet sometimes it happens. This was the case with the Peace of Ghent in 1814, which ended the war of 1812 between the United States and Great Britain. Great Britain thought it had ended the Napoleonic Wars and did not want to pour greater effort into a sideshow war in North America. By 1814, Great Britain had long since given up the hope of reconquering its wayward colonies. Any attempt to do so would surely have absorbed all of Britain's resources, and it still might not have succeeded. Since Britain was not about to make such a commitment, and since its only objective in the War of 1812 had been to safeguard Canada, why should it have fought on? Britain wanted to turn to peace in Europe and to empire in India. The United States was even more eager for peace. The war had not gone well for the United States. And now that Napoleon was cooped up on the island of Elba, and Britain had nothing more to worry about in Europe, the war could only go worse. Canada had proved difficult to conquer. Why should America continue to go after it while superior Western lands were there for the taking? The United States wanted to turn westward as much as Britain wanted to turn eastward. These peace negotiations succeeded because both sides recognized that they had better things to do than fight each other.

Nothing "greases" peace negotiations like the appearance of a greater enemy, or of larger fish to fry. In 1968, soon after the Soviet invasion of Czechoslovakia, and concurrent with the buildup of Soviet forces on the Chinese border to forty-five divisions, Mao Tse-tung decided to end all hostilities with the United States. When American officials met with Chinese leaders to arrange President Nixon's visit to China they found warm welcomes, no complications, and reassurances that China was not interested in seeing the United States lose in Vietnam. There were forty-five Russian-speaking, nuclear-armed reasons why China wanted to get close to the United States!

Most of the time, however, negotiations concern the mere modalities of capitulation. The conditions for stopping the fighting may be very different from the conditions of peace. That is not only because, as we have just pointed out, treachery almost always plays its part, but because the circumstances in which armistices are decided are too hurried, too beset by immediate problems, to grapple with the most important issues. Also, minds change as the capitulation itself changes the relative power of the belligerents.

Thus, in 1918 the German government surrendered while its armies were still on foreign soil and had by no means lost the power to resist because it believed that the Allies would be governed by President Wilson's well-advertised Fourteen Points, the thrust of which was a nonvindictive peace. Yet at the Versailles Peace Conference the Germans were forced to sign full responsibility for the entire war and to agree to pay an astronomical 105 billion gold marks' worth of reparations—certainly a vindictive peace by the standards of the day! Treachery had not been intentionally committed. President Wilson simply was not able to fully resist British and French public opinion that demanded harsher and harsher terms. By the same token, when Robert E. Lee handed his sword to Ulysses S. Grant at Appomattox Courthouse in 1865, ending the Civil War, Confederate officers were allowed to retain sidearms and horses and enlisted men their mules for plowing. No one would have expected from this courtly capitulation that the aftermath of that war would become harsh enough to pollute American life for a hundred years. But then no one could have foreseen the death of Abraham Lincoln and the rise of radical Republicans who "waved the bloody shirt."

Let us now turn to the subject of capitulation.

Capitulation

The immediate consequences of the cessation of hostilities range from the benign to the infernal. Let us descend the steps into the hell of defeat.

In the best of circumstances, the defeated nation is compelled to relinquish its objectives. When Lord Cornwallis surrendered to General Washington at Yorktown in 1781, the defeated armies marched out between files of American soldiers with full military honors as bands played sad tunes, as if to say, "Sorry, old boy." Most Americans loyal to Britain had long since gone to Canada, and calm came to both countries. King George III, ashamed of the defeat, briefly considered going back to Hanover, his German kingdom, but soon thought no more of it. Almost the same happened in 1982 when Britain fought Argentina for possession of the Falkland Islands. Argentina's troops on the islands surrendered and were promptly put on ships for home. The Argentines turned against the government that had led them into the war, blaming it more than they blamed Britain. The British had no hand in this at all. No Argentines were lynched in Britain, and the Argentine upper classes retained their Anglophile customs. There were no embargoes or blockades, and the Argentines' famous beefsteaks were as thick as ever.

Even merely abandoning political purpose, however, may bring great suffering to individuals. When France gave up its effort to hold on to Algeria (even though, by 1961, it had militarily defeated the Algerian rebels), it had to absorb, within a year, refugees from Algeria amounting to about 5 percent of the population of metropolitan France. The people of metropolitan France continued their march to prosperity as if nothing were happening. But the refugees had to start from scratch. These refugees were Algerians both of European stock, known as pieds-noirs, or of native stock, known as Harkis. All had to leave homes, farms, and businesses, lucky to escape with their lives and start life over with only the clothes on their backs. For about five years they caused political trouble in France, and even a quarter of a century later, though well integrated into French life, they remain an identifiable voting bloc.

In the second-best set of circumstances, the defeated state not only gives up its objectives but, as a condition of stopping the fighting, gives up its form of government as well. This was what happened to Germany after World War I. Germany was not occupied, except for the Rhineland and the Saar briefly. But the Allies had made it clear that they were out to do away with the monarchy, which their propaganda depicted as responsible for the war. The German military reasonably thought that a civilian government could get a better deal under President Wilson's Fourteen Points. Not incidentally, General Ludendorff also wanted civilians, rather than military leaders, to take public responsibility for the humiliation that Germany was to suffer. The humiliation and the economic privations came, and so did the German public's loathing for those civilians whom it wrongly supposed had betrayed their country by capitulating.

Even though most of Germany was not occupied, it was disarmed and at the mercy of vengeful Allies. When Germany had trouble paying reparations, it faced the threat of invasion. Once, under Prime Minister Poincaré's policy of "hands on the collar," French troops marched into Germany to collect reparations. The German government decided that it had no means of resisting, except to pay with money rendered worthless by inflation. The price of this resistance, though, was the pauperization of anyone with liquid assets. Also, the Allies had not been quick to remove the blockade that had literally starved Germany. The debauching of the German mark further retarded the resumption of normal food imports. As a consequence, Germany stayed hungry into the mid-1920s, with irreparable harm to the bodies of individuals and to the body politic.

In the aftermath of World War II the Soviet Union chose not to occupy Finland and the Finnish government remained nominally independent. But every Finn knew that the price of displeasing the Soviet Union would be occupation by Soviet troops—a disaster that every Finn wanted to avoid. The price of avoiding it was high. Finland could have no independent foreign policy and could not publicly criticize the Soviet Union, which the Finns loathed as much as they feared it. The Finns also had to pay heavy reparations, delivering to the Soviets percentages of Finnish products as part of unequal trade agreements. The Finns did not starve. But the weight of their relationship with the Soviets kept them from being as prosperous as other Scandinavian peoples.[4]

These first two sets of circumstances—in which the defeated country relinquishes war objectives or changes its form of government—are like a pleasant antechamber opening onto the far worse ills found in the hell of capitulation. The difference between the first two circumstances and the others is the fact of foreign occupation.

In the third set of circumstances, the occupation is deliberately benign. This is what happened to Italy and Japan after World War II. Here and there a foreign military governor may rule more justly and have the people's interests more at heart than any previous domestic ruler. But the very fact of foreign occupation means that the dislocation of previous patterns of doing business is piled upon the destruction that the victorious armies caused prior to the capitulation. Uncertain about what will and will not be allowed, eager not to get into trouble they won't be able to get out of, and frightened of the arbitrary power of armed foreigners who are not subject to domestic courts and who are accountable only to *their own* superiors, most occupied peoples shun large-scale economic activity at a time when such activity is especially vital. This, added to the normal dislocations of war, almost always brings hunger and all the diseases of body and soul that follow hunger.

Italy and Japan were fortunate that the American occupiers for different reasons regarded the civilians as innocent. The occupiers prosecuted only a handful of former government leaders and from the beginning did not try to make themselves substitutes for civil authorities. General MacArthur, who made it clear that he was the absolute dictator of occupied Japan, did not disband the Japanese civil administration and did not destroy the nominal authority of the emperor. He made sure that public blame was assigned to those who had led Japan to war and left no doubt that their militaristic way of life would henceforth be unprofitable. At the same time, he encouraged rather than impeded the revival of normal life. He also did not exact reparations.

Italy benefited from the occupiers' immediate sympathy—and food supplies. Nevertheless, the immediate postwar years saw both Italians and Japanese afflicted with diseases of malnutrition such as rickets and enlarged thyroids. During this period, survival and advancement came most directly from a person's ability to ingratiate himself with the occupiers. This brought to the fore some of the most distasteful elements of society and tended to diminish the occupiers' respect for all the locals. Almost a generation had to pass before Italian and Japanese statesmen could deal with the Americans on the basis of equal and mutual respect. For some people, however, the occupation meant the permanent loss of self-respect—such as the women who gave in to the temptation to prostitute themselves to foreign soldiers in order to feed their families.

The fourth category of circumstances involves all of the above ills, plus an occupation force that regards its job as cleansing the defeated society of the main element responsible for the war, punishing it, and exacting reparations. This was the lot of those parts of Germany lucky enough to be occupied by the Western Allies after World War II and of the American South after the Civil War.

It is difficult for Americans to imagine hunger in fertile Georgia. But the Union invasion of 1864–65, like most invasions, seriously disrupted planting for two years. In many cases, seeds and livestock had been burned or eaten. And so, *Gone With the Wind's* Scarlett O'Hara wept hungrily over a meager radish in her antebellum mansion, while Yankee carpetbaggers swarmed over the land backed by military governors, buying up everything of value for practically nothing, and monopolizing or taxing all attempts at economic resurgence. Meanwhile, the South's natural leaders were being jailed or banned from public or economic life because of ties to the rebellion, and former slaves were being urged to commit outrages against their former masters. This was enough to turn the South away from the gentlemanly leadership of the likes of Robert E. Lee to that of the Ku Klux Klan.

In post–World War II Germany and Austria, pitiful groups of women, children, and old men picked through rubble for rags and scraps of wood as the occupiers looked on sternly and put off definitive decisions about their future. During the two winters after the surrender of May 1945 the urban population of Germany lived virtually without heat and on the ragged edge of starvation. Mortality rates rose, and people lacked the basic nutrients necessary to dig out of the rubble and rebuild their lives.[5] For two years after the war it seemed that the country was on a downward spiral: the people were too weak to produce enough to keep from getting weaker. The victors' efforts to break the spiral did not help. For example, German coal was needed for reparations and for foreign exchange. So the miners had to be fed enough to work. But the miners were forbidden to take any of the food home to their starving families. As Konrad Adenauer, a leading German personality of the time (later to become chancellor), shivered in an unheated hotel, fully clothed and wearing an overcoat under the blankets, he thought that his people might perish.

The German economy was reduced to barter and to the use of cigarettes as currency. But the black market at least was honest. The biggest deals—the competition for the occupiers' favor, which alone could ensure food—were made by accusing one's competitors of having been Nazis. This was a prostitution far less honest than that of the poor frauleins who ate by it.

The Western occupiers were not malevolent, but they were confused. They knew that they were supposed to transform the defeated society. But they did not know how they were supposed to do it. Were they going to try to turn it into a bucolic backwater, as called for in U.S. Secretary of the Treasury Henry Morgenthau's punitive plan? Would the country be transformed into a Fabian socialist experiment, as the newly elected British Labour government wanted? Meanwhile, the occupiers, who themselves would not govern, would not allow any but local authorities to govern, and then on the shortest of leashes. And so the western zones of Germany, short of everything, including able-bodied men, and swollen with some 15 million refugees and deportees from the Soviet-occupied eastern zones, marked time. Their suffering was relieved only by charity food parcels sent from abroad. Nevertheless, as the year 1947 passed, the American, British, and French military governments, lacking any design to exploit or impose, gradually let the Germans choose liberal-minded rulers. Even though the military government officials warned the infant German economic ministry that its plans for ending rationing and for a free market would be ruinous, they stepped aside. The "economic miracle" followed immediately, and Germany was reborn. Massive American aid to Germany, without which recovery would not have been as spectacular as it turned out to be, began in 1948. When the Soviet Union started to loom as a serious threat to the United States, American leaders quickly began to see Germany not as a defeated enemy but as a possible asset. It is a rare and lucky loser whose conqueror quickly finds another enemy and starts considering him a potential ally!

The fifth ring in the hell of capitulation is much more common. The occupation not only brings on the privation and degradation mentioned above. Because the winner is out to punish, exploit, and radically reform the defeated society, the horrors are far worse. Compare Solzhenitsyn's accounts of the entry of Russian troops into East Prussia in World Wars I and II. His novel, *August 1914*, describes invading Russian troops filing into neat little German farming communities. A colonel would get off his horse, meet with the burgermeister, and arrange to camp in areas where the troops would cause the least amount of damage. The Russian officers would line up outside the barber shop and then go window-shopping. In 1945, however, the invading Soviet troops had heard Ilya Ehrenburg's call to "break the racial pride" of German women by raping them. How lucky were the women on the western front who could choose whether to prostitute themselves for bread! In the east, as one can read in Solzhenitsyn's poem "Prussian Nights," the rule was first to rape, then to torture and kill.[6] The poor civilian wretches caught by Russian troops endured almost the worst that mankind can dish out, including mothers watching their children bayoneted by the men who then raped them. A couple of weeks after conquering an area, the Soviet authorities would put a stop to the semi-spontaneous orgy of blood by conspicuously hanging a few of their own soldiers. This sort of thing was not much different from the routines of other barbarian armies throughout history.

After the semi-spontaneous killing came the programmed killing necessary to transform society. Throughout Eastern Europe, "class enemies" and "enemy classes" were rounded up, shot, or sent to the gulag. Religious leaders, landowners, members of conservative and social-democratic parties, and former military officers were wiped out. They were not accused of war crimes. They were killed not because of anything they *did*, but because of who they *were*. At Yalta, only Winston Churchill's resistance prevented agreement on Stalin's proposal to execute all German military officers in all zones of occupation. Nevertheless, the Soviets had their way wherever the Red Army ruled. Millions who were not killed were enslaved. The Soviet Union took part of its war reparations in the form of civilians shipped off to forced labor in fields, mines, and factories. Meanwhile, Soviet authorities took everything in Eastern Europe that was not nailed down, and much that was. Whole factories were dismantled and shipped eastward.

Imagine, then, the life of ordinary families in such circumstances. Some of the men have been killed in battle, the women raped, and the children brutalized. Home and possessions are gone, someone in the family has been deported. Everyone is on the edge of starvation. Everyone is at the total mercy of the occupier and his friends. The possibility of deportation hovers over everyone. The clear and present prospect of violent death drives one to do anything to get on the right side of the occupiers, and hunger drives everyone to do anything for a scrap of food. The new order that the occupier wishes to impose has one shining attraction: any kind of normalcy must be preferable to this living hell.

This is the standard consequence of capitulation in civil wars fought over what one might call life-styles, or of capitulation in civil wars caused by rebellion. Surely the capitulations in the civil war that followed the Bolshevik Revolution in 1918–21 were of this kind.[7] Indeed, the mass deportations were so large as to place it close to the horrors of the sixth category. The capitulation at the end of the Spanish civil war of 1936–39, however, unquestionably falls into the lesser reaches of that category, with 70,000 executions and perhaps 170,000 expulsions and deportations.[8]

The surrender of Cuba's military to Fidel Castro's insurgents during Christmas week of 1958 did not fit into that category at all—at first. At first it was a joyous party on both sides. Cuba's dictator, Fulgencio Batista, had not had a large following. He had been a small-time thief, and his few henchmen had left with him. The war had been neither destructive nor particularly bitter. Only a handful of killings were carried out during the first weeks after the capitulation. But after the society had been disarmed, and control had been consolidated, Fidel Castro's persecution of "class enemies" became so harsh that perhaps 20 percent of the population fled and perhaps another 5 percent were enslaved directly. This, along with hunger and yet uncounted executions, was the price the Cuban people paid for being re-formed into a Communist society.

The immediate price that South Vietnam paid for surrendering to communist North Vietnam was higher. Out of 15 million people perhaps 2 million threw themselves into the sea on anything that would float in order to escape the fate that befell perhaps 3 million of their confreres: forced labor in "new economic zones" or in "re-education camps." Under these circumstances the distinction between outright execution and slow death brought on by forced labor, or forced transit, or a "trail of tears" into exile is not terribly meaningful.[9]

The most definitive example of what happens to rebels who surrender, however, is what happened to the army of the Streltzy, a class of merchant-warriors who were hereditary servants of the czars, that rebelled and then surrendered to Peter the Great of Russia in 1712. All were tortured. All but a few were executed. The very luckiest had their heads chopped off. Most were hanged in front of their wives and children, because Peter, the great modernizer, wanted the crowd to heed the lesson. The unlucky few were broken on the wheel in Red Square and left to die slowly, cursing the good fortune of those who had been dispatched quickly.[10]

The pit of hell differs from the above only quantitatively. A vengeful occupier may want to simply extinguish the enemy's society or to reform it so radically that huge chunks of it—say, a third or more—will die. From 1915 to the early 1920s Turkish troops slaughtered the Armenian minority living in eastern Turkey. Armed resistance ended quickly. But the slaughter went on and on. Babies were cut out of pregnant women and stuck on bayonets. Rape and torture usually preceded murder. But the really big killing was done by confiscating food. Perhaps 3 million people died. This was the same technique that the Soviet government used to eliminate independent farmers in the Ukraine in the 1930s. Perhaps 10 million starved to death.[11]

All major genocides are carried out primarily by starvation. The Chinese Great Proletarian Cultural Revolution may have killed 50 million people. Disruption of planting and harvesting, combined with forced migration into areas bereft of food, accounted for the majority of deaths. Starvation played an unusually small role in the holocaust that struck Cambodia between 1975 and 1979 in the aftermath of the Cambodian government's surrender to the Khmer Rouge. After all, food grows exceptionally easily in Cambodia, and it is exceptionally difficult to create an artificial famine. The Khmer Rouge, however, performed radical surgery on society. Cities were emptied. Even amputees in hospitals were forced to crawl. They then killed everyone they could identify as, or imagined to be, professionals or tainted with Western culture, mostly by beating.

Contemplating the consequences of such surrenders it becomes possible to understand the otherwise incomprehensible Roman saying that death on the battlefield is sweet.

The degree of severity following a surrender depends on the character of the winning troops, the level of their discipline, the amount of hatred that has been built up during the war, and, above all the policy pursued by the winner.

One might wonder what would happen if the United States were to surrender after some future conflict with the Soviet Union. Given that the struggle between the United States and the Soviet Union is about the most important thing in the world, that is, how people shall live their lives, one might well expect the hatred to be high. Since it has involved proxy forces all over the world over two generations, the ranks of the winners would probably include not just Soviets but their allies from Africa, Asia, the Middle East, and Latin America. One must also keep in mind that for some two generations the staple of intellectual discourse in much of the world has been to ascribe America's prosperity to its alleged exploitation of the rest of the world and to blame America for the world's ills. Thus there would be no shortage of peoples from around the world eager to take part in an occupation of America, both to taste its delights and to punish its people. Moreover, these occupying peoples might well come from traditions inured to cruelty.

Of course, the geographic position of the United States would make it unlikely that at the moment of surrender significant numbers of foreign troops would be standing on American soil. But a surrender surely would include disarmament, and once that were accomplished, occupation might follow.

The Several Kinds of Peace

As said before, just about everyone wants peace. But human shortcomings, both intellectual and moral, lead most people to imperfect understandings of peace. Let us now look at the several kinds of peace that men try to establish through war.

THE PEACE OF THE DEAD

The prophet Isaiah warned the Jews, "Your country is desolate, your cities are burned, strangers devour it in your presence, and it is desolate, overthrown by strangers." A half-millennium later, in A.D. 70, this prophecy was realized a second time. The Romans dealt with the Jews almost as sternly as they had dealt with the Carthaginians in 146 B.C.—and for the same reason. Both peoples had been irritants for too long, and the Romans had become convinced that they could not live in peace so long as either continued to exist.

After the Romans had come to this conclusion, there was nothing the Carthaginians could do about it. In the decades before 146 B.C., Carthage tried mightily to convince Rome that it would never threaten her again. It gave Rome its finest young men as hostages. It entered into unequal arms-control agreements by which it dismantled its navy. It restricted the size of its army and paid tribute. But nothing would do. Even the most innocent things convinced the Romans that Carthage had to be destroyed. Once, when Cato returned to Rome from a trip to Carthage, he showed the senate a fruit he had picked there. The fruit had not yet rotted. This dramatized how physically close Carthage really was. Cato's fruit helped convince Rome not to rest in peace until every Carthaginian man had been put to the sword, every woman and child sold, every stone knocked off every other stone, until the plow had been drawn over the city and salt had poisoned the earth. Rome's troubles did not end in 146 B.C. Indeed, many argue that Rome's moral decline began in

the ease that followed this third and last Punic War. But after 146
B.C. no Roman lost a night's peace over the Carthaginian threat ever
again.

As for the Jews, the Romans did not extinguish them. The Romans
did not destroy Jerusalem quite as thoroughly as Carthage because
they had never feared it. Nevertheless, after A.D. 70, the Romans
believed that their peace would never be troubled by Jews again.
What a mistake! Within a generation, Rome's biggest *internal* problem was what to do about the *ideas* that had been spread by the
followers of a crucified Jew, Jesus. So, by the time the Romans had
carried out what they thought was the final solution to the Jewish
problem in A.D. 70, it was already too late to impose the peace of the
dead. The next two centuries saw Christ's church first disturb, then
divide, then conquer the Roman Empire.

Our point here is that for good or ill, the peace of the dead is a
peace of sorts. But even in the rare instances when one can kill off all
of one's enemies, their deaths do not necessarily bring peace because people do not have only biological families. Love, hate, and
commitment to a cause need only a few living carriers and often
travel well with no living carriers at all.

Of course, the power of ideas depends on their quality. When
one's enemy rules with no ideas—for instance, a Latin American
dictator such as Cuba's Fulgencio Batista during 1953–58—he is as
good as dead the moment he gives up power. But ideas, even crazy
ones propounded by a South American dictator, can outlive their
carrier. Juan Peron between 1943–55 preached that the nation owes
every citizen a living. A generation after his death, and almost two
generations after he was first overthrown, several movements still
under the banner of Juan Peron's name do not leave Argentina in
peace.

Other, more serious ideas are even more immune to death. Machiavelli was not the first to notice that while it is possible to extinguish people, fire and sword cannot extinguish memory. A conqueror will never have peace to the extent that he fails to come to
terms with the ideas that sustained a defeated enemy. If he stum-
bles, the ideas will raise a nation of enemies to overwhelm him just
as surely as if their ancestors, whether biological or ideological, had
risen from the dead. This is certainly the situation the Soviet Union
faces in Poland today. In 1949 and early 1950 the Soviets killed many
in Poland whom they thought might lead opposition to them. But

they did not kill the very notion of an independent Poland, and they could no more kill Christianity than could the Romans. And so in Poland, as elsewhere, the Communist party of the Soviet Union lives in a more precarious kind of peace—the peace of the prison.

THE PEACE OF THE PRISON

Never before in history have so many of the earth's people lived in this kind of peace. Communist countries are unique in history in that—as in prisons—they make it a serious crime to try to leave their borders, and those borders, like prisons, are fortified to keep people in rather than to keep invaders out. The wall that cuts in half the city of Berlin is only the best known of these fortified borders on land and sea, from Hong Kong to Havana.

This, too, is a peace of sorts. Both the jailer and the prisoner are at rest because both know what is expected of them. History is full of captive nations—the Jews in Babylon, the Tibetans in China, the Greeks by the Ottoman Empire, and countless others who have been conquered by empires but did not lose their identity, their memory of past glories, and the hope of future ones. For both the prisoners and the jailers, peace is neither more nor less than the policy most convenient at the moment. Although both agree on the behavior appropriate for the current balance of power and may even agree not to change it given the circumstances, neither has any illusion that they have any good in common. The imperial power exacts what it can, and the subjects give what they must. Each fears and hates the other.

The peace of the prison can be terribly stable, however. Most peoples throughout history, especially in the non-Western world, have lived as the subjects of empires. When Columbus discovered the Indies he found a relationship between the Carib and the Arawak tribes that resembled the dealings between humans and semi-domesticated animals: the Caribs would catch Arawak boys and fatten them until they ate them. Apparently it had not occurred to either tribe that their roles could or should be different. Understandably, the Arawaks did not like what was going on. But no one remembered it ever having been different. Even when such people remember having had other masters, the only question that has meaning for them is *which* master they shall have in the future. For example, the various Central Asian peoples, the Kazakhs, and the

Uzbeks, have been reasonably content to be part of the Mongol Empire, Tamerlane's empire, the Ottoman Empire, and the Russian Empire. They have always retained their identity while being passed from master to master.

Observers from Alexander the Great to Machiavelli have noted that such empires, while they appear solid, are actually quite brittle. If the master is defeated in a major battle the peace between him and his subjects is broken. If the subject people do not instantly take out their grievances against the master's officials, at the very least they will stop obeying them.

The peace of the prison is even more precarious when it involves people who have known freedom or when the idea of freedom has somehow entered their heads. It is easy for a superior military power to threaten an inferior with annihilation and carry out its threat. But it is far more difficult for the superior power to know *what to demand* as the price for its restraint.

When the Western Allies faced the problem of achieving victory over Germany in 1919, all too few thought of the obvious: Since nobody was proposing to draw the plow Roman-style over the land and impose the peace of the dead, was it conceivable that Germany could be indefinitely held down by force? Was it not probable that the effort to hold it down would stimulate its people to rise up again? The Allies of 1919 did the most thoughtless thing possible. They imposed a prison regime for the people of Germany while neglecting any effort to change their minds. Their simplistic dogma—monarchy equals war, democracy equals peace—blinded them to the fact that war and peace are in the hearts of men and in the preferences of society, and not found in legal institutions. Thus, Germany between 1919 and 1939 will remain the textbook example of how an ingenious people used every bit of elbow room in its prison to reestablish its independence and power.

The prison that the Soviet Union has established for the conquered peoples of Eastern Europe is incomparably more binding than that established by the Treaty of Versailles. Nevertheless, as time has passed the Polish, Hungarian, Czech, and other subjects have wiggled more and more room for themselves. Granted, they have so far not been able to do what Germany accomplished in 1919–39. Moreover, it is impossible to foretell how significant the degree of autonomy they have managed to establish will stand up to future developments, or whether it will have any significance at all.

But that is just the point. The Soviets had hoped to establish an empire that would be far less vulnerable to circumstances. While they have succeeded as no one else has in modern times in establishing the peace of the prison, they have failed to establish a peace based on cultural conquest.

THE PEACE OF CULTURAL CONQUEST

"France," Charles de Gaulle correctly tells us in the opening sentence of La France et Son Armée, "was made by strokes of the sword." But the various provinces were not united by force alone. Today the struggles between the Ile de France, Brittany, Burgundy, and Provence are mere episodes of ancient history because the kings of France and subsequent regimes made Frenchmen out of all whom they conquered. They trained them to forget what once divided them. Thus they conquered them more definitively than the sword alone could do. Burgundy will never fight France again because it has ceased to exist as something capable of doing that. Today's Burgundians read the stories of their days of independence, but they are not stirred to be anti-French. Quite the contrary.

Not quite as final, but nevertheless just as impressive was Douglas MacArthur's cultural conquest of Japan after 1945. Like all wise conquerors who want their achievement to outlive them—or who merely want not to have to play the jailer—MacArthur set about making his subjects like what had happened to them. This is difficult but not impossible to accomplish. Rather than destroying Japanese culture, MacArthur turned it toward emphasizing another aspect of itself, commerce. Discipline, Japan's outstanding cultural trait, could find at least as satisfying an outlet in trade as in war. MacArthur discredited one facet of the Japanese way of life, accredited another, allowed exponents of the new order to root themselves in power, and then faded from the scene. It is possible that someday Japan will turn its disciplined soul back toward war. But for a half-century it has turned away. No one can make anyone else change his mind, but MacArthur used the power and prestige of his sword to persuade Japan to want to choose his way.

Alexander the Great, the Romans, and later, to a lesser extent, Napoleon followed their military conquests with cultural ones. They brought to conquered lands a superior way of life, and the conquered for the most part seized the chance to take full part in it. In the second century B.C., elites from Persia to Egypt were proud to argue with one another in the Greek language and thought patterns that Alexander had brought, and to forget the traditions of Babylonians, Hittites, Persians, and Pharaohs. Two centuries later, the same peoples, plus Gauls, Celts, Germans, Iberians, and Jews could say, "*Cives Romanus sum*" ("I am a Roman citizen") along with the Jewish apostle Paul, who proudly claimed the full protection of Roman law. Soon thereafter the Roman Empire was itself conquered. But today the descendants of the Gauls and Germans, not to mention the descendants of the Goths, Franks, and Longobards, who reconquered them, think in categories, worship the God, and speak in the terms that the Romans taught them. Indeed, Machiavelli shrewdly noted that while the barbarians were riding up and down the Italian peninsula seizing things, they were naming their sons Peter, Paul, Matthew, Mark, Luke, and John. In this case, those who were conquered militarily accomplished a far more lasting cultural conquest. But our point is more general: only such accommodation can bring a peace more genuine than the peace of the prison, whichever the direction in which cultural accommodation occurs.

"Our ancestors, the Gauls"—such words, read aloud in perfect French by classrooms of black children in northern and western Africa testify to the peace that followed France's nineteenth-century conquests there. A century and a half after those conquests Frenchmen and French-speaking Africans have more in common with each other than French-speaking Normans and Saxons did two centuries after the Norman victory at the battle of Hastings in 1066. The cultural accommodation that made England a single society out of separate classes of Norman lords and Saxon serfs came slowly and required adjustment on both sides. We do not mean to imply that cultural accommodation occurs primarily in the direction of the culture that is inherently more advanced or in the direction of the culture that holds military supremacy. To the extent that it occurs, the process is a combination of both force and reason. Its result, however, regardless of who changes the most, is that both sides come to refer to the same standards of behavior and hence recognize a common good. That is peace indeed!

It is very difficult to accomplish cultural conquest without this openness no matter how hard one tries. Consider by way of contrast the efforts of the Soviet Union and of generations of Islamic conquerors. No modern imperial power has paid more attention to cultural matters than the Soviet Union. No less than France, it has imposed the study of its own language on conquered peoples. It has also imposed the study of Marxism-Leninism on all categories of people—from workers required to attend indoctrination sessions to schoolchildren who must learn basic grammar and arithmetic by manipulating only Communist symbols. Moreover, advancement in Soviet-conquered societies is strictly and formally regulated by the Communist party. Nevertheless, in Communist countries—as opposed to some Western university faculties—few outside the Communist ruling classes pay more than lip service to communism.

Islam did not have to try so hard. It is true that it gave conquered rulers no choice but to proclaim the One God or die. But in accordance with the Koran, Islamic conquerors allowed ordinary infidels to live undisturbed as second-class subjects. The muezzin atop one of the minarets of a mosque would call people to forsake their former ways of life and follow the law by which the new Muslim rulers lived. Millions responded, and the Muslim conquest of northern and coastal Africa, as well as much of southern Asia, is solid. Islam's conquests succeeded because it represented a good shared by both conqueror and conquered.

Despite all of communism's cultural efforts, Communist conquests have given no sign of transcending the peace of the prison. Because Marxism-Leninism is a doctrine of universal struggle, it has successfully attracted people from around the world who see themselves playing the role that Lenin created for them as the all-powerful vanguards of historical change. But without having read Marx or Lenin, anyone in contact with Marxists realizes that they are engaged in a struggle without logical end, and that anyone at anytime is liable to be cast as the enemy with whom there can be no peace. No amount of submission, not even joining the Communist party, ensures peace, because Marxism-Leninism denies the very possibility of a good that is common to any two individuals and, hence, of peace.

Thus, we conclude that cultural conquest, although it may contain various admixtures of force and love, nevertheless always produces a kind of tacit agreement between the winners and losers that, whatever happened in the past, things now are more or less as they should be. This is remarkable testimony to the power of real peace, if given time, to heal wounds and to justify even the victory of unjust causes.

The Tranquility of Order

Whether agreement between winner and loser to live life on a mutually satisfying basis comes at the time of a peace treaty or long afterward, or is tacitly accepted in the absence of a treaty, only such an agreement can be the basis of peace among living and free men. As we mentioned at the beginning of this book, it is impossible to define peace because peace is a kind of satisfaction and different people can be satisfied in different ways. Saint Augustine, knowing that war is the struggle for different conceptions of peace, summed up the matter by saying that peace is "the tranquility that comes of order." No one can mistake this as including the peace of prison. By "order" Augustine meant something far more solid:

> The peace of the body lies in the ordered equilibrium of its parts; the peace of the irrational soul, in the balanced adjustments of its appetites; the peace of the reasoning soul, in the harmonious correspondence of conduct and conviction; the peace of body and soul taken together, in the well-ordered life and health of the living whole. Peace between a mortal man and his Maker consists in ordered obedience, guided by faith, under God's internal law; peace between man and man consists in regulated fellowship. The peace of a home lies in the ordered harmony of authority and obedience, between the members of a family living together. *The peace of the political community is an ordered harmony of authority and obedience between citizens. . . . Peace in its final sense is the calm that comes of order.*[12] [Italics added]

The classical tradition had taught Augustine that different people have different capacities for participating in the order of nature. So, just as there can be no perfectly ordered human body, or any perfectly ordered family, or for that matter, any perfectly ordered polity, there can be no perfect order among polities. Perfect peace, the perfect tranquility that comes from perfect order, exists only in the City of God. On earth, an approximation of the right order, whether of the body or of the polity, would have to be sought in finite, imperfect circumstances.

Again, this does not mean that all earthly solutions are equally good. Quite the contrary. The order of the City of God was to be the standard by which all earthly solutions would be judged. Approaching this harmony, he argued, is perhaps man's deepest natural desire. "According to the poor limits of mortal life, in health, security, and human fellowship," peace is "the loveliest of all lovely things on earth" because it allows men to partake of all other lovely things, both temporal and eternal.[13] But Augustine knew that God guarantees not the achievement but only the longing for peace and the freedom to pursue it—wisely or unwisely.

For Saint Augustine, only one thing was certain. Any peace established on earth, in addition to being imperfect, would last only as long as it was defended. As the French philosopher Etienne Gilson has commented, "the only force capable of preserving a thing is the force which created it."[14] But alas, the force that creates peace—victory in war—is typically inclined less to creating a harmonious order than to satisfying the victor's passions.

Assume for a moment that the winner of a war wants to establish a peace as just and stable as possible. What would he have to do? Both history and common sense point to the need to avoid two extremes. On the one hand, the winner must not fail to consummate the victory, to make sure that the issues of the present war have been thoroughly resolved and that at least *that* particular set of troubles will not arise again. By the same token, it also should not fail to retain the military power necessary to enforce the settlement and to guard the new order against the new and different threats that will inevitably arise. A country that thinks of the finished war as the last and the settlement as the beginning of a costless tranquility is setting itself up for another war, which it will lose. On the other hand, it should not dare to impose a peace so harsh as to preclude the loser from reconciling himself to the new order. To forget Churchill's dictum "in victory magnanimity, in peace goodwill" is to throw away the fruit of peace for the sake of which the war was fought.

Is it possible to avoid these extremes? Often it is possible, but never in the same way twice and never to the same extent twice. Sometimes it is not possible at all. Everything depends on the nature of the vanquished foe, how well the victor understands it, and how competently the victor deals with it. In 1945, for example, there was no shortage of Americans who believed that the Japanese people were unfit partners for a harmonious world order. And indeed, the Japanese had shown quite enough cruelty, dishonesty, and fanaticism so that a reasonable case could have been made that only the peace of the prison or of the dead was possible for them. But some saw the possibility that the humiliation of one side of Japanese culture together with the promotion of another would produce a different Japan. This possibility was made into reality. But, under less skillful direction than Douglas MacArthur's, it might not have been. Given the wrong set of incentives, it might not endure.

In our time, Israel has repeatedly defeated Arab attempts to destroy it. Israelis would dearly love to establish an arrangement under which they could live in the land of the Covenant in peace. Although Israel has defeated Arab armies and crushed countless mobs, it has not been able to gain leverage over the politics of Arab nations and turn them away from their goal: the elimination of Israel. In Israel's case the exceptions prove the rule.

In 1967, Israel captured the Sinai peninsula from Egypt, the Golan Heights from Syria, and Jordan's lands west of the Jordan River. Since that time, the seemingly obvious path to peace has been Israel's return of the lands in exchange for the Arabs' genuine acceptance of Israel's right to exist in peace. But with the exception of Egypt, which traded a halfhearted peace treaty for Israel's (demilitarized) return of the Sinai, the Arab states for their own reasons have continued to mobilize their citizens to annihilate Israel and assassinate those among themselves who think otherwise. Pointedly, Egypt's leader, Anwar Sadat, was assassinated for having made peace. So, as Arabs in the occupied territories seethe with hatred of Jews, and any Arab who might disagree fears for his life, what can Israel expect were she to withdraw to less defensible borders in exchange for paper promises of peace? This seems to be a case where the peace in the hand, though it be the peace of the prison—and of the garrison—is better than the one in the bush, which might well turn out to be no peace at all. The U.S. State Department has repeatedly urged Israel to "take chances for peace." But the other side of the chance is defeat in war—and at whose hands!

The Arab-Israeli struggle is the clearest example in our time of an unconsummated war—a *bellus interruptus.* When the issues that gave rise to a war have not been resolved and when one side has not given up its objectives it is dangerous to think the war is over. In 1919 the German people never came to terms with their defeat and were not averse to resuming the fight when they could. Today's world is filled with unresolved conflicts: between Greeks and Turks for control of Cyprus, between Afghans and Soviets for control of Afghanistan, between Iran and Iraq, between Kurds and Arabs, as well as between rival factions in Cambodia, Angola, and Central

America. Above them all looms the greatest unresolved conflict of all, that between the United States and its allies and the Soviet empire. To suggest that these conflicts can be resolved through a "peace process," the only solid feature of which is to assume the tractability of intractable emotions, is both practically harmful and intellectually dishonest.

Why then would anyone have kind words for a *bellus interruptus*? Because by disregarding or denigrating the very idea of victory, by declaring that stopping the fighting is more important than who wins, one avoids difficult questions such as which side is right? And on what or whose basis is peace to be built? Hence, the formula familiar to contemporary Americans: the adversaries must go to the bargaining table. They must arrange a cease-fire or an agreement to limit certain kinds of weapons, and possibly interpose unarmed "observers" and inspection teams. Create a committee where the two sides can charge each other with violations, award the mediator the Nobel Peace Prize, and hope that *somehow*, even though the "peace process" did not resolve the questions that set the belligerents to killing each other, those questions will fade away after the killing has stopped. But this familiar formula for *bellus interruptus* constrains only those who wish to be constrained, while the other side licks its wounds and prepares for an honest-to-goodness victory. The *bellus interruptus* usually is a smart tactic for one side and a stupid one for the other.

Happily, this is not always so. It is conceivable that the forty years' "time-out" enforced by the United States in the war between China's Communists and Nationalists may have allowed bases for peace to develop that had not existed before. For more than a generation beginning in 1949, while Nationalist China (Taiwan) was integrating itself into the world economy and even moving toward being that most un-Chinese of things, a democracy, mainland China seemed to retain a particularly harsh and isolated brand of communism. But in the 1980s, mainland China began to change. It of course remained a tyranny, but by then the tyranny appeared not so different from what China has long known. Moreover, that tyranny was surely loosening and opening itself to the world. Most important for the future, it seemed that Marxism-Leninism had sunk very shallow roots in China after all. By 1989, then, a harmonious relationship between the mainland and Taiwan was no longer inconceivable. Time had moved on and seemed to have pushed the causes of hatred into a chapter of history that could conceivably lead to a real peace.

But this sort of thing cannot be *counted on* to produce peace. Time can be counted on only to kill the current generation. Ordinarily, in the world of the living the tranquility of order can only be built by intelligent choices backed by victorious arms. Given good choices and good arms, time and the amnesia that may accompany it can be an ally in achieving both victory and peace while minimizing bloodshed. Abraham Lincoln, for example, sought to head off the looming Civil War by allowing time to settle the issue of the war, namely, shall the United States be all free or all slave. To safeguard peace, Lincoln wanted to reassure slave owners that he would strenuously oppose anyone depriving them of their slave property. He would not wage war to free the slaves. Nevertheless, he would do all things necessary to demonstrate to the public that slavery was "in the course of ultimate extinction."[15] Lincoln hoped to do this by what in contemporary jargon might be called "containment." Slavery would not be allowed to expand, every incentive would be given to slave owners to sell their slaves into freedom, and the moral weight of a nation in which slavery would have been a shrinking backwater would finish off the "peculiar institution." If the southern states had agreed to let time run under these circumstances, Lincoln's peaceful victory would have come about. But the South started the Civil War precisely because time would have been working against it.

Our own age is dominated by the unresolved conflict between the Soviet empire and what is often called the Free World, led by the United States. The conflict, a true world war, has been raging since 1945 by all means short of direct clashes between the belligerent's major military units. Small clashes have occurred. Proxies for both sides have fought and millions have died. The arts of political and economic warfare have been raised to new levels of sophistication because of this conflict. And of course, preparations for the possibility of decisive clashes continue all the time.

How are the issues of this war to be resolved? Whose peace shall prevail? If one merely listened to rhetoric one would conclude that both sides were following similar strategems. The United States has called its strategy "containment" and the Soviet Union has called it "peaceful coexistence." The essence of both—at least on the declaratory level—is the same as Lincoln's strategy for winning the peace without fighting the war. The opponent is to be prevented from expanding. He is to be stripped of friends and allies. Then, in time, isolated, poor, and morally defeated, he will gradually give up his designs and his objectionable features. It is really remarkable how much the documents that outline these approaches resemble each other. George Kennan's 1947 article, "The Sources of Soviet Conduct," in *Foreign Affairs*; Stalin's speech to the 17th Party Congress in 1927; and Khrushchev's speech to the 20th Party Congress in 1956 each declare that time can be made to work for its own side and against the opponent, and each professes to believe that military superiority, indeed, *ever-increasing* military superiority, is the shield behind which it can observe the other side's internal decay. Similarly, only arms can insure that the other side in its death throes will not recoup its losses with one deft military move.

Indeed, both the Americans and the Soviets are correct—in principle. But struggles for a preferred peace, or a preferred order, are not decided abstractly. There is an art to war, an art we have sought to explain in these pages. Its essence lies in making day-to-day decisions in light of the fact that the purpose of war is victory and that any action that deviates from that purpose leads to defeat. In other words, the primary requirement of this art is concentration of the mind, not to say single-mindedness.

Our purpose here has been to describe the ways in which exemplary winners and losers have struggled for differing kinds of peace. Our reflections mean to inform our students and fellow citizens that everything we do that influences the foreign policy or the defense posture of the United States will have a bearing on the outcome of this struggle. Our reflections do not prescribe recipes for conducting this struggle for peace. We do not rule out any means—including appeasement—because appeasement sometimes does appease. Circumstances arise in human affairs in which even normally disastrous measures are required. But the very purpose of these reflections has been to redirect thoughts away from arguments over recipes and toward the stark fundamentals of peace and war. What can possibly satisfy the enemy? What means does he have to ensure his own satisfaction? How much do we value our own kind of peace? What, then, do we have to do to make sure that it prevails? These fundamentals deserve our single-minded attention.

The Soviet Union has mastered the art of war as competently as any regime in history. But so long as it is Communist, it will not be at peace with itself. It will oscillate between talk of the heavenly "socialist commonwealth" on earth and the practical pursuit of the peace of the prison, or the peace of the dead. Our civilization, following Augustine, prizes the tranquility of order. But for us to see war as anything but the other side of the coin of that tranquility is to misunderstand it, to suffer it, and ultimately to lose it.

NOTES

Introduction

1. R. J. Rummel, "War Isn't This Century's Biggest Killer," *Wall Street Journal*, 7 July 1986, p. 12. Rummel's numbers are 119.4 million people killed by governments, 35.7 million people killed in war. The number of people killed by governments does not include those executed for nonpolitical criminal acts, nor does it include deaths from either the Soviet famine of 1921–22 or the Chinese famine of 1958–61, both of which were caused in large part by forced collectivization and state planning of agricultural production. See also Antony Sutton, *Western Technology and Soviet Economic Development*, 3 vols. (Stanford: Hoover Institution Press 1968–1973).

2. International Institute of Strategic Studies (IISS), *The Strategic Balance* (London, 1986).

3. See James L. Payne, *Why Nations Arm* (London: Basil Blackwood, 1989), pt. 1, chap. 3.

4. Ibid., pt. 1, chap. 1.

5. Numa Denis Fustel de Coulanges, *The Ancient City* (Garden City, N.Y.: Doubleday, 1956), bk. 3, chap. 1. Originally published in Paris in 1864.

6. Saint Augustine, *The City of God* (Garden City, N.Y.: Image Books, 1958). Augustine writes in bk. 19, chap. 13 that "the peace of the political community is an ordered harmony of authority and obedience between citizens."

7. The Prophet Mohammed's injunctions about war and peace, including the jihad (holy war), have been stressed by Iranian Shi'ites in the Iran-Iraq war. For the faithful, *jihad is the means of separating the people of Paradise from all others*. The Prophet said, "Jihad is necessary for you even if you prohibit it. . . . God buys property and life of the faithful in exchange for Paradise, for they fight and kill and get killed for God. . . . One hour of jihad is better than sixty years of worship." See Sepehr Zabih, *The Iranian Military in Revolution and War* (London: Routledge and Kegan Paul, 1988), pp. 139–40. See also Bernard Lewis, "The Language of Islam," *Encounter* (May 1988): 39–45; and Daniel Pipes, *In the Path of God* (New York: Basic Books, 1983).

8. For a classic Hindu text on war, see Kautilya's *Arthasastra*, trans. R. P. Kangle (Bombay: University of Bombay Press, 1960). For a Chinese text on war, see Sun Tzu's *The Art of War*, trans. Samuel B. Griffith (Oxford: Oxford University Press, 1963).

9. See Frederick Engels, *The Origin of the Family, Private Property, and*

the *State* (New York: International Publishers, 1942); and Karl Marx, *Critique of the Gotha Programme* (New York: International Publishers, 1972).

10. Thucydides, *The Peloponnesian War* (New Brunswick, N.J.: Rutgers University Press, 1975), bk. 2, pp. 79–81. The passage includes and follows the account of the revolution in Corcyra.

Chapter 2

1. F. E. Adcock, *The Greek and Macedonian Art of War* (Berkeley: University of California Press, 1957), p. 2.

2. Quincy Wright, *A Study of War* (Chicago: University of Chicago Press, 1942), pp. 1261–83.

3. See Donald Kagan, "The Pseudo-Science of 'Peace,' " *The Public Interest* 78 (Winter 1985): 43–61. See also Bruce Bueno de Mesquita, *The War Trap* (New Haven: Yale University Press, 1981).

4. Henry Ashby Turner, Jr., *German Big Business and the Rise of Hitler* (New York: Oxford University Press, 1985).

5. James Payne, *Why Nations Arm* (London: Basil Blackwood, 1989), pt. II, chap. 9.

6. Such sentiments animate those who seek to introduce peaceable sentiments into educational curricula and to eliminate instructions, content, or behavior suggestive of combat in order to induce exemplary peaceable behavior in children. Several years before Pearl Harbor, Eleanor Roosevelt urged American toymakers to "turn their attention from tin soldiers, cannon, tanks and battleships and other warlike toys and make instead armies of foresters and farmers and mills with modern workmen" (Jason Berger, *A New Deal for the World* [New York: Social Science Monographs, 1981], p. 7). Disputes on this matter are revived in the pre-Christmas buying season every year.

7. See Reinhold Niebuhr, *The Irony of American History* (New York: Scribner, 1952), 84–86.

8. See Michael Howard, *War and the Liberal Conscience* (New Brunswick, N.J.: Rutgers University Press, 1978), chaps. 1 and 2.

9. Ibid., 29–30. See also Felix Gilbert, *To the Farewell Address* (Princeton: Princeton University Press, 1961).

10. The victims of this "classicide" until the mid-1950s were chiefly, but not exclusively, Russian and Chinese victims of Stalin's and Mao Tse-tung's purges. The blood baths in Indochina, which followed the Vietnam War in 1975, bear witness that this form of peacemaking knows no boundaries. That *economic* theories can be more brutal in their logic than other modern ones is ironic. They are a truly dismal science, indeed, graveyard socialism.

11. Payne, *Why Nations Arm*, pt. II, chap. 8.

12. Geoffrey Blainey, *The Causes of War* (New York: Free Press, 1973), p. 133.

13. Ibid, pp. 141–42. The pathetic young protagonist of Theodore Dreiser's *American Tragedy*, Clyde Griffiths, exemplifies such a man. Having elabo-

rately plotted the murder of his pregnant girlfriend, at the critical moment his will fails, yet he accidentally drowns her.

14. During the above-mentioned Russo-Japanese War, the commander of a Russian navy ship sailing from Murmansk on its long voyage to the Far East mistook a fleet of British fishing vessels for hostile Japanese warships and shelled them, causing many casualties. A real accident! This "Dogger Bank Incident," as it was called, briefly jolted but scarcely harmed Anglo-Russian relations. British policy already was moving strongly toward detente with St. Petersburg for reasons of state. However, had such an accident happened a generation before or after, it easily could have been a *casus belli*.

15. Carl Schmitt, *The Concept of the Political*, trans. George Schwab (New Brunswick, N.J.: Rutgers University Press, 1976), pp. 27–29.

16. Plato, *The Republic*, trans. Harold Bloom (New York: Basic Books, 1968), pp. 147–52.

17. Schmitt, *Concept of the Political*, pp. 30–33.

18. Winston Churchill, *The Second World War* (Boston: Houghton Mifflin, 1948), vol. 1, p. 667.

19. See Patrick Glynn, "The Sarajevo Fallacy," *The National Interest* 9 (Fall 1987): 30.

20. Ibid.

21. Quoted in Martin Gilbert, *Winston Churchill: The Wilderness Years* (New York: Macmillan, 1981), p. 267.

22. Regarding Roosevelt's state of mind see Robert Dalleck, *Franklin Roosevelt and American Foreign Policy 1932–1945* (Oxford: Oxford University Press, 1979), p. 316. Ironically, the war in the Pacific started in Japanese surprise and ended in American surprise, the bombing of Hiroshima and Nagasaki.

23. *Abraham Lincoln's Speeches*, compiled and edited by L. E. Crittenden (New York, 1895), p. 19.

24. Gilbert, *Winston Churchill*, p. 267.

25. See Charles de Gaulle, *Memoires de Guerre* (Paris: Plon, 1954), vol. 1, chaps. 1 and 2.

26. See Paul B. Henze, *The Plot to Kill the Pope* (New York: Scribner, 1985).

Chapter 3

1. Quoted in Isaiah Berlin, *Russian Thinkers* (New York: Penguin Books, 1984), pp. 60–62.

2. Bruce Catton, *Terrible Swift Sword* (New York: Doubleday, 1966; New York: Washington Square Press, 1967), p. 429.

3. Hans Mark, *In Search of the Fulcrum* (Berkeley: Institute of International Studies, 1988), pp. 65–66.

4. U.S. Department of Defense, *Soviet Military Power: 1988*, pp. 109–16, and *Annual Report to the Congress for Fiscal Year 1989*, pp. 29–34 (Washington, D.C.: U.S. Government Printing Office, 1988).

5. Carl von Clausewitz, *On War*, ed. and trans. Michael Howard and Peter Paret (Princeton: Princeton University Press, 1976), p. 579.

6. Western strategic theorists since the 1950s, envisioning future great-power wars, have directed their attention to constraints and limitations. These compunctions, however, are not shared by Soviet strategists. While the Soviets are quite concerned about the uncertainties of war, they tend not to be paralyzed by them. The standard Soviet view is expressed by Marshal V. D. Sokolovskii in his authoritative work, *Soviet Military Strategy* (New York: Crane, Russak, 1975): "It is entirely clear that both gigantic military coalitions will put out massive armed forces in a future *decisive* world war; all modern powerful and long-range means of combat, including multi-megaton nuclear-rocket weapons, *will* be used in it on a huge scale; and the most decisive methods of military operations will be used" (pp. 187–88).

7. This is particularly true of military surprises, such as Pearl Harbor, which have inspired a rich literature. Some of its post hoc wisdom resembles the old adage about locking the barn after the horse has been stolen. See Roberta Wohlstetter, *Pearl Harbor: Warning and Decision* (Stanford, Calif.: Stanford University Press, 1962). See also Klaus Knorr and Patricia Morgan, *Strategic Military Surprise* (New Brunswick, N.J.: Transaction Books, 1983). New sophisticated surveillance technologies, at least for the superpowers, lessen the risk of certain forms of surprise attacks, but they are vulnerable, delicate, and especially subject to deception. Therefore, they increase rather than decrease uncertainty.

8. Ingenuity can compensate for C3 inadequacies. During the recent Grenada invasion, a U.S. Army unit was briefly trapped by enemy fire, without communications to request support from offshore naval forces. With a personal AT&T credit card, its commander cleverly placed a call through to Fort Benning, Georgia. Help was forthcoming. This sort of thing happens frequently in wafare but one cannot count on it. That is the paradoxical nature of warfare.

9. *Standard Encyclopedia of Southern Africa* (Capetown: NASDOU, 1975), vol. 11, p. 44.

10. See Georges Fauriol and Eva Loser, *Guatemala's Political Puzzle* (New Brunswick, N.J.: Transaction Books, 1988).

11. Albert Speer, *Inside the Third Reich* (New York: Macmillan, 1975), pp. 220–21, 320.

12. Ibid., pp. 225–28.

13. Edward Teller, *Better a Shield than a Sword* (New York: Macmillan, 1987).

14. David E. Sanger, "U.S. Chooses Martin Marietta for Simulation of 'Star Wars,' " *New York Times*, 23 January 1988.

15. Robert MacNamara, "Speech to the Democratic Party Convention of 1964, Washington, D.C., 17 August 1964," *Vital Speeches of the Day*, 30: 10.

16. Alexander Orlov, *Handbook of Intelligence and Guerrilla Warfare* (Ann Arbor: University of Michigan Press, 1963), p. 10. Orlov, a general in the NKVD (one of the earlier incarnations of the KGB, the Soviet intelligence agency) originally wrote this book in the 1930s as a textbook for the educa-

tion of Soviet military officers and party cadres. After he defected to the West, he rewrote it from memory.

17. See *Transcript of Defense Secretary Laird's News Conference, Washington, D.C., Monday, November 23, 1970* (U.S. Information Service, Press and Publication Branch, Document no. 70–125). See also the *New York Times*, 29 November 1970, p. 1; *The Economist*, 28 November 1970, pp. 14–16; and the *Washington Post*, 24 November 1970, p. 1.

18. Winston Churchill, *The Second World War* (Boston: Houghton Mifflin, 1948), vol. 3, p. 393.

19. Niccolo Machiavelli, *The Prince* (New York: Penguin Books, 1962), chap. 7.

Chapter 4

1. Roy P. Basler, ed., *Collected Works of Abraham Lincoln* (New Brunswick, N.J.: Rutgers University Press, 1953), vol. 6, p. 409.

2. Winston Churchill, *The Second World War* (Boston: Houghton Mifflin, 1948), vol. 1, pp. 311–14.

3. Edward Luttwak, *The Pentagon and the Art of War* (New York: Simon and Schuster, 1984), p. 86.

4. Ibid., pp. 17, 44–45, 55, 153, 271.

5. Annual Report of the Chief of Staff, U.S. Army, for the fiscal year ending 30 June 1933.

6. Charles de Gaulle, *Memoires de Guerre* (Paris: Plon, 1954), vol. 1, p. 427.

7. B. H. Liddell-Hart, *History of the Second World War* (New York: Putnam, 1971), pp. 622–28.

Chapter 5

1. See Hitler's plan, "Operation Barbarossa," quoted in Winston Churchill, *The Second World War* (Boston: Houghton Mifflin, 1948), vol. 2, pp. 559–89. See also B. H. Liddell-Hart, *History of the Second World War* (New York: Putnam, 1971), pp. 141–70.

2. Hart, *History of the Second World War*, pp. 639–59.

3. The geometric formula for calculating how far away the horizon is from any given altitude is $z = (2Eh)**1/2$, where E is the earth's radius and h is the altitude above the earth.

4. Arthur H. Westing in E. W. Pfeiffer, "The Cratering of Indochina," *Scientific American* (May 1972): 20–29. By the end of 1971, the United States had dropped 6 million tons of bombs on Indochina, three times the tonnage dropped by air forces in all theaters of World War II. Some 3.6 million tons of these bombs had been dropped on South Vietnam. See also Phillip B. Davidson, *Vietnam at War, the History: 1946–1975* (Novato, Calif.: Presidio Press, 1988), p. 589.

5. Churchill, *Second World War*, vol. 4, p. 732. See also Albert Speer, *Inside the Third Reich* (New York: Macmillan, 1970), pp. 247–51.

6. U.S. Department of Defense, *Soviet Military Power* (Washington, D.C.: U.S. Government Printing Office, 1985), pp. 40–41.

7. U.S. Naval Institute, Proceedings, *The Maritime Strategy* (Washington, D.C.: U.S. Government Printing Office, 1986).

8. Churchill, *Second World War*, vol. 2, p. 182.

Chapter 6

1. A. A. Sidorenko, *The Offensive*, trans. and published by the U.S. Air Force (Washington, D.C.: U.S. Government Printing Office, 1971) p. 24.

2. Winston Churchill, *The Second World War* (New York: Houghton Mifflin, 1948), vol. 2, p. 46.

3. Ibid., p. 289.

4. Frank C. Carlucci, Secretary of Defense, *Annual Report to Congress, Fiscal Year 1989* (Washington, D.C.: U.S. Government Printing Office, 1988), pp. 29–34.

5. Ibid. p. 55.

6. See John Lehman, "Rebirth of a U.S. Naval Strategy," *Strategic Review* (Summer 1981): 9–15; Thomas Wilkerson, "Two if by Sea," *U.S. Naval Institute Proceedings* (November 1983): 34–39; and James L. George, *The U.S. Navy: The View from the Mid-1980s* (Boulder, Colo.: Westview Press, 1985).

7. Michael M. McCrea, *U.S. Navy, Marine Corps, and Air Force Fixed Wing Aircraft Losses and Damage in Southeast Asia, 1962–1973* (Arlington, Va.: Center for Naval Analyses, 1976).

Chapter 7

1. Bernard Brodie, ed., *The Absolute Weapon* (New York: Harcourt Brace, 1946).

2. Ibid., p. 80. See also Richard Pipes, "Why the Soviet Union Thinks It Could Fight and Win a Nuclear War," *Commentary* 64 (July 1977): 21–39; also Brodie's editorial letter of reply (pp. 6–7) and Pipes's rejoinder (pp. 20, 22) in the September 1977 issue.

3. General Daniel Graham, *Shall America Be Defended?* (New Rochelle, N.Y.: Arlington House, 1979), p. 36.

4. Samuel P. Huntington, *The Common Defense: Strategic Programs in National Politics* (New York: Columbia University Press, 1961), p. 298.

5. Samuel Glasstone, ed., *The Effects of Nuclear Weapons*, U.S. Atomic Energy Commission (Washington, D.C.: U.S. Government Printing Office, 1961), p. 135. One thousand feet from the center of a one-kiloton blast, the peak overpressure is ten pounds per square inch, enough to blow away frame houses but not enough to kill unprotected human beings except by means of flying debris.

6. U.S. Department of Defense, *Soviet Military Power*, 8th ed. (Washington, DC: U.S. Government Printing Office, 1985), p. 55.

7. Ships are seriously damaged or sunk by overpressures exceeding ten pounds per square inch. This means that a ship cannot allow a cruise missile with a warhead of twenty kilotons to get closer than about 4,000 feet. Larger warheads require a greater keep-out range. See Glasstone, *Effects of Nuclear Weapons*, p. 255.

8. "As I have explained . . . in previous years, this question cannot be answered precisely. . . . I would judge that a capability on our part to destroy, say, one-fifth to one-fourth of her population and one-half of her industrial capacity would serve as an effective deterrent. . . . It is precisely this mutual capability to destroy one another, and conversely, our respective inability to prevent such destruction, that provides us both with the strongest possible motive to avoid a strategic nuclear war" (Robert S. MacNamara, *Annual Report to Congress for Fiscal Year 1969* [Washington, D.C.: U.S. Government Printing Office, 1968], pp. 47, 49).

9. Robert MacNamara later described his thinking most concisely in his *Statement of Secretary of Defense Robert S. MacNamara before the Senate Armed Services Committee on the Fiscal Years 1969–73 Defense Program and 1969 Defense Budget* (Washington, D.C.: U.S. Government Printing Office, 1969), esp. pp. 47–50.

10. Richard Pipes, "Why the Soviet Union Thinks It Could Fight and Win a Nuclear War." See also Frank C. Carlucci, Secretary of Defense, *Annual Report to the Congress, Fiscal Year 1989* (Washington, D.C.: U.S. Government Printing Office, 1988), esp. last paragraph of p. 28.

11. Leon Sloss and Marc Dean Milot, "U.S. Nuclear Strategy in Evolution," *Strategic Review 12* (Winter 1984): 19–28. See also Albert Wohlstetter, "Bishops, Statesmen, and Other Strategists on the Bombing of Innocents," *Commentary 75* (June 1983): 15–35.

12. David S. Sullivan, *The Bitter Fruit of SALT: A Record of Soviet Duplicity* (Houston: Texas Policy Institute, 1981). In 1974, Kissinger responded to a reporter's question at a press conference saying, "What in the name of God is strategic superiority? What is the significance of it operationally, politically, militarily . . . at these levels of numbers? What do you do with it?" (p. 32).

Chapter 8

1. Paul Smith, *On Political Warfare* (Washington, D.C.: National Defense University Press, 1988), p. 1.

2. *United States Foreign Broadcast Information Service Daily Report: Middle East and Africa*, 7 October 1981.

Libyan President Qadaffi used Sadat's death to threaten other less radical, less pro-Soviet Arab leaders in a statement over Tripoli radio: "The sound of the bullets [that] resounded firmly and courageously in the face of Sadat this morning was in fact saying 'this is the punishment of those who betray the Arab nation; this is the punishment of those who betray the martyrs' " (p. Q2). "After this day, whoever dares to sign an agreement of capitulation with the enemy, in Egypt or elsewhere, the Arab nation will be laying in wait for him" (p. Q3). "His end will be the end of anyone who follows the path of treason and treachery, the end of King Abdallah, Wasfi al-Tall and Sadat, the path of treason . . . which Sadat called the march of peace" (p. Q4). "It is the right of the progressive forces to assume authority and to restore Egypt to its progressive socialist march, the anticolonialist front" (p. Q5). "Death always to the traitors" (p. Q9).

Syrian radio reports followed in the same vein, threatening moderate Arab leaders and praising the Soviet Union: "Today, it is Sadat's turn; tomorrow, it will be [King] Husayn, afterward Saddam Husyan and Numayri until all traitors are wiped out for good from our Arab homeland" (p. H1) ". . . particularly in our Arab region, the friendly Soviet Union constitutes today the most important guarantee of the march of freedom in the world at large" (p. H2). "The U.S. road forced Sadat to concede the Palestinian issue, the pan-Arab issue and to play the role of serf to U.S. imperialism in the Arab homeland, Africa and Afghanistan" (p. H3).

Baghdad radio drew parallels between Sadat's assassination and the downfall of the shah of Iran, using both as examples of the fate that will befall those leaders who cooperate with the United States in the quest for peace in the Middle East: "The death of Sadat is an eloquent historical lesson which once again confirms that those who betray their people and nation believing that they can continue their traitorous behavior forever are greatly deluded no matter how long they remain" (p. E1). "The Egyptian Army will not become the region's policeman as Sadat planned with the United States after the disappearance of the Shah of Iran" (p. E2).

On the same day that Algerian President Chadli Benjedid signed a protocol with the secretary general of the Spanish Communist party, Algiers radio also described Sadat's murder as the inevitable fate of those leaders who seek peaceful coexistence with Israel and cooperate with the United States: "Sadat betrayed Egypt and the Arab cause and entered into an alliance with Zionism and imperialism against the Arab nation. The action taken today by certain men of the armed forces to eliminate Sadat was an inevitable consequence in the confrontation of the regime of treason" (p. Q1).

3. Georgi Arbatov and other members of the USA–Canada Institute in Moscow frequently visit the United States and are widely received by the press and other media. The institute reports directly to the Central Committee of the Communist party.

4. Joseph Finder, *Red Carpet* (New York: Holt, Rinehart, Winston, 1983), pp. 292–314. See also Steve Munson, "Armand's Story," *The National Interest* 9 (Fall 1987): 98–103.

5. Herman Rauschning, *Hitler Speaks*, as cited in Allan Bullock, *Hitler: A Study in Tyranny*, rev. ed. (New York: Bantam, 1961), p. 188.

6. Quoted in Albert Weeks, ed., *Soviet and Communist Quotations* (Washington, D.C.: Pergamon-Brassey, 1987), p. 313.

7. Colonel Harry G. Summers, Jr., *On Strategy: A Critical Analysis of the Vietnam War* (Novato, Calif.: Presidio Press, 1982), esp. part 1. Summers recounts a conversation he had with a North Vietnamese general after the American withdrawal: "You know you never defeated us on the battlefield," said the American colonel. "That may be so," said the North Vietnamese general, "but it is also irrelevant" (p. 1).

8. V. I. Lenin, *Collected Works* (New York: International Publishers, 1927).

9. Vladimir Bukovsky, "Peace as a Political Weapon," in *Soviet Hypocrisy and Western Gullibility* (Washington, D.C.: Ethics and Public Policy Center, 1987), p. 9.

10. Gustav Hilger and Alfred G. Meyer, *The Incompatible Allies: A Memoir-History of German-Soviet Relations 1918–1941* (New York: Macmillan, 1953), p. 241.

11. The extensive use of combined political warfare operations may sometimes be crudely overdone. A huge Soviet-inspired propagandistic "peace campaign" in Western Europe against NATO installation of intermediate-range nuclear forces miscarried in the 1980s when Western public opinion backlashed against its crudities. See Alex R. Alexiev, "The Soviet Campaign against the INF," *Orbis* 29, no. 2 (Summer 1985): 319–50.

12. *New York Times*, 15 December 1984, p. 1.

13. Malcolm Wallop and Angelo Codevilla, *The Arms Control Delusion* (San Francisco: ICS Press, 1987).

14. Bruce Weinrod, ed., *The Arms Control Handbook* (Washington, D.C.: Heritage Foundation, 1987), pp. 86–89.

Chapter 9

1. Quoted in Tom Shachtman, *The Phony War: 1939–1940* (New York: Harper and Row, 1982), p. 129. King George's source for these moving words was an obscure book by Minnie Louise Haskins, *The Desert*, published in 1908.

2. B. H. Liddell-Hart, *Thoughts on War* (London: Faber and Faber, 1924).

3. Frank Barnaby, *The Automated Battlefield* (New York: Free Press, 1986).

4. Sterling Seagrave, *Yellow Rain* (New York: M. Evans, 1981).

5. William Colby, *Honorable Men* (New York: Simon and Schuster, 1978).

6. Shachtman, *Phony War*.

Chapter 10

1. Thomas Jefferson to Thomas Leiper, 12 June 1815, in *The Works of Thomas Jefferson*, ed. Paul L. Ford (New York: Putnam, 1905), vol. 2, pp. 477–78.

2. "Only 4 percent died among the 260,000 British and American prisoners captured by the Germans" (Ronald H. Bailey, *World War II Prisoners of War* [Arlington, Va.: Time-Life Books, 1981], p. 14).

3. Arnold Krammer, *Nazi Prisoners of War in America* (New York: Stein and Day, 1979), pp. 256, 266.

4. "Of 5.7 million Russians taken prisoner, 3.7 million died in German hands" (Bailey, *World War II Prisoners of War*, p. 122). Eight hundred thousand Russians (prisoners and émigrés), especially cossacks and non-Slavic minorities, fought with the Nazis as the Russian Liberation Army (p. 128). Most of these were killed when they were forcefully repatriated to Russian

authority. Altogether, only a small number of those Russians who were taken prisoner in World War II ever returned to their homes.

Chapter 11

1. Edward Gibbon, *The Decline and Fall of the Roman Empire* (New York: Heritage Press, 1946), vol. 2, pp. 975–76.

2. Robert Murphy, *Diplomat Among Warriors* (Garden City, N.Y.: Doubleday, 1964), chaps. 5–6. The German military authorities at Reims believed that they were acting as representatives of their government, while the Allied military authorities there contended that the Doenitz government did not exist, and that in any case they did not make deals with the German government but were merely accepting the unconditional surrender of the German armed forces. This position, however, contained a contradiction: the Allies were demanding from the German high command an order for a simultaneous cease-fire on all fronts, clearly a political act.

3. Max Hastings, *The Korean War* (New York: Simon and Schuster, 1987). "1,319,000 Americans had served in the Korean theater and 33,629 did not return. A further 105,785 were wounded. Forty-five percent of all U.S. casualties were incurred after the first armistice negotiations with the Communists took place" (p. 329).

4. DOR Sekretariatet et al., *Economic Growth in a Nordic Perspective* (Copenhagen, 1984). The gross domestic products per capita in U.S. dollars at current prices and exchange rates in 1960 were $1,200 for Finland, $1,400 for Norway, and $1,800 for Sweden.

5. Konrad Adenauer, *Memoirs: 1945–1953*, tr. Beate R. von Oppen (Chicago: Henry Regnery, 1966).

> Statistics showed that in March 1946 men weighed on the average seven kilograms below normal. Their weight had sunk to 9.1 kilograms below normal by June—that is thirteen percent below normal weight—while the inmates of old people's homes averaged as much as twelve kilograms or twenty percent below normal. . . . More than fifty percent of the pupils in our elementary class that was tested in the spring had tuberculosis.
>
> While there had been 11.8 deaths registered per thousand inhabitants in 1938, the number was already up to 15.1 in April 1946 and had risen to 18 by June 1946 (pp. 58–59).

6. Aleksandr Solzhenitsyn, *"Prussian Nights": A Poem*, trans. Robert Conquest (New York: Farrar, Straus and Giroux, 1977).

7. John J. Dziak, *Chekisty* (Lexington, Mass.: Lexington Books, 1980), pp. 19–39. See also Richard Pipes, *The Russian Revolution*, vol. 1 (forthcoming). See also Robert Conquest, *Harvest of Sorrow* (Oxford: Oxford University Press, 1987). This is the definitive account of the artificial famine in the Ukraine that broke resistance to communist collectivization at the cost of perhaps 10 million lives.

8. For a good account of the aftermath of the Spanish civil war, see Stanley

G. Payne, *The Franco Regime: 1936–1975* (Madison: University of Wisconsin Press, 1987). Franco's Nationalists executed 70,000 to 72,000 Republicans from 1936 to 1950, almost exactly equal to the number of Republican executions of Nationalists during the civil war (p. 217). In addition, Spain lost approximately 162,000 Republicans to permanent exile (p. 220). However, Payne notes that conditions undoubtedly would have been worse had the Republicans triumphed under the Communist hegemony created in 1937–38. He adds that Franco's was the second most clement resolution to any revolutionary civil war in the twentieth century, the resolution of the Greek civil war of the early 1950s being the most clement.

9. See Jacqueline Desbarats and Karl D. Jackson, "Political Violence in Vietnam: The Dark Side of Liberation," *Indochina Report*, no. 6. (April–June 1986): 22–28 especially; and Richard M. Nixon, *No More Vietnams* (New York: Arbor House, 1985), pp. 86–88 especially.

Casualty figures are always tricky. In this case two baseline numbers exist. In 1978 Vietnamese premier Pham Van Dong claimed to have released over one million people from re-education camps, lending weight to claims that far more than that number went in. Also some 600,000 Vietnamese who fled by sea reached safe haven, and enough bodies and wreckage have been found to support the estimate that on the order, only one out of two boat people survived the sea. Desbarats and Jackson limit themselves to estimating actual executions. They estimate 320,000 reports and divide that number by an arbitrary factor of four. But in such situations, execution is the least of the causes of death.

10. The name Red Square, which existed at the time of Peter the Great, is not an allusion to communism. The Russian adjective "red" sometimes means "beautiful." See Michael Glennon and John L. Moore, eds., *The Soviet Union* (Washington, D.C.: Congressional Quarterly, 1982), p. 4.

11. See Conquest, *Harvest of Sorrow*, pp. 309–11.

12. Saint Augustine, *City of God* (Garden City, N.Y.: Image Books, 1958), p. 456.

13. Ibid., p. 458.

14. Etienne Gilson, in Saint Augustine, *City of God*, p. 34.

15. Roy P. Basler, ed. *Collected Works of Abraham Lincoln* (New Brunswick, N.J.: Rutgers University Press, 1953), vol. 2, p. 461.

BIBLIOGRAPHY

Arendt, Hannah. *On Violence*. New York: Harcourt, Brace, and World, 1970.
————. *The Origins of Totalitarianism*. New York: Meridian Books, 1963.
Aron, Raymond. *The Century of Total War*. Garden City, N.Y.: Doubleday, 1964.
————. *Clausewitz: Philosopher of War*. Englewood Cliffs, N.J.: 1984.
Augustine, Saint. *The City of God*. Garden City, N.Y.: Image Books, 1958.
Blainey, Geoffrey. *The Causes of War*. New York: Free Press, 1973.
Bozeman, Adda. "Statecraft and Intelligence in the Non-Western World." *Conflict* 6 (1985): 19.
Brodie, Bernard. *War and Politics*. New York: Macmillan, 1975.
Carr, Edward Hallett. *The Twenty Years' Crisis, 1919–1939*. London: Macmillan, 1946.
Churchill, Winston. *The Second World War*. 6 vols. Boston: Houghton Mifflin, 1948–1953.
————. *The World Crisis*. New York: Scribner, 1923.
Clausewitz, Carl von. *On War*. Ed. and trans. Michael Howard and Peter Paret. Princeton, N.J.: Princeton University Press, 1976.
Cohn, Norman. *Pursuit of the Millenium*. New York: Oxford University Press, 1970.
Cox, Richard. *Locke on War and Peace*. Washington, D.C.: University Press of America, 1982.
Craig, Gordon. *The Politics of the Prussian Army*. Oxford: Clarendon Press, 1955.
Creasy, Edward S. *Fifteen Decisive Battles of the World*. New York: Dorset Press, 1987.
Crozier, Brian. *A Theory of Conflict*. London: Hamilton, 1974.
de Gaulle, Charles. *Memoires de Guerre*. Paris: Plon, 1954.
Deane, Herbert. *The Political and Social Ideas of Saint Augustine*. New York: Columbia University Press, 1963.
Dulles, Allan W. *The Craft of Intelligence*. New York: New American Library, 1965.
Earle, Edward Meade, ed. *Makers of Modern Strategy*. Princeton: Princeton University Press, 1943.
Erasmus, Desiderius. *The Complaint of Peace*. Trans. Margaret Mann. New York: Garland Publications, 1972.
Feierabend, I. K., and Betty Newhold. "The Comparative Study of Revolution and Violence." *Comparative Politics* (April 1973).
Fischer, Fritz. *Germany's Aims in the First World War*. Trans. London: W. W. Norton, 1967.
Fitzgibbon, Constantine. *Secret Intelligence in the Twentieth Century*. New York: Stein and Day, 1977.
Fuller, J. F. C. *The Conduct of War, 1789–1961*. London: Minerva Press, 1968.

Fussell, Paul. *The Great War and Modern Memory*. London: Oxford University Press, 1975.

Gilbert, Felix. *To the Farewell Address*. Princeton: Princeton University Press, 1961.

Gilbert, Martin. *Winston S. Churchill: Road to Victory, 1941–1945*. Boston: Houghton Mifflin, 1986.

Glynn, Patrick. "The Sarajevo Fallacy: The Historical and Intellectual Origins of Arms Control Theology." *The National Interest* 9 (Fall 1987).

Godson, Roy. *Intelligence Requirements for the 1980's: Intelligence and Policy*. Washington, D.C.: National Strategy Information Center, 1979.

———— (ed). *Intelligence for the 1990s*. Lexington, Mass.: Lexington Books, 1989.

Grant, Ulysses S. *Personal Memoirs*. 2 vols. New York: 1885–86.

Grotius, Hugo. *Prolegomena to the Law of War and Peace*. Indianapolis: Bobbs Merrill, 1957.

Hinsley, Francis Harry. *British Intelligence in the Second World War*. New York: Cambridge University Press, 1979.

Hobbes, Thomas. *Leviathan*. Ed. Michael Oakeshott. Oxford: Oxford University Press, 1957.

Howard, Michael. *War and the Liberal Conscience*. New Brunswick, N.J.: Rutgers University Press, 1978.

————. *War in European History*. London: Oxford University Press, 1976.

Huntington, Samuel P. *The Common Defense: Strategic Programs in National Politics*. New York: Columbia University Press, 1961.

————. *The Soldier and the State: The Theory and Practise of Civil-Military Relations*. Cambridge, Mass.: Harvard University Press, 1957.

Iklé, Frederick. *Every War Must End*. New York: Columbia University Press, 1971.

Johnson, Paul. *Enemies of Society*. New York: Atheneum Press, 1977.

————. *Modern Times*. New York: Harper and Row, 1983.

Kagan, Donald. "World War I, World War II, World War III." *Commentary* (March 1987).

Kahn, David. *The Codebreakers*. New York: Macmillan, 1967.

Kahn, Herman. *On Thermonuclear War*. Princeton: Princeton University Press, 1960.

Kautilya. *Arthasastra*. Trans. R. P. Kangle. Bombay: University of Bombay Press, 1960.

Kecskemeti, Paul. *Strategic Surrender: The Politics of Victory and Defeat*. Stanford: Stanford University Press, 1959.

Keegan, John. *The Face of Battle*. New York: Viking Press, 1976.

Kissinger, Henry. *A World Restored: Europe after Napoleon*. Boston: Houghton Mifflin, 1973.

Krebs, Richard [Jan Valtin]. *Out of the Night*. New York: Alliance, 1941.

Lefever, Ernest W., ed. *Ethics and World Politics: Four Perspectives*. Washington, D.C.: Ethics and Public Policy Center, 1988.

Lenin, V. I. *Collected Works*. New York: International Publishers, 1927.

Liddell-Hart, Basil. *Strategy*. New York: Frederick A. Praeger, 1962.

Lincoln, Abraham. *Abraham Lincoln's Speeches*. Comp. L. E. Crittenden. New York: 1895. Includes his first and second inaugural addresses and his letter to Mrs. Bixby.

Luttwak, Edward. *The Grand Strategy of the Roman Empire*. Baltimore: Johns Hopkins University Press, 1976.

———. *Strategy: The Logic of War and Peace*. Cambridge, Mass.: Harvard University Press, Belknap Press, 1987.

———. *The Pentagon and the Arts of War*. New York: Simon and Schuster, 1984.

MacArthur, Douglas. *Reminiscences*. New York: McGraw Hill, 1964.

Machiavelli, Niccolo. *The Prince and Other Works*. New York: Penguin Books, 1962.

Mahan, Alfred Thayer. *The Influence of Seapower in History*. New York: Hill and Wang, 1957.

Mao Tse-tung. *Selected Military Writings*. Beijing: Foreign Language Press, 1963.

May, Ernest. *Knowing One's Enemies: Intelligence Assessment Before the Two World Wars*. Princeton: Princeton University Press, 1984.

Murphy, Robert. *Diplomat Among Warriors*. Garden City, N.Y.: Doubleday, 1964.

Nef, John. *War and Human Progress: An Essay on the Rise of Industrial Civilization*. Cambridge, Mass.: Harvard University Press, 1952.

Nicolson, Sir Harold. *The Congress of Vienna*. New York: Harcourt, Brace, 1946.

———. *Diplomacy*. Oxford: Oxford University Press, 1955.

———. *Peacemaking, 1919*. Boston: Houghton Mifflin, 1933.

Niebuhr, Reinhold. *The Children of Light and the Children of Darkness*. New York: Scribner, 1944.

———. *Moral Man and Immoral Society*. New York: Scribner, 1960.

Nixon, Richard. *The Real War*. New York: Warner Books, 1980.

Orlov, Alexander. *Handbook of Intelligence and Guerrilla Warfare*. Ann Arbor: University of Michigan Press, 1963.

Orwell, George. *Homage to Catalonia*. New York: Harcourt Brace, 1956.

Osgood, Robert E. *Limited War: The Challenge to American Strategy*. Chicago: University of Chicago Press, 1957.

Osgood, Robert E., and Robert W. Tucker. *Force, Order, and Justice*. Baltimore: Johns Hopkins University Press, 1967.

Paret, Peter, ed. *Makers of Modern Strategy*. Princeton: University of Princeton Press, 1986.

Payne, James. *Why Nations Arm*. London: Basil Blackwood, 1989.

Pike, Douglas. *PAVN: The People's Army of Vietnam*. Novato, Calif.: Presidio Press, 1986.

Preston, R. A., S. F. Wise, and H. O. Werner. *Men in Arms: A History of Warfare*. New York: F. A. Praeger, 1962.

Ramsey, Paul. *The Just War: Force and Political Responsibility*. Washington, D.C.: University Press of America, 1968.

Richardson, Lewis. *Statistics of Deadly Quarrels*. Ed. Quincy Wright and C. C. Lienau. Pittsburgh: Boxwood Press, 1960.

Schmitt, Carl. *The Concept of the Political*. Ed. George Schwab. New Brunswick, N.J.: Rutgers University Press, 1976.

Seabury, Paul, and Patrick Glynn. "Kennan: The Historian as Fatalist." *The National Interest* (Winter 1985–86).

Smith, Adam. *The Wealth of Nations.* London: George Routledge, 1893. (See esp. bk. 5, chap. 1, pt. 1: "Of the Expense of Defense.")

Smith, Paul A., Jr. *On Political War.* Washington, D.C.: National Defense University, 1989.

Sokolovskii, Marshal Vasili. *Soviet Military Strategy.* New York: Crane, Russak, 1975.

Summers, Colonel Harry G., Jr. *On Strategy: A Critical Analysis of the Vietnam War.* Novato, Calif.: Presidio Press, 1982.

Sun-Tzu. *The Art of War.* Trans. Samuel B. Griffith. London: Oxford University Press, 1963.

Taylor, A. J. P. *The Struggle for Mastery in Europe, 1848–1918.* London: Oxford University Press, 1954.

Thomas, Hugh. *The Spanish Civil War.* New York: Harper and Row, 1986.

Thucydides. *A History of the Peloponnesian War.* New Brunswick, N.J.: Rutgers University Press, 1975.

Tuchman, Barbara. *The Guns of August: August 1914.* New York: Macmillan, 1962.

Tucker, Robert W. *The Just War.* Baltimore: Johns Hopkins University Press, 1960.

Tucker, Robert C., ed. *The Marx-Engels Reader.* 2d ed. New York: W. W. Norton, 1978.

Valtin, Jan. *See* Krebs, Richard.

Van Crefeld, Martin. *Supplying War: Logistics from Wallenstein to Patton.* Cambridge, England: Cambridge University Press, 1977.

Vargas Llosa, Mario. *The War of the End of the World.* New York: Farrar, Straus, Giroux, 1984.

Waltz, Kenneth. *Man, the State, and War.* New York: Columbia University Press, 1964.

Walzer, Michael. *Just and Unjust Wars.* New York: Basic Books, 1977.

Washington, George. *Farewell Address.* Albany, NY, 1810.

Weigel, George. *Tranquilitas Ordinis: The Present Failure and Future Promise of American Catholic Thought on War and Peace.* Oxford: Oxford University Press, 1987.

Wiskemann, Elizabeth. *Europe of the Dictators.* New York: Harper and Row, 1966.

Wright, Quincy. *Study of War.* 2 vols. Chicago: University of Chicago Press, 1942.

Xenophon. *The Anabasis.* Trans. Alpheus Crosby. New York: Potter, Ainsworth, 1875.

Zabih, Sepehr. *The Iranian Military in Revolution and War.* London: Routledge, Kegan and Paul, 1988.

Zhukov, Georgi. *Memoirs.* New York: Delacorte Press, 1971.

Zim, Herbert. *Codes and Secret Writing.* New York: William Morrow, 1948.

INDEX